To Own a Fig Tree

To Own a Fig Tree

From Shetland Crofters to New Zealand Settlers

Written by

Wendy Hamilton

ZealAus Publishing

To Own a Fig Tree
From Shetland Crofters to New Zealand Settlers

Copyright © 2021 by Wendy Hamilton

www.zealauspublishing.com

All rights reserved. No part of this book may be reproduced or transmitted in any form or by any means without written permission of the author. Attitudes expressed in this book are not necessarily the attitudes of Wendy Hamilton or ZealAus Publishing.

ISBN: 978-1-925888-87-4 (e)
ISBN: 978-1-925888-88-1 (hc)
ISBN: 978-1-925888-89-8 (sc)

Contents

An Unpromising Land 1
No Cash No Choice 17
An Evil System. 25
The Meeting 30
 Changes Afoot 35
Anderina Makes Up Her Mind 48
Preparations 51
Farewell Shetland 68
The Ocean Mail 74
A Great Start 81
Misery 86
Happier Times 93
Nelson 102
The Hostel and Hope of Land 108
An Odd Place 115
The Meeting 122
High Hopes Are Dampened 128
Difficulties 136
Black Sunday 142
Karamea Jack 146
A Way of Escape for Some 153
O'Connor Saves the Day 156
A Big Surprise 163
A Temporary Solution 167
Only Bare Necessities Please 171
A Wonderful Discovery 176
Land at Last 181
Building Our First House 186

Shifting In	193
A Damp Home and Castles in the Air	199
O'Connor Has Doubts	203
A Letter and a New House	209
Progress	216
Robert Surprises Us	221
A Bullock, Baby, and New Tracks	227
The First School	234
Truck Rears its Ugly Head	240
Disaster	246
Sickness and Theft	250
The Steamer Arrives	257
Lost, Saved, and Found	263
A Miserable Anniversary	268
Camp Life	274
Political Sabotage	281
An Unsettling Letter for Samuel Friend	286
The South Terrace is Abandoned	294
House Moving	300
A Wedding	312
The Second Anniversary	320
God's Provision in a Tight Spot	332
Big Trouble	338
Worse Trouble	343
A Petition is Sent to Parliament	347
The Hearing	352
The Great Flood	362
Be Fruitful and Increase	368
Two Sorts of Blindness	377
The Dairy Cooperative	384

Robert buys a boat 390
The Settlers Get a Boat. 397
Captain Johnson Solves the Problem 405
Safety Precautions are for the Rich 409
Shipwreck. 414
Tragedy. 420
Glossary 431
References 432

Acknowledgements

Thanks to Dulcie McNabb, who was very helpful and generous with her time. Her book 'Karamea a Story of Success,' was a source of valuable information. Also, the late Elva Bett. Her account of the Johnson family's history in her book, 'The Robert Johnsons and Karamea,' was foundational in piecing this story together.

The cover photos of Simpson's Hotel, and the Johnson family and their cattle are courtesy of the Karamea Museum.

Introduction

This is a story of a little 'fish' who rode a big wave.

In 1870, the Colonial Treasurer of New Zealand, Julius Vogel, instigated his great Public Works policy to develop the new country through railways, roads, telegraph lines and immigrants. A year later, the first official inquiry into the oppressive truck system in Shetland was presented to the British Parliament. The opportunities for agricultural workers in the southern hemisphere, coupled with the semi-serfdom in the northern hemisphere, created a mighty wave of emigration from Shetland to New Zealand.

When the big wave came, Shetland crofter, Robert Johnson, wrapped his four-year-old son, William, in a knitted blanket, and sailed with his family to New Zealand. William was my great grandfather, and I met him when I was two and he was ninety-four. I remember him dimly, an old man in a wheelchair surrounded by a dark room. Sadly, I asked no questions about his early life; the rag doll my grandmother produced from the hall cupboard was infinitely more interesting than New Zealand history. Over fifty years later, however, William and his family have emerged from the shadows. Historical records, combined with family stories and imagination, bring them to life.

In a book such as this, it is important to know where the lines between fact and fiction lie. The plot is historical, the characters are historical, the conversations are imaginary.

The attitudes and human-interest stories (such as Robert's pipe and the missing cows) are tales handed down to me by my father, Arthur Johnson, or gleaned from Karamea's locals.

My cousin has William's knitted blanket, my sister owns Anderina's clock, and I have the 'almost-pirate' chest that stored their luggage during the voyage. But better than these are the freedom and opportunities I and many others enjoy; all because Robert Johnson and a multitude of other little 'fish,' rode the big wave of Julius Vogel's vision.

Micah 4:4

But they shall sit everyman under his vine and under his fig tree, and none shall make them afraid: for the mouth of the Lord of hosts hath spoken it.

King James Version (KJV)

W.E. Hamilton

An Unpromising Land

I had heard of trees but the nearest I came to seeing one on our barren island was the timber from the shipwrecks that washed onto the beach. I could see a ship's rib on the shoreline, rocking in the waves.

"Look Dad," I shouted, running towards it. "A beam to fix the broken rafter."

"Aye, the Lord heard our prayers and has sent us a grand one," said my father, as we pulled it out of the water and carried it towards our croft. "This is better than the one the gale tore off."

"Will we fix the roof or the stonewall first, Dad?"

"The roof. Always take care of your roof, Robert, for there are no poorhouses in Shetland, and often the roof is the only thing a crofter owns. When you are too old to work, you may take it."

I stopped and dropped my end of the beam. "Will the house leave Brindister and go to another village?"

"Not the house, Robert, you and the roof. It is not much of a shelter but it is better than nothing."

I stared at my father as he put the beam on the ground and sat on it.

"Now you are twelve, my boy, and have an account at the store, I'll not shield you from reality. I'll be honest with you," my father paused and looked sadly over the windswept land,

To Own a Fig Tree

"your future is unpromising."

I was more shocked by his sitting down than his words, for it was not dinnertime. I dropped beside him and Dad rubbed his hand over his youthful-looking face. His strong shoulders sagged as he leaned forward with his elbows on his knees and slumped his bearded chin into his cupped hands.

"Not promising at all," he repeated. "The lairds and their *factors*[1] have realized the sea is more valuable than the land, so they are dividing the crofts into smaller and smaller units. You as the eldest may scratch a living from crofting, but Arthur will have to fish for survival."

I wanted to cheer my father up, so I said, "Arthur can farm; I don't mind fishing."

"Fishing is not the problem, my son. The fishermen must sell their fish to the factors at the prices they set, and then we spend the money in the shops run by the same factors at prices they demand."

"Do you mean, Mr Hay and his brother, who own the store and the fish curing factory?"

"That's right, Hay and Company. They are also the factors we rent our land from."

"What about the farmers?"

"The crofters are bound to sell their sheep and cattle to the factors in exchange for goods. Almost everyone in Shetland is hopelessly in debt, and we are little more than slaves."

I thought of the new Sunday suit lying in its cardboard box in the cupboard, and drew back my shoulders proudly.

"Now that I am old enough to go to church and start work, Dad, I'll help out." I clenched my fist into a ball and flexed my

---

1   agents

arm. "And when I grow bigger, I promise I will go whaling and bring home enough money to make us rich."

My father sighed and gently pushed my arm down. "It's a kind thought, Robert, but if you did Mr Hay would evict us from our home."

"Couldn't we go elsewhere?"

"Mr Hay is the factor for the Earl of Shetland, and as such, has control over a quarter of the Shetland Isles." My father shook his head sorrowfully. "It grieves me to think your Sunday suit is your entrance to a lifetime of bondage."

I was puzzled.

"How does my suit cause trouble?"

"How did you pay for the suit, Robert?"

"I am starting as a beach boy on Monday, so Mr Hay's brother at the store let me have it ahead of time. I will pay for it at the end of the fishing season."

"That is right," my father nodded. "But no matter how many *ling*[2] you salt and dry, or how well the season goes, by the end of it you won't have paid off your suit, the Hay brothers will make sure of that. You will be in so much debt you will have to sign up for next year's season. Maybe you'll get your suit paid off by the time you are old enough to fish the *haf*[3] for them. Then they will provide you with a boat and lines for fishing. Along with five other men you will sign up for a sixth of the value of the equipment, which will take at least three years to pay off, for the laird will take two-thirds of your wages. In the meantime, you have to eat, and if you marry, provide for your family, and so the endless cycle of debt and bondage begins.

---

2   fish
3   Deep Sea

To Own a Fig Tree

The only way out is death."

We sat in silence for a few minutes. Finally, I said in a small voice, "Do you want me to take the suit back, Dad?"

"Mr Hay would not take it back, and even if he did, they would get you some other way. I am sorry for spoiling your pleasure over your first suit, my boy," he said with an apologetic sigh. "As bondage is inevitable, let it be for the sake of Christ, though I am sure the Lord would not have it so." Dad patted me on the shoulder. "I have no worldly goods to pass on to you, Robert. I do, however, have something of greater value. The world's treasures are fleeting. Look beyond this world for the hope that lasts an eternity. God has promised a home and fig tree in the new earth and heavens to all who love him."

"What are figs like, Dad?"

"I don't know, but they must be wonderful. Hold fast to this promise, Robert, and you will taste them, for God never breaks his word. He sees our misery and will deliver us at the right time, just as surely as he delivered the children of Israel from the hand of Pharaoh."

"When will that be, Dad?"

My father gazed into the distance as if he was peering into the future. "I do not expect to see it in my lifetime, but it will certainly come."

He stood up and squared his shoulders. "Nobody can steal this hope, Robert, not even the laird or the factors. I have passed it on to you, even as my father passed it to me, and his father to him..." He picked up his end of the beam, and scrambling to my feet, I picked up the other end. "Never forget this, for it will save you from despair." He twisted his head to look at me as we walked, and his eyes suddenly twinkled. "That and a good woman. If you choose your wife wisely, she will not *allow* you to despair or forget. Come, let us show your mother and sisters the marvellous beam God has sent."

It was a short walk from the beach to the town and the cluster of cottages and byres huddling at the end of their crofts, was soon in sight. I saw women digging in their long strips of land, or knitting as they carried loads of peat in wooden cradles on their backs. Like all the other cottages, a huge pile of dung dwarfed our house. It sat like treasure in the front yard. My younger brother, Arthur, was hard at work in the potato patch. Over the grass dyke beyond him, our cow grazed on the common land, while nearby chickens scratched under a clothesline, where socks and fillets of fish flapped in the wind. We passed through the gap in the stonewall surrounding our land, and carried the beam up the narrow path between the house and the dunghill, and set it on the ground beneath the damaged roof.

"Run and tell your mother of our find, Robert," said Dad, "while I check that Arthur is mounding the dirt around the *taities*[4] properly."

I nodded, and opening the door that once hung on a captain's cabin, stepped inside. The cottage was a single room with whitewashed walls and two deep-set windows. As expected, my mother sat at the spinning wheel, her hands gently teasing a cloud of wool into a strand as the wheel whirled and clattered. Above her head, hanks of yarn hung from the rafters, while dried fish dangled in profusion from the rest of the beams, for being August, *piltock and saithe were plentiful in the tideway. In the centre of the room was a peat fire, over which a caldron

---

4   potatoes

To Own a Fig Tree

dangled from a chain attached to the roof. On each side of the fire stood a wooden sofa, on one of which, my sisters Margret and Barbara sat. Nearby, my other sisters, Grace and Mary, were feeding a lamb.

"Come and look at the beam Dad and I found, Mum."

"Ooo, let me see," cried Barbara and Margret, throwing down their knitting.

"Careful girls," scolded my mother, slowing her wheel with her hand. "You'll lose stitches." She lowered her voice to a whisper, "I know a woman willing to smuggle knitting to Lerwick. If we give her some of our hosiery, we can exchange it for cash instead of ribbons and fancy goods. Do you want to go all winter without sufficient oats because you were careless with your knitting? Our harvest won't last all year; potatoes and dried fish get pretty boring by themselves?" She wound her yarn around the spindle to stop it from untwisting, and taking the carded wool from her coarse apron, stood up.

Barbara and Margret shook their heads, and after checking their knitting, put it down carefully.

Grace, meanwhile, hoisted the toddler onto her hip as she stood up. "Come on, Mary, let's see what our big brother has brought home."

The lamb trotted behind them as they followed me outside.

"See," I said, throwing back my shoulders, and placing my foot on the timber like a mighty hunter.

The girls squealed and immediately started mincing along the rib, carefully following its curve as they placed one foot directly in front of the other, arms outstretched.

I knew by the sudden glow in her eyes that my mother was very pleased, but all she said was: "Humph, don't drop bits of

W.E. Hamilton

turf in my pot while you're clambering on the roof, we're not the Jamieson's with one of those fancy lids for their cauldron. And wear your *beanie*[5], for the wind is chilly."

"Aw, Mum, it's summer," I protested, my shoulders slumping forward.

"Don't backchat, Robert," said my mother, giving me a hard look. "You need your hat, for even a summer wind is cold in *Zetland*[6]. And tell your father to check the wall while he's at it, for I feel a draught in that direction. Come, girls, time to get back to work." She turned, and the girls jumping off the beam, followed her inside.

"What did your mother think?" said Dad, coming up the path carrying a ladder.

"She was pleased, but asked us to check the wall for a draught."

He nodded, and between us we jiggled the ladder about in the narrow corridor between the house and the dung-pile, until we had it leaning against the wall. Then, Dad, after embedding the bottom of the rails in dung, squinted speculatively at the ever-present clouds.

"We'd best hurry. It's been two days since it last rained, we can't expect the dry spell to last much longer."

There was no need for me to hold the ladder, for it was near impossible to move,ced as it was between the house and the wall of manure. I stood below, and watched my father stump up the rungs until his waist was level with the top stones.

"I see the problem," he said, peering into the cavity between the inner and outer walls of rock. "Water has got in and some

---

5   a knitted close-fitting hat.
6   The old name for the Shetland Isles

To Own a Fig Tree

of the dirt has washed out." He came down the ladder. "Get a bucket, Robert, we need more soil."

I ran inside and grabbed a wooden bucket.

"What are you doing?" Mum cried, as I tipped potatoes on the clay floor.

"Dad needs this to insulate the wall."

"Alright, but put your *beanie* on like I told you to," she said, pointing at the woollen hats hanging by the door.

I yanked one off a peg and pulled it on as I sped outside. Dad met me by the garden and handed me a spade.

"Fill the bucket while I scout around for the right kind of rock."

I did as he said, and by the time I finished, he had found a tapering one with a flat bottom. It was short work to fill the cavity, for the subsidence was not great. Dad pounded the soil with his rock until the dull thuds changed into ringing sounds.

"That will do," he said, throwing the rock down before clambering onto the roof. "Hand me the beam, Robert."

I dragged it along the narrow path to the ladder, and summoning all my strength, hoisted an end as high as I could. Dad leaned down, gripped it with his powerful hands, and hauled it onto the roof before lashing one end to the ridgepole and the other end to the eves that barely cleared the wall.

"That feels firm," he said, "shaking the unyielding rafter."Hand me the roofing boards."

I skipped to a neatly stacked pile of timber and pulled an armful of boards off the top. Dad was halfway down the ladder by the time I got back. He twisted down, took the pile from me, and placed it on the roof near the hole. When we had enough, Dad sent me to cut squares of grass from the pasture while he made the repair. When he finished, we covered the bald spot with turf, and covered the turf with thatch. Then we stretched ropes over the roof and weighted everything down with stones. Mum had milked the cow and dinner was ready by the time we tied a flagstone onto the end of the last rope.

"There!" said Dad, lying the stone on the thatch. "The weather can do its worst, but no wind or rain will get through *that*." He picked up the ladder. "Time for supper. Wash the bucket before you take it back to your mother."

I nodded and sped to the well that stood a small distance from the house. When I got in, Mother was at the table dishing potatoes, turnip tops, and fish onto six plates. I hung my hat on the peg by the door, put down the bucket, and slid into the chair beside Margret.

"Your turn to eat last, Robert," said Mum, looking at me apologetically.

"It's alright, Mum, I don't mind. When I am grown up, I will buy you an entire dinner set with twelve big plates, twelve little plates, and even twelve bowls."

Barbara gasped. "What will you *do* with so many?"

"A plate each is enough," said Mum, "eat don't talk, we need to bait the *daibodi*[7] before sunset."

"Aw, do we have to?" whined Margaret. "I'm sick of fishing every night."

Mum gave my sister a hard look as she spooned potato and fish on her plate.

"Stop that silly talk, Margret. Everyone has to pull their weight. We can't rely on the oats or *taities*[8] before the harvest

---

7   a fishing trap
8   potatoes

To Own a Fig Tree

is gathered. An unexpected storm could wipe everything out, and then where would we be? The good Lord sends fish abundantly at this time of year to save us from starving.

Margret subsided like a sail when the wind drops, and her face looked fearful.

"Cheer up, Maggie," I whispered, "famines only come every four years. Next year is the time to worry."

At this, Margret cheered up, because a year was a long way away.

Mum put the cauldron next to the large Bible in the centre of the table and nodded at Dad.

"Let us give thanks for this food," said Dad.

At this cue, we dropped our heads and closed our eyes.

"Thank you for this food dear Lord. Amen."

"Amen," we chorused.

I took a shell from my pocket and looked at it while I waited.

"That's pretty," said Margret.

"Where did you get it?" said Mum, fear flooding her face.

"I found it on the beach."

"Don't let the factor catch you," said Dad. "Slip it back when we go fishing."

"Why?"

"Shells, stones, and seaweed belong to the laird. We can't take them for ourselves. If you want a shell, you must buy it."

I sighed and put the shell back in my pocket as Arthur scraped the last of his food from his plate.

"Here you go, Robbie," he said, handing it to me.

"You can have the rest in the pot, Robert," said Mum, as Dad reached for the bible. "I left you the *taito*[9] with the extra

---

9   potato

bulge on it as a treat for being last."

I smiled as I lifted my dinner from the pot. "Thanks, Mum."

"Oh, Laurence!" said Mum, as Dad opened the big black book. "Couldn't we skip 'Family Alter' just once? We are already late, much longer and we will miss out on lots of fish."

"Man does not live by bread alone, Elizabeth," said Dad, turning the thin pages. "But by every word of God. If our stomachs get a little less because our souls have a little more, it is a good trade."

"Quite right," said Mum, subsiding.

"Exodus chapter three, verse seven," read Dad. *"And the Lord said, I have surely seen the affliction of my people... and have heard their cry by reason of their hard taskmasters; for I know their sorrows, and I am come down to deliver them... and to bring them up out of that land unto a good land flowing with milk and honey."*[10] Dad shut the bible. "Let us pray."

At this, we bowed our heads and closed our eyes.

"Dear Lord," said Dad, "look down on Shetland and save us from our hard taskmasters. Amen."

"Amen," we echoed.

There was silence for thirty seconds before the room exploded into activity. Some talked, while others shouted. Plates clattered, and everywhere arms reached for garments and hats.

"Grace, get the fish and the clothes off the line in case it rains overnight," Mum cried, as she wrapped a shawl around Mary. "Arthur, lift the kettle off the fire and pour the hot water into the enamel bowl for Barbara to wash the plates."

"Bring the fishing lines, Robert," called Dad, putting on

---

10   Taken from the King James Bible

To Own a Fig Tree

his hat, and picking up a large deep basket made of cornstalks. "I've got the *dabodi*[11]."

I ran to one of the cupboards covering the walls, and opening a door, grabbed a pile of sticks. Unfortunately, some of the lines of horsehair had unravelled and several fishing lines had twisted into a snarled lump. By the time I had picked them apart and rewound the line, my family had gone. So, snatching my hat off its peg, I ran after them. The evening air intensified the chill in the wind, and I shivered as I pulled the door behind me and slid the wooden catch shut. Dad, giving Arthur the *dabodi*, swung Mary onto his shoulders and gripped her ankles. She sat astride his neck and played with the pompom on his hat. My mother, looking solid and strong, plodded beside my father in silence. As we walked over the hillocky land towards the beach, families emerged from their cottages until a number of us arrived at the small bay where boats bobbed in the water.

"When you've got your limpets, meet your father and I back here," said Mum, handing us each a sack.

The girls nodded and raced off to their friends who were knocking limpets off the rocks. I slipped my shell onto the beach when nobody was looking, and then Arthur and I ran to join a group of boys. The limpets were plentiful in the rock pools and it did not take long to collect a great quantity of them. Once our sacks were heavy with shellfish, we went back to Mum and Dad. Then we pulled the soft flesh from the conical shells, and chewed them before spitting them into the darbodi. When the basket was full enough, Dad threw it into the tideway and dragged it through the water. Meanwhile, the rest of us uncoiled the hair on our sticks, baited our lines with

---

11   trap for fish

limpets and fished off the pier. The families already fishing with lines and *dabodi's* were hauling out fish swiftly, for the *piltocks*[12] were plentiful on the surface of the water. The big boys trawling lines through the riptide, however, were even more successful.

"Why don't we go over there, Mum?" I said, pointing towards the mouth of the inlet.

"Not until you are older and bigger, my son. The rip tide is dangerous and not worth the risk. We are doing alright here."

And indeed, we were, for by eleven pm, our darbodi was full to the brim with fish. I took one side of the basket and Dad took the other and we started for home. We were almost at our door when cheerful fiddle music floated through the strange light of the summer night. My mother sniffed and hitched up her shawl.

"That will be that infidel family with their godless music," she said.

"They are lucky the minister has not smashed their fiddle," giggled Barbara.

"It's nothing to laugh about," Mum chided her. "Fiddling while there are fish to be caught is an idle, fleckless way of living."

"Your mother is right," said Dad. "A teacher in Out Skerries went to propose to a young woman, but when he got to her cottage he saw through the window, her dancing to the fiddle while the rest of her family unloaded a boat full of peat."

"What happened," said Barbara?

"He changed his mind, for a poor man needs a sensible hardworking wife."

---

12   A young saithe or coalfish

To Own a Fig Tree

"Then I shall marry a rich man," said Barbara. "Dancing is nicer than carrying peat."

My mother snorted. "Then you'll die an old maid, for there are no rich men to be had in these parts."

"And you'll still have to carry baskets of peat on your back," said Arthur with a smirk. "For if you don't marry, you'll never leave home."

"You might not marry either," said Barbara, pulling a face at her brother.

"I can marry whoever I like," said Arthur cockily, "because there're twice as many girls as men."

"But if you don't choose your wife carefully, Arthur," said Dad, seizing the moment to impart a spiritual truth, "you will end up worse than the proverbial man who lived in the corner of his rooftop."

"And there are two girls for every man because half the males drown while fishing the *haf*"[13]," said Barbara, scoring a bitter-sweet victory over her brother.

Arthur (looking subdued) nodded as Dad and I dropped the basket beside a large flat stone a small distance away from the dunghill.

"I'll put Mary to bed," said Mum, swapping the sleeping toddler from one hip to the other. "When you have finished cleaning the fish, I'll have the kettle boiled."

"Very good," said Dad. He tipped the fish on the ground and slapped a *saithe onto the stone as Mum and the girls went inside. Then, in three swift movements he removed the head, slit the belly, and pulled out the guts. Once that was done, Arthur removed the liver and I scraped away the scales. When

---

13   Deep sea

we finished, we threw the fillets back into the basket, but the livers were washed and left to drain through a bed of straw.

"That will do," said Dad, pushing guts into the dung heap. "Mum can boil the oil out of the livers tomorrow."

"Will we get enough oil this season to pay the rent? Dad," I asked.

"The Lord willing, we will. I think so, but it will take every last drop we scoop off the water."

Arthur opened the door and Dad and I carried the basket inside and dropped it next to a barrel of salted herrings. Without a word, Mum lifted the kettle off the fire and poured hot water into the teapot, which she swivelled around on its base.

"That's right, Mother," said Dad, "show it to the pictures on the wall."

It was true there were many pictures about the room, but I knew my father was referring to a good brew of tea rather than the pencil sketches. I wrapped my fingers around the cup with the broken handle and drank from the side opposite the chip. The girls were asleep in two of the box beds that stood like cupboards against the walls, I could see them huddled together through the open doors of the beds as I drank my tea. When I finished, I pulled off my boots and jersey before slipping my nightshirt over my head and loosening the string around my trousers.

"Don't leave your clothes lying on the floor," said my mother, as my trousers dropped. "Put them where they won't get damp."

I folded my clothes and stuck them at the foot of the bed Arthur and I shared. My brother, half asleep, scooted closer to the wall as I climbed in and lay down. The mattress was thin

To Own a Fig Tree

because the straw inside the ticking had crumbled.

I yawned. "I'm looking forward to Mum and the girls replacing the straw in our mattress."

Arthur pulled the rough knitted blanket up over us.

"I'm not, harvesting is hard work. When I am grown up, I'm going to be so rich I will be like the laird and have others harvest my land."

"I'm not so sure about that."

Arthur sat up and his eyes popped open. "Why not, Robert? You always said when we grow up we will be rich and have plenty to eat. Why the sudden change?"

I was about to tell him what Dad had told me, but his eyes were wide in his face. He was only ten. He deserved two more years of hope.

"Nothing, forget I said anything, Arty, go to sleep."

And with that, Arthur slumped back and fell into a deep sleep. But despite my tired limbs, I lay awake for a long time, thinking about my unpromising future in our treeless land.

W.E. Hamilton

No Cash No Choice

Time played her age-old trick of moving swiftly while pretending to meander. I heeded my father's advice and for the next sixteen years worked on his tenure. In between farm work, I grubbed for stones to build a *but-and-ben*[14] cottage, and in 1852, (aged twenty-eight) I married Anderina Nicholson, daughter of John and Mary Nicholson from the seafaring village of Clousta, over the hill. She was a good woman who bore poverty and hardship as the will of God, and by 1874, we had eight children. Robert junior, was twenty-one and his sister, Mary, a year younger, while John was sixteen and Elizabeth twelve, Margret was nine and Laurence six. That left four-year-old William and James. James, my heart sank as I thought of the frail two-year-old. I feared James would receive his eternal reward long before he reached ten. Anderina was also thinking of our youngest as we trudged along the road to the store.

"Do you think James will be alright?" she said.

"Don't fuss, woman, Elizabeth is capable of looking after him and William. We won't be away long."

Anderina nodded, but the troubled expression did not leave her face. "I'm not really worried about them."

"What's bothering you then?"

---

14 A two-roomed dwelling with one door. The but end was the outer room and the ben the bedroom.

To Own a Fig Tree

Anderina switched her basket to the other arm. "Oh, Robert, is it wise to ask for cash for my knitting? Mr Hay is unlikely to agree, and we risk losing our land."

"He won't throw us out. We have paid our rent and done all the improvements imposed upon us."

"He might if he knows we are in the group calling Her Majesty to further investigate the *truck* system[15]."

I hitched up the canvas bag I carried. "We will be alright; Hay has no names or proof. Now, remember, you want cash for your goods."

"Yes." Anderina gave a nervous sigh. "And I will take the usual reduction for cash."

I nodded. "Six shillings for every ten, but *only* if he gives you *actual* money that we can use to pay off some of our debt. Never take a promissory note or you'll end up with nothing."

"Like the time I tried to cash in his I.O.U for *worsted*[16]," said Anderina bitterly. "He wouldn't honour his own note, said I had to pay for it in cash. I lost a lucrative order because I had no money."

"That is exactly why he refused to give it to you. He doesn't want you knitting for anyone other than himself."

"If he offers me an I.O.U, what do I do?"

"Turn him down and barter for grain. It's unlikely he will agree, but if you could pay for the oats, it will keep the General Account lower."

"If he says no, then what?"

"Cut the value out on tea, sugar, and soap."

"I'll try, but he will probably push me to take useless fancy goods."

15   Cashless barter
16   yarn

"Then I will talk with him."

By now, we were almost at the store. Anderina plucked a hair off my coat and twitched her shawl into place as I pushed the door open and stepped inside.

The factor and his goods stood behind a long counter. I took off my hat.

"Good morning, Mr Hay."

"Good morning, Robert and Anderina, what can I do for you today?"

"I have knitting to sell," said Anderina, putting her basket on the counter before lifting out lacy shawls and veils.

I loosened the drawstring of my canvas bag and added hat's, jumpers, and long underwear to the pile.

"Very nice," said Mr Hay. He opened a large ledger, and counting the garments, wrote a figure before shutting the book.

"Now Anderina…" he paused, and like a man at a carnival sideshow, spread his hands towards the items behind him. "What will you have in exchange? You have enough for a dress and a couple of fancy goods."

Anderina hesitated.

"Come now, don't be shy." He lifted a gaudy hat with feathers in its band. "Perhaps a new hat to go with the dress?"

"I would like cash, Mr Hay."

"You realize, my dear, you get less value if you take cash?"

"Yes, I know."

"Unfortunately, I've no money on me. I'll give you an I.O.U note." He smiled urbanely. "Would that be alright?"

I cleared my throat and twisted the cap in my hands. "Mr Hay, instead of cash, we wish to pay off some of the debt owing on my General Account?"

To Own a Fig Tree

"I'm sorry, Robert, credits from your wife's account cannot be transferred to your account."

"But I am concerned it is getting very high."

"Don't worry about it."

"Can I see how much I owe?"

"There's no point bothering about it until settling time at the end of the year, my boy. I'll see you right as I always have. You came to me empty-handed as a lad, and I've kept you from starving all these years. Unless of course," he paused and his eyes bored into me. "You are one of those ungrateful ones calling for another investigation?"

I clenched the hat in my hands and stuffed down anger.

Anderina shot me a warning glance.

Swallowing I said, "I am not ungrateful."

"I'm pleased to hear it!" Mr Hay turned back to Anderina. "Now my good woman, what will you have?"

"If I can't have cash, I will take grain instead."

"Mrs Johnson, we have been over this before. You have a Woman's Account, and as such, you cannot have grain. Only men may purchase grain through their General Account. Women may, however, purchase tea, sugar, and soap."

"I'll take it all in tea, sugar, and soap."

"Bulk purchases are not allowed, but certainly you can have a packet of tea, a pound of sugar, and two bars of soap instead of the hat. Would you like the black or navy dress?"

Anderina turned to me uncertainly. "I don't need another Sunday dress, but I could get Elizabeth's first Church-dress instead."

"How old is Elizabeth?" said Mr Hay.

"Just turned twelve."

"Then I am sorry, she will need her own account. You cannot use a Woman's Account to purchase clothing for children over twelve."

Anderina's shoulders slumped. "That was six months' worth of work, I want *something* of lasting value for it."

"If you won't take a dress, I have a nice selection of gloves, ribbons, and silk flowers," said Mr Hay.

I slid my wife a sad smile of defeat. "You love your home, dear, choose something for the house."

"What about a print to hang on the wall, or a sea chest?" said Mr Hay, waving his hand at a selection of household goods.

"I have enough sea chests," said Anderina, regarding the items. She pointed at a black mantel clock; its rectangular shape with two columns on either side of its face made me think of a Roman temple. "Can I have a look at that clock?"

"A chiming clock is a wonderful choice," said Mr Hay, lifting it down from the shelf and placing it on the counter. "This is a high-quality clock."

Nothing in the shop was good quality, but Anderina and I overlooked the blatant lie because there was no alternative. He wound it up.

"Listen to the sound of the pendulum. There is nothing like the tick-tock of a clock to make a house feel homely."

"Alright, I'll have the clock."

"You have ten shillings left, what will you have now?"

"Tea, sugar, and soap."

Mr Hay put them next to the clock. "You have eight shillings. What will you take?

"A yard of grey calico."

He cut the fabric from a bolt of cloth and folded it up.

To Own a Fig Tree

"That leaves you with two pennies. Which sweeties do you want?"

"A penny's worth of toffees and the rest in barley sugars."

Mr Hay dropped a few sweets into a small paper bag, twisted the top and put them beside the other things. Then he opened the woman's-book and deducted figures from the amount next to Anderina's name. Anderina put the groceries and fabric into her basket, while I folded the empty bag I had hoped to fill with oats.

"Before you go," said Mr Hay, shutting the book with a bang. "I notice you are not bringing in your usual number of eggs, Anderina. Have your chickens died? I could advance you a loan to get more."

"No, no, Mr Hay," Anderina stammered, "I've been feeding eggs to our youngest child because he is frail and needs building up."

"I see," said Mr Hay. He pointed his finger at Anderina and fixed a gimlet eye on her. "Is that the only reason your egg count is low? If you are selling them on the sly, admit it, and if the numbers go back up, we will say no more about it."

"I promise you, Sir," said Anderina, trembling, "I have not sold my eggs or butter, or knitting to anyone other than you, Sir."

"Very good," said the factor, putting his finger away. "Make sure you keep it that way because if I find you have been lying…" he pressed the tips of his fingers together, "I shall know what to do about it."

"And you, Robert," he said, as I picked up the clock. "Don't be foolish and sell your sheep on the sly." He tapped his nose. "It is easy to catch someone defrauding me. All I have to do is look for the man with money or a bank account."

He took a gold watch from his pocket and swung it back and forth on its chain.

"On to happier things. Give my regards to your father, and congratulate him on his recent appointment to *magistrate*[17]. He is a good man and cares about the well-being of his fellow man. I am sure as a man of peace he won't want the unrest another government inquiry into *truck*[18] would bring."

He stopped speaking, and opening the watch, wound it slowly. I slid my eyes over the headline of a nearby newspaper as we waited for dismissal. At last, he spoke.

"Tell your father, to get me the names of the agitators, and I will make it worth his while." He glanced at the watch with a meaningful look before snapping the lid shut and putting it back in his pocket.

"Yes, Sir," I nodded. "Is that all?"

"That is all. Good day to you both."

"Good day, Sir," Anderina and I replied as I put my hat on and shuffled out.

Neither of us spoke until we were sure we could not be overheard.

"At least I got tea, sugar and soap," said Anderina. She pulled a face. "You can tell a poor woman by her appearance - she has twice the dress, and half the weight of the laird's wife."

I was not in the mood for jokes. "Yes, but they were not your first choice," I burst out. "The clock has cost you hours and hours of toil. I hate being treated like a foolish child. I want to be self-reliant and beholden to no man."

---

17   Justice of the Peace
18   Cashless bartering system

To Own a Fig Tree

Anderina heaved a sigh. "It's been this way for three-hundred years. There is no point fuming over that which we are powerless to change."

"We could escape by going South. I wish we had gone to New Zealand last year. Such a pity we could not get to London to take up Reverend Barclay's offer of assisted passage." I shot a glance at my wife. When she said nothing, I added, "I saw in the newspaper the Reverend is back, and he is holding a meeting in the Parish-hall next week."

The expression on Anderina's face turned hard. "There is Scotland-south, and the bottom-of-the-world-south. I don't want to go down that track again! There is no point thinking about it, Robert. The fare to Scotland for you is unobtainable, let alone money for the entire family to go to London. Even if the Reverend was to make the offer a hundred times over, it would do us no good; ten pounds is impossible to get. This is our life and we must bear our heavy load with patience. I told you last year I don't want to hear another word about it."

"But we have prayed for deliverance for generations. Surely God wishes to set us free…"

Anderina held up her hand. "Not another word, Robert, it is hopeless and that is the end of it."

I looked at the clock in my hands; I was powerless to choose oats. My wife was right, escape was hopeless.

W.E. Hamilton

An Evil System

Mary was spreading compost on the garden when we got home. When she saw her mother and me, she put down her spade and bucket of dung.

"How did you get on?" She looked at the clock in my hands. "I see you didn't get cash or oats."

"Aye, it would have been a miracle if we had," said Anderina. "I see no use for a clock other than its cheerful sound, but it was the best of my choices."

"Take it inside for me, Mary," I said, handing it to her. "I have a message from Mr Hay for Granddad."

Mary's eyes flew open.

"What about?" she said, wiping her hands on her coarse apron.

"Nothing much."

My parent's cottage was close by. I strode along a narrow path through the garden until I got to the entrance.

"Hello," I called, as I pushed the door open. My parents were white-haired and stooped by now, but other than that, little had changed since my childhood. Dad was sitting at the table surrounded by papers while Mum was cleaning dirt off eggs.

"Hello, dear," said Mum. She put a clean egg into her shopping basket before swinging the kettle over the fire.

Dad lowered the page he was reading and looked up.

To Own a Fig Tree

"Hello, Robert. You are just the person I want. Now I have become Magistrate, I have access to The Commissioners Report, and I am discovering some very interesting things."

I pulled out a chair and sat beside my father. "That's the reason I've come."

Dad raised an eyebrow of enquiry, while Mum took the steaming kettle from the fire and filled the teapot.

"I've just been to the store."

"Oh?"

"Mr Hay wants the names of the agitators pushing for a further inquiry, and says he will make it worth your while."

The pleasant smile on Dad's face disappeared, and his blue eyes turned icy. "Did he now!"

"I wanted to punch him for believing you would betray men for the sake of trinkets."

"You can't blame him for that, my son. Men judge others according to their own hearts. A man like Hay is easily bought, and assumes others are the same."

"Hay wants you to supress agitators and discourage a further inquiry.'"

"Then I am afraid Mr Hay will be disappointed," said Dad, as Mum placed tea before us. "I am encouraging Shetlanders to unite against this evil system."

"How did Anderina get on with her knitting?" said Mum, wiping another egg.

"The usual fiasco. She asked for cash or oats, and we ended up with a clock."

Dad nodded.

"Heads I win, tails you lose; it's all part of the rigged system."

W.E. Hamilton

"Everyone knows it is rigged! What I don't understand is how did it get that way, and how do we escape?"

"It is because we have no vote, no land, no cash, and no rights to the fish, sand, shells or kelp."

"It says in the Good Book God owns the cattle on a thousand hills, it is a pity one of the hills is not in Shetland," I said dryly.

Dad's eyes twinkled as he replied:

"Aye, there's no room for the Lord's cattle in *Zetland* because of the Laird's sheep."

After we had laughed a little, Dad got serious again.

"Because we have no rights to anything, we are constantly empty-handed, and the lairds and the factors work together to make it stay that way. Listen to this…" Dad shuffled through his papers until he found a spot heavily underlined. "This comes from a transcript of the 1871, *Truck* Court Hearing." Dad cleared his throat and read: *'"The success of a merchant in Shetland consists in being able to accumulate such an amount of bad debts about him as to thirl[19] whole families in his neighbourhood, and then he succeeds. I have brought for your information the case of a merchant who did not succeed because in a few years he was only able to get five-hundred people in debt to him…"'*

"Five hundred," exclaimed my mother.

"It gets worse," said Dad, listen to this next bit:

'"He came to grief in consequence of not having enough bad debts…if he could have carried on until he had two-thousand pounds worth of bad debts, he would have had a flourishing trade because then they keep going in a circle."'

"A circle of what?"

---

19   enslave

To Own a Fig Tree

"Debt, of course."

I stroked my beard thoughtfully.

"So that is why Mr Hay did not want me to reduce my debt."

"Exactly. And that is why men, women, and children have different accounts. The knitting is lucrative for they get a shawl for five shillings and sell it in Scotland for thirty."

I gave a whistle of surprise. "That is a profit of twenty-five shillings."

"That is right, all in cash. And yet the fishing is even more lucrative. The fishermen get all the toil and danger while the laird and his factor cream off the profit. They don't want the women or the children joining together and using their earnings to buy necessities because they want the men to remain in debt, and therefore bound to fish for them."

"But even if a man got free from debt," I said, "the factor has the leverage of throwing him out of his home."

"Yes, but if the man had even a small amount of money in the bank, he and his family could flee to Scotland where he could find paid work."

"Speaking of fleeing," I said, "I saw when I was at the store that Reverend Barclay is back and he is holding a meeting in Lerwick next week."

"I know." Dad shuffled through papers and pushed a handbill over to me. "While you were out a lad delivered this."

My heart rate quickened as I ran my eye over the advertisement calling for dairy women, domestic servants, and agricultural workers.

"I'm surprised he's trying again," said Mum, tipping a cheese curd into a cloth and wringing out the whey. "He recruited so few last year."

"I think he was surprised by the small numbers because the interest was high," said Dad.

"He obviously is unaware of our peculiar difficulties regarding money," I said bitterly. "The few who left were the ones with hidden cash."

"True," Dad nodded. "Nevertheless, I'm going to the meeting, for who knows, God may do something miraculous and if he does, I want to see it."

I looked my father in the eyes. "If you could emigrate, would you?"

"If I was younger, yes. But now I am old. Moreover, the people need a just magistrate to represent them. My place is here. But, Robert, if the way should open for you and your family to leave, do not hesitate. After three hundred years of bondage there is a portal of escape, and who knows how long it will remain open?"

I sighed, Anderina doesn't want me to go to the meeting and get my hopes dashed again. She says the fare to London is impossible to find, and she is right."

"Go anyway," said Dad clapping me on the shoulder. "And don't lose hope, for the Lord has promised in his Good Book, *'that which is impossible with man is possible with God.'*"

"It is indeed," I said. And tucking this truth in my heart, I bid my parents goodbye and went home.

To Own a Fig Tree

The Meeting

The man in charge of advertising Reverend Barclay's itinerary, did his job well. In addition to newspaper adverts and handbills, every Post Office in the country displayed a large poster announcing the dates and times of forthcoming meetings. On the afternoon of an appointed day, a large group of men gathered in the parish hall in Lerwick. I took a seat, and staring through the gap between Benjamin and Peter Coutts sitting in front of me, saw a table with a glass of water and a pile of booklets on it. Near the table sat Reverend Barclay. When the hall was so packed men were crowding out the doors, the Reverend stood up, unfurled two maps and pinned them to the wall behind him. Then picking up a pointer he said:

"Gentlemen, thank you for coming. I present to you, New Zealand." He ran the point of his long stick down the map of three islands (two large and one tiny.) "A land of opportunity for hard-working men." He moved his pointer onto the world map marked with marine distances. "New Zealand enjoys a fine commercial position," he swirled his stick in a circle. "Note how close it is to the South American, Indian and Australian markets. The land is long and narrow, so export is easy. It is a land blessed with fertile soil, abundant timber and mineral wealth. In this new land, a man may better himself." He stood his stick on the floor and leaned on it in a friendly manner. "Labour and toil are necessary of course," he smiled, "for you must plant a fig tree before you gather figs."

At the mention of figs, I sat up and listened intently.

"But unlike Shetland," he whipped up his pointer and smacked it on the South Island. "This soil is good and once the tree is planted, it will grow and flourish, *merely tickle the land with a hoe and it will laugh a harvest.* What's more, your labour won't be in vain, for there are no lairds and factors to steal the fruit of your toil."

"Who owns the fish, the shells, and the seaweed?" a voice shouted.

"They are free for the taking, as are the wild birds and everything in the rivers. In New Zealand, Joe is as good as his master. If you do well, you may buy land."

A murmur of astonishment burst from our lips.

The Reverend spread out his arms and leaned forward. "An industrious man can build a good life for himself. In New Zealand, unlike here, you can gain a profitable farm, a pleasant home and education for your children. You may even vote."

"Vote!" Astonishment rippled around the room.

"How do we know this is true?" called out another voice.

Barclay unfurled a beautiful watercolour landscape and pinned it up. There was another murmur of excitement. "I have been there myself. I testify the land is a Garden of Eden, and working men eat well." He pinned up a picture of a smoking joint of mutton.

At the sight of the meat, we burst into cheers and stomped our feet. The Reverend took a sip from his glass of water.

"What about single women?" shouted Benjamin Coutts, as the noise subsided? "Are there any opportunities for them?

"Wonderful oportunities. Women and children are never

To Own a Fig Tree

employed in outdoor occupations, and they don't carry heavy loads on their backs as they do here. Instead, the children go to school while the single women are employed as servants. Wages for women are eight to ten shillings a week, with everything provided except clothing." He smiled. "But whether working or living with their families, very soon single women marry and get homes of their own, for there is a great shortage of women."

Benjamin turned his head and beamed at me. "Maybe there is hope for my girls at last."

"I've heard the natives are cannibals," came another shout.

There was an oo noise as we collectively sucked in our breath.

"False rumours," said Barclay, waving his hand dismissively. "The Maori people did occasionally practice cannibalism, but that was long ago." He laughed, "I assure you, you'll not end up in a cooking pot." He picked a booklet off the table and held it in the air. "This is a book I have written called '*Notes on New Zealand for the use of Emigrants.*'" He passed the pile to Benjamin Coutts, who was nearest to the table. "It's free. Pass these around and if you are interested, take one. In here," he held his book up again, "you will find thirty pages of information, including the discovery and settlement of New Zealand, its size and position, mineral wealth and the customs of the Maoris. Also, a collection of papers by experienced colonists on the colony including several provinces." He picked up a fistful of pamphlets. "And these are excerpts from the *Labourers Chronicle and Union*." He gave them to Benjamin. "Take one of these as well."

By now, the room was buzzing with talk. I took a book

and flicked through it eagerly. Reverend Barclay sat down and sipped his water, allowing the excitement within the room to build. Once the few remaining books were returned to the table, he stood and the room fell quiet.

"I know more Shetlanders would have taken up the offer of assisted passage last year, if it were not for the cost of getting to the docks in London." He paused until the quiet turned into expectant silence. "I am happy to announce New Zealand's colonial treasurer, Julius Vogel, has authorized the payment of passages from London to New Zealand again. Plus, New Zealand will foot the bill for the journey from Lerwick to London."

Cheering broke out.

"In addition," Barclay shouted over the hubbub, "ten pounds for travelling expenses will be paid to the head of each family."

At this, the cheering turned into roaring, stomping and whistling.

Barclay held up his hand for quiet. When we settled down, he said, "This is a big step. The journey is dangerous, and leaving loved ones will be difficult. If you are lazy, don't sign up. This offer is not for the fainthearted, or men unwilling to get stuck into hard labour. The rewards are great, but you will be tested often. Go home and think about what you have seen and heard tonight, and tomorrow I will be here to pray with any of you who are thinking about taking this step, for you will need the strength of God to embark on this glorious adventure."

We clapped, and as he sat down one of the leading brothers stood up.

"Thank you, Reverend Barclay, for that enlightening talk.

To Own a Fig Tree

The elders and I are calling for a day of prayer and fasting, that we may earnestly enquire the Lord's will in this matter. Anyone interested in emigrating, meet here tomorrow morning."

With that, he dismissed us and we went home.

———————

W.E. Hamilton

Changes Afoot

I pushed the door of my cottage open, and the pungent smell of fish and burning peat engulfed me as I stepped into the outer room. My home differed little from my parent's house. Like a spiralled time-warp, Anderina sat at the spinning wheel. Hanks of yarn hung from the rafters above her head, but only a few dried fish dangled from the roof, for it was May, the beginning of the fishing season. Mary stood by the fireplace, skimming oil from boiling livers with a ladle made from a shell and a stick.

"Well, Robert, how was it?" Anderina shot an enquiring look at me without breaking the rhythm of her hands and feet.

I hung my hat and coat by the door.

"It was a good meeting."

"Humph, I don't know why you bothered going. I hope you haven't got your hopes up."

"There was a good turnout," I said, sitting on a wooden sofa.

"I'm surprised Reverend Barclay came back," said Anderina. Her foot kept peddling the spinning wheel. "The man has character, I'll give him that, even if he is a dreamer, for travelling from England by foot or pony takes toughness; especially as last year he only recruited seventeen families from *Zetland*."

I picked up a half-finished boot and plunged an awl through

To Own a Fig Tree

the edge of the leather. "Many will go this time," I said.

The spinning wheel stopped abruptly, and my wife stared into my eyes before sucking her breath in sharply. *"Robert, you are thinking of going!"*

"It is a chance of a lifetime, Anderina," I burst out. "You should have seen the watercolour pictures Reverend Barclay showed us: a beautiful land of mountains and streams, and huge smoking joints of mutton."

My wife started her wheel with her hand and turned back to her spinning. "That's all very well, Robert, but we've gone through this before. Assisted passage to New Zealand does not mean we can afford to emigrate. It's impossible to find ten pounds for the passage to London. Even if we found buyers for the cow, the sheep, and my spinning wheel, we'd only clear what we owe the store."

"That is where you are wrong, my love," I said triumphantly. "I have seen a miracle today. This year the colonial treasurer, Julius Vogel, will pay our fares from Lerwick. It will not cost a penny to get from our door to New Zealand. Plus, we get ten pounds for expenses."

The spinning wheel stopped again, and my wife looked at me with a dazed expression. "How could we leave family and friends?"

I put down the boot and leaned forward.

"Peter Henry and his family are going."

"What about Peter's brother and sisters?"

"They are thinking about it, too. As is the Moffatt family, the Williams, and Alfred Burton."

"Alfred Burton!" said Mary, spilling oil over the side of the flagon she held. Her cheeks flushed a pretty pink. "Is he the only single man going?"

My wife's eyes focused, and her mouth settled into a grim line as she noted the rising flush on Mary's cheeks. "We are a Godfearing family. I'll not have my daughters thrown into close quarters with a bunch of reprobate sailors and heathens!"

"Reverend Barclay is a preacher; he would suggest nothing improper," I intervened hastily. "He assured us precautions are taken to ensure nothing untoward happens. The ships are divided into three areas, one for the single women, one for the single men, and one for families, moreover, the divisions between the three groups are strictly kept."

"What about the cannibals?" said Laurie, throwing pebbles up and down.

"Cannibals" exclaimed Anderina.

I frowned at Laurence.

"There are no cannibals," I said, glossing over the rumour. "*Listen to what the Labourers Union and Chronicle* says. I pulled the pamphlet from my back pocket and read aloud:

"*'Not a farm labourer in England but should rush from the old-doomed country to such a paradise as New Zealand. A good land, a land of oil, olives, honey, and figs: a land wherein thou mayst eat bread without scarcity. Away then, farm labourers, away, New Zealand is the promised land for you.'*"

I let the words sink in as I put the pamphlet back in my pocket.

"Anderina," I said gently, "this is the chance we thought we'd never live to see, our chance to own land and fig trees in this life. If we stay here, we will continue being little more than slaves for the lairds and factors, but if we go, we can become self-reliant, beholden to no man."

To Own a Fig Tree

My wife stopped peddling and the wheel slowed to a halt. The puff of wool in her hand was sucked into the shaft of the spindle, but Anderina took no notice. She stared into the air with a preoccupied look.

"We cannot better ourselves here," I continued, "for you know our toil is not rewarded. When we improve the croft, the factor raises our rent. If we stay, we live with the constant threat of being thrown out of our home to make room for the laird's sheep. As I see it, we don't have a choice, we have to go."

The last sentence was a mistake. My wife shook herself and gave me a hard look. "Of course we have a choice, Robert. God gives us the strength to bear what we must, and looks after us in times of trouble."

"That is true, but should we spurn his deliverance when he makes a way of escape?"

My wife stared into the air again. The water in the pot of potatoes bubbled over the top and hit the fire with a hiss of steam, but she took no notice. Elizabeth, seeing her mother was distracted, rolled up her knitting and took the pot off the hook.

"Anderina," I said, taking her hands. "Have you forgotten the poor folk of the Garth estate whose laird took away their ancient grazing rights? These last seven years, they have barely survived without sheep. Yell and Unst are near us, if our laird stops our sheep grazing on the Common, we will starve."

The door opened, and Margret came in, carrying a pail of milk. At this, my wife shook herself and retrieved the wool jammed in the spindle.

"It is dinner time. Stop juggling, Laurie, and set the table."

W.E. Hamilton

Lawrence put his pebbles in his pocket, and laid spoons and plates on the table. Anderina left her spinning wheel, and dropping potato and fish into a cup, mashed them into a smooth mixture. Then, calling the family to dinner, she lifted James onto her knee as she sat down.

I took the head of the table opposite her, with our children between us. When everyone was quiet and their heads bowed, I prayed:

"Dear Lord, thank you for giving us food. May it make our bodies strong. Protect Robert as he sails to the Continent, and bring John and the other fishermen back from the *haf'* safely. Amen."

"Amen," came the echo, before spoons clattered on plates.

The older children ate quietly, their ears flapping, aware momentous things were afoot. Only Willie ate his potato and fish with whole-hearted concentration. He was a sturdy little chap, small but strong like a young calf, quite the opposite of wispy James, who listlessly supped potato from his mother's spoon.

When she finished eating, Anderina poured the tea into cups before turning to me with the light of battle in her eyes.

"And what about the children's schooling? For two years now, schooling has been available for all children. I don't want the girls growing up illiterate like me."

"Reverend Barclay says there are schools in the new colony, and I promise you, if we find ourselves in a place where there are no schools, I will teach the youngsters to write just as I taught our older children."

"Even the girls?"

"I promise."

To Own a Fig Tree

"Humph," said my wife. She was silent for a few minutes while she drank thoughtfully. The children and I kept quiet, watching her from the corner of our eyes while we ate and drank. At length, Anderina looked up and stared at me.

"We are getting too old to up stake and move to the other side of the world, Robert. I am forty and you are forty-five."

"And fit as a fiddle. Why, forty-five is nothing! Benjamin Coutts is keen to go."

My wife's eyes flew open. "What, old Benjamin and Barbara?"

"That's right."

"They must be in their sixties."

"Seventies," I said triumphantly, "Benjamin is seventy-nine and Barbara is seventy."

"Why would they go?"

"Three dependant daughters, two of them over forty. With women outnumbering men two to one here, most women will never marry, whereas, in New Zealand, even Clementina and Elspeth will find husbands, for the shortage is the other way around."

"Yes, but what kind of husbands? Godless-heathens I expect."

"Not so, my dear. New Zealand is only calling for people who are sober, industrious, of good moral character, of sound mind and in good health. They take nobody without a certificate of character from employers and clergy." I leaned forward and pulled the pamphlet from my pocket once more. "Listen to this: *'We are now offering free passage to all who can pass the selection. We do not want paupers or infirm people, but able persons willing to work. All kinds are in urgent demand, especially good domestic servants, and agricultural workers. Wages in New Zealand are good and employment abundant, and no accumulation of a depraved idle class, while squalor and poverty are not seen.'"*

Anderina said nothing, but I could see she wore her 'thinking face.' As everyone had finished eating, I reached for the bible in the centre of the table and opening it, read to the next generation:

"Exodus chapter three, verse seven. And the Lord said, I have surely seen the affliction of my people... and have heard their cry by reason of their hard taskmasters; for I know their sorrows, and I am come down to deliver them... and to bring them up out of that land unto a good land flowing with milk and honey."[20] Then I shut the Bible.

"Dear Lord, thank you for seeing our affliction. Give us the courage to take your window of escape. Amen."

"Amen," said everyone but Anderina.

Then, just as the days of my youth, the room exploded with talking and shouting. John took the *daibodi*, Elizabeth took the fishing lines from the cupboard, while Mary and Anderina pulled jumpers and hats on William and James. Once we were outside, I swung William up onto my shoulders and grabbed his ankles. Anderina lifted James onto her hip, and we fell into step as Elizabeth, Margret, and Laurence ran ahead of us. Mary and John kept a respectful distance behind, far enough to let their mother and I feel like we were talking privately, but close enough to be within earshot. The *toonie-dog* barked and turning our heads we saw a small collie herding straying sheep away from the crops.

---

[20]   King James Bible

To Own a Fig Tree

"Do you really think it's possible the laird might take away our ancient right to graze the *skattald*[21], Robert?" said Anderina, regarding the dog.

"Not possible, Anderina, *probable*. Since when did the lairds do anything for anyone other than themselves? If they think they will make more money by grinding the poor harder, they will surely do it. Consider the fishing. The profit from fishing falls to the rich, while the toil and danger fall on the poor."

"What does your father think?" said Anderina.

"If he didn't have the duties of a magistrate, he would go himself, for he has been praying for this all his life and is glad he's lived to see it. But his duty and care for the islanders keep him here."

"Dear Dad Johnson," said Anderina, "he's a good man. Does he think we should go?"

"Yes. We would go with his blessing."

"What about your brother, Arthur?"

"He is not leaving, for his wife is not willing. If we go, he won't have to fish the *haf'* for he can take over our croft."

My wife stopped as if her legs were rooted to the ground. "You speak as if it is definite and you have already signed up, Robert."

"I have not signed anything, my love, for I will not force you. If you absolutely refuse to go, I will stay here."

Anderina plodded down the slope towards the beach once more.

"I suppose Arthur will have to keep fishing for a living if we don't go."

---

21   common land

"Don't worry about that. If he doesn't get our croft, it is likely there will be plenty of others to choose from, for a great multitude of Shetlanders are thinking of taking up the offer. So many, the leading brothers have set aside tomorrow as a special day of prayer and fasting, and Reverend Barclay has promised to pray with anyone thinking about going to New Zealand."

"Are you going to the meeting, Robert?"

"Certainly, for we need guidance to stay as much as we need guidance to go."

We were almost at the beach by now. Elizabeth, Margret, and Laurence skipped about the shore playing with their friends. As in the days of my youth, the early birds had their darbodis in the tideway, while others spat limpets into baskets. The thunder rumbled, and every head turned skyward.

"I don't like the look of those dark clouds," said Anderina. "It's Friday. The men should be back for the weekend by now. Robert, your eyes are better than mine, can you see the boats?"

I squinted into the distance. "I see nothing other than seabirds riding on the wind."

"I hope they won't risk staying out too long for the sake of their hooks," said Anderina. "Lives are worth much more than fishing tackle. Those open boats are little protection in the deep ocean if a storm blows up."

"Don't fret, Anderina, John will be fine," I said, lifting William off my shoulders. He stood on his sturdy little legs, looking at the water as he sucked two of his fingers. "There are few boats as buoyant as those sixerns. Many times, when I was little more than a boy, I and five other men rowed forty-five miles out to sea and never drowned once."

To Own a Fig Tree

But my wife was not in the mood to be comforted.

"Yes, and what about the great gale of July 1832, when seventeen boats and one-hundred-and-five men were lost!"

"All the more reason for emigrating to New Zealand," I said, as Mary handed us sacks. "If we work hard, one day we might own land, and our sons will not have to go to sea. But if we stay here, they will all have to fish." I saw my wife waver, so I added, "Their lives will be hard; they will cart herrings to the Continent like Robert, or like John, live in primitive huts among offal between fishing trips. If the weather is fine, they'll stay out on the ocean two or three nights at a time, with little sleep, and insufficient oat cakes and water. We could lose all our sons in one storm, and if they survive the sea, the British press gangs will pluck them from their boats."

Anderina shivered. "I know, I know, you are not telling me anything I don't know and dread."

The children came running up with their bags filled with shellfish.

"Well, what do you all think about emigrating to New Zealand?" I said, as I pulled a limpet from its shell. "I want to sail on a big ship," mumbled Laurence, through a mouthful of limpets.

Elizabeth spat her limpet into the *daibodi*. "I want to go."

Mary was eager for adventure, and Margret wanted to see whales, while William and James were too young to care.

I spat a limpet into the *daibodi* and grinned. "Looks like you are outvoted, Mother."

"That will be the day!" snorted Anderina with a hint of a grin. "My vote carries more weight than the lot of you put together."

W.E. Hamilton

By now we had chewed enough bait, so the subject was dropped, for we were too busy catching fish or scanning the horizon to speak of it. Just as the sun set and the light turned into a weird haze, a shout came from the beach:

"I see boats!"

And sure enough, when I squinted, the small smudges way out at sea turned into little square sails.

Nobody waited for them to come in, for we knew it would be sometime before the boats landed on the beach. Nevertheless, it was reassuring to know they were in sight. When we got home, Anderina put the younger children to bed, while Elizabeth, Mary, and I cleaned the fish. When we finished, I carried the *daibodi* into the byre behind the cottage, and put it beside a barrel of salted herrings. When I got back to the house, I passed the bed beside the peat fire in the outer room, where James and William were asleep. I could see by the light of the iron lamp they had kicked off their blanket. I pulled it over them before going through to the best room on the other side of the wooden partition.

Unlike the utilitarian *But*-end of the cottage, the *Ben* had a wooden floor and a ceiling of lathe and plaster. Moreover, the medley of cupboards lining the *But* were missing. Instead, white plastered walls peeped between box-beds and sea-chests. On the mantelpiece above the glowing fire at the end of the room, sat Anderina's clock. And on either side of the clock was a jar of sweeties, and a vase of silk flowers. I sat on the bench facing the fire, and took off my boots before walking towards the largest box-bed. Anderina's woollen dress and shawl lay folded on a chair, and the door of the bed was ajar. Her hair, that she usually wore in a bun at the back of her head, was

To Own a Fig Tree

neatly plaited and the long braid hung down her chemise. I stripped down to my knitted underwear, and (taking the candle with me) pushed the door open and climbed in beside her.

"There is no point trying to sleep until John gets back," I said, setting the candle on a small shelf jutting from the wall at the foot of our bed.

Anderina nodded. "There will be no sleep until we know he's safe."

"Robert..." Anderina paused as Mary and Elizabeth came into the room. "Shut the door, I need to talk in private."

I leaned out and pulled the door closed.

"What about James?" she whispered, "I see there are advantages to leaving, but what about James? How far away is New Zealand?"

"About twelve-thousand miles."

"That's a long way. How long do you think it would take to get there?"

"Well, it depends on the wind, but I think two-and-a-half months is normal."

Anderina spoke slowly and softly. "Many children die on those voyages."

"Yes, they do."

We were both silent for several minutes. Finally, Anderina said, "I fear James will not survive a sea voyage."

"If it is God's will for James to die, my dear, land or sea makes no difference to the outcome." I sighed as I remembered our dead children.

There was another long silence before she said, "You are right; nothing saved our first Elizabeth and Laurence."

"We lay in silence, watching the flickering candlelight

until we heard John come in. I opened the door of our bed and handed him the candle as he came close.

"Praise be to the Lord you are back safe and sound, my son."

Anderina leaned across me, and poking her head out briefly, said: "Fish and potatoes in the pot on the bench, John, I saved you some. Blow out the lamp when you are done."

John dropped his tackle-box on the floor wearily. "Thanks, Mum."

"How was the trip?" I said.

"The usual grind. Did anything happen while I was away?"

"Yes, something *has* happened. I will tell you all about it tomorrow." I reached for the handle of the bed's door.

"Goodnight Mum and Dad," said John.

"Goodnight, John," I said. And pulling the door shut, I blew out the candle.

To Own a Fig Tree

Anderina Makes Up Her Mind

It was Saturday, not Sunday, nevertheless, John and I put on our sabbath clothes, and (without eating) walked to the parish hall in Lerwick. When we got there, the place was crowded with men, mostly the heads of families. Some like me, had brought their older sons along. The atmosphere was charged with hope, and as we milled about talking, excitement rose. When the hall was so packed there was standing room only, Reverend Barclay called for silence and addressed us.

"Gentlemen, we have come to seek the will of God concerning emigration. It is a big step and not for the faint-hearted. If after prayerful consideration, any of you want to go to New Zealand, I will be at the back of the room for you to sign up. So, without further ado, let us draw near to God in prayer."

Every man (his hat in his hand) bowed his head.

"Dear Lord," said the Reverend, "we bring this serious matter before you. Freedom is so important you gave us the choice to choose or reject you. Give these men the courage to flee their oppressors. Amen."

The Reverend's prayer resounded in every man's heart, and by now the collective mood was electric. Then the leading brothers prayed one by one, and after them the rest prayed. Hours passed as we devoutly sort the will of God, and as we prayed, fears gave way to a growing sense of destiny. Soon it was clear, God Almighty himself, had paid our fare to New Zealand, and by the end of the day, a long queue waited at the Reverend's desk.

I wanted to sign up there and then, but I was not willing to without Anderina's consent. It was after lunch by the time we got home.

"Do you still want to go?" said Anderina.

"Yes, and God (through the New Zealand Government) will foot the bill of one-hundred-and fifty-two pounds fifteen shillings and sixpence to get us from Lerwick to Nelson."

"That is an enormous amount, Robert," Anderina cried. "We might get a huge bill when we get there!" At the sound of her raised voice, James (who was having an afternoon nap) stirred. She stopped speaking and stared unseeingly through the window. "I've not held as much as a pound note before," she whispered. "We could never pay it back!"

"Reverend Barclay assured us there is no charge. Moreover, the wages are high in New Zealand and we will easily find work. Indeed, he even showed us advertisements in a Nelson paper calling for labourers and farm hands."

"They are paying big money, Mum," said John, "a week's wage is worth more than a season's fishing."

"And best of all, it is cash," I said, "no more slaving under this evil system of truck. We don't have to swap our labour for goods from the laird store."

"When would we be going if we went?" said Anderina, flicking back to practicalities.

"After Robert takes his able seaman exam," said John.

"August!" Anderina's voice was loud again. "So soon?"

To Own a Fig Tree

"Eighty-four people are leaving in three weeks. Compared to that, August is heaps of time, Mum," said John.

Anderina said nothing.

The front door opened and Mary and William came in. Mary leaned her spade against the wall.

"Are we going?" she asked, her face aglow with excitement.

"Mum doesn't want to," said John.

Mary's face fell.

"Am I the only one who doesn't want to leave Granny and Grandpa and all the aunties and uncles?" Anderina cried. "Don't you realize we will never see them again? What if the natives are wild and fierce? If we hate New Zealand we can never return!"

I sighed. "The advantages of emigration are enormous, but leaving your family is a lot to ask. I won't force you." I took the spade from beside the door and went out to the potato patch. I did not dig long before Anderina came and sat on a nearby rock.

"Robert, do you really think God wants us to go?"

I stopped digging and leant on my spade.

"I do," I said fervently. "It is a chance to escape three hundred years of bondage. A chance for our sons to escape drowning, and our daughters to find husbands and homes of their own."

I almost stopped breathing as I watched my wife fiddling indecisively with the tassels of her shawl. Finally, she spoke.

"You win. If you think it is the right thing, I'll go."

"Thank you, thank you, my love," I cried, throwing down my spade. Then, for fear she might change her mind, I ran all the way back to Lerwick to sign the emigration papers.

W.E. Hamilton

Preparations

I got back from Lerwick so late the younger ones were in bed.

"Well, I've done it. We are going."

"So much to do," said Anderina.

Mary laid a hand on her mother's shoulder. "I can help with the packing, Mum."

I pulled some sheets of paper from my pocket. "Reverend Barclay is going to help us through the maze of administration involved. He gave me a pack of information to help us prepare for the journey." I sheafed through the pages and handed some to my wife.

"There is no point giving them to me, Robert. You know I can't read. Give them to Mary and she can read them to me tomorrow. And that is another thing," she added gloomily, "I suppose it is written in that silly English."

"Of course it is, Mum," said John, "our Gaelic dialect is not a written language."

"And I will have to speak English in New Zealand."

"You will be fine. You speak English as good as anyone," I said.

"Aye, but I don't enjoy it."

"It won't matter, half of Shetland is coming with us. You'll have plenty of opportunities to speak our comfortable old language with friends."

To Own a Fig Tree

"It's all too much to think of. I'm going to bed," said Anderina. "Mary, bring your candle and come with me. You men, leave your dishes on the bench when you are finished. Elizabeth can wash them tomorrow."

The next morning when the news broke, the entire household was excited. That sabbath, the talk after the church meeting was all about emigration. Many of the congregation were going. As was our custom, we spent the Sabbath resting. The next day, Margret and Laurence set off for school and I spread a wad of forms over the table.

"Time to start the paperwork," I said. "Reverend Barclay said to fill out as much of the forms as we can, and he will help us through the difficult bits."

"Shall I read you the paper Dad gave me last night, Mum?" said Mary, seeing her mother pick up her knitting."

Anderina nodded. "A good way to spend a wet day."

"Emigration regulations," read Mary. *"The ships employed to bring out immigrants are carefully chosen and thoroughly inspected before starting."*

"That's good," said Anderina.

"They are all under the provisions of the Passenger Act."

"What does that mean?"

"Something to do with the law," I chipped in, as I wrote, *'Robert Johnson born, 1825,'* on a form.

"There is a doctor on board, and a matron in charge of the single women..."

"A matron, that's good. I suppose you, (being of age) will be with the single women, Mary."

"I suppose so."

"I'm pleased to hear there is a doctor on board," said

W.E. Hamilton

Anderina, "I must take my midwifery bag, he might need help."

"An excellent idea," I said,

Mary bent her head over the papers again, "...*these along with the captain, on arrival in port, receive according to their efficiency and good conduct, gratuities from the Government.*"

"What on earth does that mean?" said Anderina. Her nimble fingers deftly knitted a snowflake pattern.

"Yes, Dad," said Mary, swivelling to look at me. "What *does* that mean?"

"Hmm, gratuities… I think it's money. "Read it again."

"*These with the captain, on arrival in port, receive according to their efficiency and good conduct, gratuities from the Government.*"

"Ah, I've got it now. If we say they have run a good ship, they get bonus money. If we complain, they don't."

"That's fair," said Anderina, "it means they'll be careful to treat us well."

"*The 'tween-decks' of all the ships are divided into three compartments, kept carefully distinct and separate, for single men, married couples, and single women.*"

"As it should be, all good and proper."

"*A liberal scale of rations has been adopted, under which each immigrant receives beef, pork, preserved meat, vegetables, tea, coffee etc, and bread. Children under twelve years of age are specially provided for.*"

"I wonder what children under twelve being specially provided for means?"

"Perhaps it is rations of milk and eggs," I said.

Anderina nodded. "You'd best look into it, Robert, for James needs extra nourishment."

To Own a Fig Tree

Mary continued:

"*Immediately after the sailing of an immigrant ship from England, the Agent-General for New Zealand forwards to the Colonial Government, by overland mail...*"

John snorted. "How can it be forwarded to New Zealand over land?"

"*A list is forwarded,*" said Mary, frowning at her brother, "*containing the names and occupations of all on board. A summary of this list is published in the local papers...*"

"See my love," I interrupted, "Robert, John and I will start earning as soon as we get there."

"*...With an advertisement stating that applications for the classes of labour therein specified will be received by the Immigration Department,*" continued Mary. She looked at me over the top of the page. "What does *that* mean?"

I wasn't sure, but I didn't want to admit it so I said, "it doesn't concern women, don't worry about it."

"*Each immigrant ship is, on arrival, immediately visited by the Health Officer and Immigrations Commissioners. If the state of the health is satisfactory, the Commissioners go on board and inspect all the arrangements. The immigrants are mustered, and inquiries are made as to comfort, discipline, and general conduct of all on board.*"

"That must be when we get to report on them," said my wife with satisfaction.

"*The immigrants are asked if they have any complaints to make, either of the quality or quantity of the provisions and water supplied to them, and generally if they have been comfortable and satisfied on the voyage.*"

Anderina nodded. "I told you so."

W.E. Hamilton

"All the compartments of the ship, the surgery, hospitals, lavatories, closets, etc, are inspected and any defects noted. In case of complaints or bad conduct on the part of either the officers or of the immigrants, a strict inquiry is instituted before the report of the Commissioners is sent in."

"That's reasonable."

Mary shuffled the paper to the back of the wad. "This next one is advice about what to take."

Anderina nodded.

A great mistake made by many emigrants, particularly those with little money..."

"That's us," said John.

"The mistake," repeated Mary, *"arises from the supposition that nothing can be obtained in the colony, or at any rate everything is very dear in price. This is not so."*

A sigh of relief passed through the room.

"Purchase nothing you can do without, but bring your capital in cash. Clothing brought from England is very frequently unserviceable in the New Zealand climate, and English agricultural implements are unsuited to the requirements of a bush farm."

"If they don't use spades, what do they use?" burst out John.

"Garden hoes. Don't you remember Reverend Barclay saying, 'tickle the land with a hoe and it will laugh a harvest?'" I said. "Perhaps New Zealand is so fertile you just scratch the dirt and scatter seeds."

"Fancy that! Growing potatoes without having to carry fertile soil from the common," said Anderina, beaming. "No more heavy loads to bend my aching back."

To Own a Fig Tree

"Emigration is sounding better and better," said John.

"Carry on, Mary," said Anderina.

"Very little furniture goes a long way at first in the colony. You will be astonished at the variety of uses to which packing cases and boxes can be turned. A few stretchers, in leu of beds, can be obtained cheap, and a form or two may replace chairs for a short time until you have begun to count your savings."

"Very good," I said, "we won't take any household goods."

Anderina's face crumpled into dismay. "What about my spinning wheel and clock, Robert?"

"We will sell them. The cow and the butter churn will be sold as well, but we'll keep them until the last moment for the sake of James. We can leave the beds for Arthur, along with the peat and manure pile."

Anderina drew her shoulders back and her eyes bored into me. Apprehension filled me, for I knew that look all too well.

"You can sell the cow and the spinning wheel, Robert, and Arthur will value the dung, but nobody's going to waste money on a frippery like that clock. It cost me a great deal of toil and sacrifice. If the clock does not go, I do not go!"

"We'll take it," I said hastily.

"We can also sell the sheep," said John, steering the conversation away from the clock. "And if we sell them in July, we get June's wool harvest."

"That's right," I looked out the window furtively and lowered my voice. "But if we wait until August, before selling the sheep and wool, we can trade them for cash."

"Sell the sheep to someone other than the storekeeper?" echoed Anderina, her eyes flying open fearfully. "We will be evicted like all the others who sold their goods for cash!"

"Eviction won't matter because we are going," I whispered. "If we get cash, we can pay our account off. I'm not risking Hay blocking us from leaving because of unpaid bills."

"Everything familiar is slipping away," said Anderina, trembling. "We don't even know if Robert wants to come."

"It's alright, love, Robert will relish the adventure," I said. I rose from my chair, and going over to my wife, put my arm around her. "I know how you feel."

Anderina swivelled her head and looked me hard in the eye. "*Do you,* Robert?"

"Of course. Do you think it is easy for me to defy the storekeeper, or leave the house I built with my own hands on the land where I grew up?"

"I suppose not."

"At the moment we can only see the losses, but when we are in the promised land you will have two cows, an even bigger spinning wheel, land and a fig tree. You will look back on this time and be glad we took the opportunity of a better life."

When I finished speaking, the room was silent for a few minutes before Anderina sighed and said:

"You are right, Robert. Now, Mary, read me the next bit."

I went back to the table as Mary continued.

"Apparel can only be safely bought out in soldered tin cases. In ordinary boxes, the moth and damp make sad havoc, and the owner on arrival at the port will probably find most of his or her clothes spoilt."

"All those sea chests we had to take instead of oats will come in handy after all," I said.

Anderina nodded and pointed her knitting at John. "Make yourself useful, son. If you are not going to dig the garden, get a pen and paper, I need a list."

John roused himself from the hearth where he was sitting, and searched in a cupboard until he found a pen and paper.

"What do you want me to write," he said, dipping his pen into my bottle of ink?

"*Pack clothes in the soldered tin cases, use wooden sea chests for other things,*" read Mary. "*The immigrant should bring out little if any clothes that cannot conveniently be taken out and aired occasionally during the voyage.*" Mary shifted the sheet to the back of the pile in her hand. "This one is advice to single women from a girl who has made the journey."[22]

"Make a separate list for Mary, John."

"*Bring as few things as you can, luggage being one of the most troublesome things possible for single women.*"

"Very sensible."

"*Each of you must have one box you can get at, once a month during the voyage.*"

"*A box each!* I'll buy one more trunk and that is all. The youngest only need two trunks between the four of them.

"*Into it put all your best things. Each must also have a large carpet bag with a good lock.*"

"Carpet bags, John."

"*In it put twelve shifts, to save washing, for if you have to wash them with salt water it spoils them.*"

"*Twelve shifts!* I don't think so. Salt water will have to do. Write three shifts each, John."

"*Also, eight to ten pairs of stockings…*"

"*Ten stockings!* Three is ample of anything. One for best,

---

22   Advice to single women taken from Chamber's Journal Feb. 14th 1874.

one off, and one in the wash."

John dipped his pen in the inkwell and scratched 'three stockings' on Mary's list as she read:

"Two flannel petticoats besides the one you have on, so that you may have enough to last through the voyage. Have also a red flannel jacket to wear at night."

Anderina's lips went thin.

"Not red, but a flannel jacket for the night is a good idea."

"Bring plenty of pins and needles with you, as well as any work you could bring to do during the voyage, knitting or sewing, thread for tatting or anything you can get. Each must have her own bag, which you will be allowed to keep in your berth, and you will get to them when you like. Let the boxes be properly addressed and stitch an address on each of the bags."

"Pins, needles, knitting, sewing, stitch name tags on all bags, John."

"You should have a small box of three-shilling tins of baking powder, or you will have nothing to eat but ship's biscuits. You get your flour weighed out to you and you can mix the powder in it and it will make very good bread. Don't omit that. Carbonate of soda and tartaric acid might do, but not so well as the baking powder. A large tin of biscuits would be a good thing to bring. Some brandy and a little ginger wine are also good to have."

"Baking powder, biscuits, and medicinal brandy." My wife switched her attention to me. "We must use some of the money for expenses to purchase a proper medicine cabinet, Robert. I would feel much easier about the trip if I knew we were properly prepared for sickness. I've seen pictures of nice ones in the catalogues."

To Own a Fig Tree

"That is an excellent idea, my love. Next time you go to the store, get them to order us one."

"The female emigrants are divided into messes of six or eight persons, and each mess has a table. You must keep a good lookout for yourself and keep all your things locked up. Be frank, obliging, and kind to all, but make a friend of no one, and keep your tongue still for there is always some scandal and bother going on: so be advised, and keep to yourself on the voyage."

"Sensible advice."

"Wear a hat when you board the ship and have a dress in your bag to wear on Sunday, with collar and cuffs. You must also have some light print frocks to wear in the tropics. You will need three, which you can have in your box, as you will get them out, there being a general turn-out of boxes to let people get their light things for the heat."

"Two dresses will do."

"After that comes the cold for which you must have worsted cuffs, and a good warm jacket to wear all day, also a shawl or cloak to take round you for the cold is severe. All your dirty clothes you will get washed at the immigration barracks when you land. Have some little bits and things to put around your neck because you soon start to look shabby and they help to make you look tidy."

"Shawl and cloak." Anderina's fingers stilled, and she looked into the air thoughtfully. "Severe cold. Hmm. Write down 'extra blankets', John." John dipped his pen in the inkwell as Anderina's fingers resumed their rapid movements.

"Above all, do not answer any letters that may be written to you by any of the sailors or young men, for as they are not

allowed to speak, they write. You know they dress and go to church on board just the same as on land. Be sure to have your Bible and some of Spurgeon's sermons handy to read. Also, have a coarse apron to put on when it is your turn to wash up the dishes for your mess."

"Excellent advice, our spinning aprons will do very well."

"We don't have any of Spurgeon's sermons," said Mary, looking troubled.

"'We have the Bible and Foxe's Book of Martyrs," said Anderina, "and that is enough for anyone."

"I am relieved to hear they keep the sabbath aboard," I said, pausing in my task.

"Indeed," said Anderina. "Does it say what the men need, Mary?"

"Six shirts, three Guernsey or flannel shirts, six pairs of stockings, one pair of good stout boots, one pair of good stout shoes, one suit of warm winter clothing, one suit of light clothing and an extra pair of trousers, one light cap, and one warm cap or sou'wester."[23]

"I think half the number of shirts, but no shoes, homemade boots will do well enough."

"The sou'wester is a good idea, though," I said.

"Yes," nodded Anderina."

I looked at the page before me and scratched my head. "What years were the children born?"

"Robert was 1853, Mary 1854, John 1858, Elizabeth 1862, Margret 1865, Laurance 1867, William 1870, and James 1872." Anderina's lips curved slightly. "I can't write, but I remember

---

23   Taken from the 19th-century Emigrant experience NSW State Library

the dates my babies were born. And not only my children, I know the birthday of every child I delivered into this world," the curl turned into a smile of satisfaction. "And I have not lost a single one." A look of pain crossed her face as she thought of two little graves in the churchyard. "At least none at birth."

The door opened and Elizabeth came in with her little brothers.

"Willie did half of the milking this morning," she said, carrying the pail of milk over to the bench. "And James managed a couple of squirts into the bucket."

"What good boys," said Anderina, putting down her knitting and scooping James onto her knee. She glanced at Elizabeth, "Pour some of that into a pitcher before you set the rest aside, Liz, I want James to have cream in his milk."

Elizabeth nodded, and taking a blue enamel jug from a shelf on the wall, tipped a quantity of thick creamy milk into it. Then she poured the rest into a preserving pan and covered it with a clean cloth. Meanwhile, my wife lifted hanks of wool down from the rafters with a hook on the end of a pole.

"We have a lot to do before we go. John, get the long knitting needles, seeing it's so wet, you can start knitting blankets. The girls and I will knit the smaller ones for the younger children and some lightweight ones, but you men will have to knit the heavy ones as usual." Anderina picked out all the greenie-brown hanks of coarse yarn. "We will use the kaki wool, take the finest white wool with us, and trade the rest."

"Why does the wool go green?" said William.

"The seaweed makes it that colour," said Mary. "When the grass is hard to find, the sheep eat seaweed."

Anderina finished selecting wool and put the pole away,

as John took the yard-long wooden needles from the corner where they lived.

James pulled his thumb out of his mouth. "I see sheeps on the beach eating weed."

"Yes, you have seen the sheep on the beach," said Mary, lifting the butter churn onto the table while Elizabeth skimmed the cream off yesterday's milk. "And Mummy, is going to knit you a nice warm blanket from their wool."

There was a lull in the conversation as the girls took turns churning the butter, and my older sons cast hundreds of stitches on their needles. Meanwhile, I wrote 'born in Brindister Aisting,' beside my and my children's names, but next to Anderina's name I wrote 'born in Clousta Aisting, 1831, married, 1818, at Twatt, Aithsting.'

The day thus occupied passed swiftly, and before long Laurence and Margret arrived home from school, bursting with excitement.

"Laurance and Robert Sinclair say their folks are emigrating," said Laurence.

"And Mary and James Moffat say their family is going too," said Margret.

"So are the Kelly's and the Henry's and the Lawrenson's."

"Jessie's mother swapped a basket of knitting for trunks and packing cases," said Margret.

"And George says..." Laurence's eyes grew round with wonder, "his family won't be fishing for pitlock tonight, because there is no need to gather fish for the winter."

This was shocking, but several families must have thought the same way because that evening, only a few people fished from the wharf, and the number of boys dragging *daibodis* through the riptide were significantly less. And that was not the end of it. Already the patterns and habits of centuries were altering. Men who year in and year out fished the *haf'*, and sailed the herring ships, were not reenlisting. Among them were John and Robert.

"Of course I want to emigrate," said Robert, when he came home and heard the news. "I'll tell the laird I'll do one more trip." He grinned. "I never thought I would have a chance to see the Southern Ocean. I can't wait to see if the tales of monstrous waves are true."

"Monstrous waves?" said Anderina, her eyes flying open as she sucked in her breath sharply.

"Just sailor's tall tales," I soothed, "you know how men are when they get together."

Anderina's face relaxed, and she nodded. "The fish stories get bigger with each telling."

"That's right," I said, frowning at my son.

Time moved swiftly and at the end of May, the village infidels farewelled the first eighty-four emigrants with music and dancing, while the Godfearing prayed for their safe voyage every sabbath. Between minimal fishing and farming duties, Anderina and I sorted out our few possessions. Some we gave away, some we traded, and some we set aside to take with us.

And changes were not confined to the home and farm. At the store the unheard of was happening; women bought calico and steamer trunks with cash, and men settled generations of debt by selling sheep and cattle.

"That has to be one of the best moments of my life," I said to Anderina, as we walked away from the laird's store. "I never thought I would see the day we would pay for travelling supplies with cash."

"Aye, we stretched the allowance and still have money left. That will tide us over in the new country." My wife looked at the wooden cabinet in her arms. "This medicine chest is a beauty. I feel safer now we have tonics for James and plenty of quinine for the tropics." She sighed, "I wish I'd had it when the first Elizabeth and Laurence were sick."

There was a sad pause before I said, "It is handsome. Are you sure it is not too much for you? All those glass bottles make it heavy."

Anderina shook her head. "I'm fine. This is easy work compared to grubbing thistles and toting rocks. I've wanted a medicine chest for years, but never thought I'd get one."

"This is just the beginning, my dear. Today it is a medicine chest, in the new world it will be land and fig trees."

But land and fig trees were too far in the future for Anderina. Her mind was still on the treasure in her arms.

"The little drawer where the scales and the mortar and pestle are kept, is ingenious," she said. Her shoulders went back and she held her head high. "I bet the medicine chest in the laird's big house is not as good!"

"Aye, and the boxes behind his carriage are not a whit better than this one," said Robert, pulling the trunk on his shoulder forward a little.

Margaret giggled and hitched up a bundle of canvas bags. "It looks like a pirate's chest with its big padlock and wooden ribs."

"No, it doesn't," said Laurence, swinging an iron camp oven. "Pirate's chests have rounded tops, ours is flat."

"Will we have enough time to make our travelling clothes,

To Own a Fig Tree

Mum," said Mary, glancing down at the bolt of green and white calico she clutched?

"Certainly. You girls and the littlies will look smart in checked frocks. The important thing is to finish them in time for a family photograph before we leave."

"A photograph!" I said, "why are we wasting money on a photograph?"

"To record this moment in history. I will have copies made for our parents; it will make the parting a little more bearable for them."

"Yes, yes, you are right," I said, feeling a little ashamed that I had not thought of it myself.

"So much to do, so little time left," Mary sighed. "Before we know it, we will leave *Zetland* forever. I'm excited about going, but it makes me sad."

And indeed, we all seesawed between excitement, hope, fear, and sadness. Daily we rode the emotional rollercoaster as we prepared to leave. Stitch by stitch, name tags were fastened to canvas and carpet bags, and fabric turned into dresses and trousers. Row by row, wool was knitted into blankets, hats and jumpers. Little by little, tea-crates were filled with bits and pieces; the camp oven, a large pot, the iron lamp, and the milk pitcher. Warm clothes went into soldered tin trunks while the medicine chest and midwifery bag, a hymn book and concertina, Robert's able seaman's certificate, and last of all the clock, were locked in the almost-pirate chest. This last box troubled Anderina.

"It's foolish to pack medical things in a trunk that will be stowed in the hold," she said, eyeing it thoughtfully. "We should keep them in our hand luggage."

"You could carry your midwifery bag," I said.

"Yes, but not the medicine cabinet. It won't fit in a carpetbag."

"What about this, Mum," said Robert, lifting a suitcase off the top of a cupboard?

Anderina smiled and nodded. "That would work well."

I scratched my head thoughtfully. "My squeezebox and the hymn book shouldn't be in there either; we need them for the Sabbath."

Robert sat the case on the floor and opened it. "There's enough room for them as well."

So, we swapped the four essentials into the case, and topped up the chest with bits and bobs. And that was not the end of the shuffling. My wife, with nervous energy, packed and repacked during the months we hung in limbo, our bodies in Shetland, our minds already sailing the sea. With growing detachment, we plucked wool from the sheep in June, and the family portrait was taken in July. At the beginning of August, we sold the wool and the sheep, then we sold the spinning wheel, and after that, we let go of the cow. Then we dressed in our travelling clothes, and settled our debt in full, because the day to depart had finally arrived.

To Own a Fig Tree

Farewell Shetland

Anderina roused the family at daybreak.

"Get up, we're not leaving without saying goodbye to Laurence and Elizabeth-the-first."

"Why?" grumbled Laurence-the-second, "they are in the land of fig trees, not the grave."

I glanced at my wife and shot my son a quelling look.

"Quite right," I whispered to him. "But today is not the day to point it out. Just humour your mother."

We dressed and hurriedly ate a bowl of oatmeal. Then Anderina took the silk flowers off the mantlepiece, and we went over the grassy dyke to two small mounds on the common.

"Goodbye, my little ones," said Anderina, as she set the vase between the two headstones. "I will never forget you."

Then we made haste, for the carts taking us to Lerwick had arrived, and the villagers were gathering to see us off. After the luggage was loaded, we hugged our loved ones, goodbye. Some of the women and children cried. Not my Anderina, however. Anderina never cried; not when she put a fish hook through her finger, not when I fell down a cliff, not when our children died. Her heart was full, but her eyes were dry as she said goodbye to her parents and siblings.

"Come Mary and Elizabeth," she said, "get on the cart, blubbing won't change a thing."

The girls sniffing, wiped their eyes with hankies and did as she bid. Then, with hands waving, and rumbling wheels, we left.

The city of Lerwick was bewildering for the women and children, who seldom ventured beyond our isolated town. One-hundred-and-sixteen of us milled about the dock like lost lambs. We were not left floundering for long. Reverend Barclay strode into our midst like a saviour. Single-handedly he retrieved order from chaos, shepherding us through the labyrinth of departure procedures.

"Did you write the name of your ship on all your boxes, Robert?" he said.

"No, I forgot."

"Here, do it now, we don't want your trunks going to China."

"Reverend Barclay, Reverend Barclay," shouts rang out.

"I'll be with you in a minute."

He thrust a brush and paint-pot into my hands. "Write, '*Ocean Mail*,' and your name in big letters."

"Reverend Barclay!"

"Coming," he cried, bustling off.

And his help did not end there; he accompanied us on the first leg of the journey, and settled our nerves so effectively that by the time the hooter blew and the paddle-wheels churned the water, we were calmly lined along the rails of the deck, silently staring at our homeland for the last time.

"To think we will never see it again," said Anderina, swapping James to her other hip as the dock reseeded.

Elizabeth squeezed William's hand and sighed. "We will never set foot on dear old *Zetland* again."

But Mary, staring back, softly quoted an old Oradian poet:

To Own a Fig Tree

"Land of the whirlpool, torrent, foam,
Where the oceans meet in maddening shock;
The beetling cliff the shelving holly,
The dark insidious rock;
Land of the bleak, the treeless moor;
The sterile mountain, seared and riven;
The shapeless cairn, the ruined tower,
Scathed by the bolts of heaven;
The yawning gulf, the treacherous sand..."

As Mary's voice faltered, Anderina and I joined in, and together we finished the poem.

"I love thee still, my native land."

We stood silent until there was nothing other than sea to look at. Then Anderina put James down, sat on a nearby seat, and opened her carpetbag.

"No point wasting emotion. Emigration is no reason for idle hands, girls," she said, taking wool and knitting needles from her bag. "Finally, we can sell our shawls for cash. In New Zetland, I won't have to choose a clock or sweeties instead of grain."

"New Zealand, my dear," I corrected, "not New Zetland."

Anderina sniffed. "Zealand, *Zetland*, take your pick. Let the rest of the world say New Zealand, it is New Zetland to me."

"Lambie," said James.

Anderina rummaged in her bag once more. "Here you go, love." She handed him a battered woollen toy before unwinding a length of yarn, fine as cotton thread.

Elizabeth let go of William's hand as she and Mary followed their mother's example, and I grabbed him as he ran towards the railing.

"Where are the others?" said Anderina, rapidly casting on stitches.

"Robert was talking to one of the sailors and they've gone to see the engine room," said Mary, "and the others went to find their friends and explore."

I thought exploring and talking to friends was more interesting than knitting. I cleared my throat and said, "I will take William for a walk, my dear."

Anderina nodded, counting softly as she multiplied stitches. So, taking my son with me, I wandered off.

For the next two days, other than mealtimes, I saw little of my family. The women knitted, the children played with friends, and I talked to the men. Everyone, apart from Robert, took turns minding William and James. Of Robert, there was no sign; for once the crew knew he had his able seaman's certificate, they were happy for him to expand his knowledge by helping out.

In this way, the time passed pleasantly, and soon we arrived at the Granton docks in Edinburgh. Once again, Reverend Barclay was a lighthouse in a storm. Without his guidance, I don't know how we would have found our way to the train. The big city and bustling station were overwhelming, but the Reverend got all one-hundred-and-sixteen of us onto the right train at the right time. Then the whistle blew and with a jerk, we moved forward, slowly at first, through the station, faster, faster, past the backyards of tenement slums until we got clear of the city. Then we clattered along at the tremendous speed of thirty miles an hour. There were plenty of things to see as we careered through the countryside pocked with small towns, for

To Own a Fig Tree

every hill and each bend brought land and streams we had not seen before. Nothing, however, caught our attention like the trees. There were so many I could not count them.

"Are they fig trees, Dad?" said Margret, her eyes wide with wonder?

I did not want to admit ignorance, so I said, "You will know when you are older."

Margret frowned. "But I want to know now, by the time I am two minutes older, these trees will have gone."

Reverend Barclay leaned across the aisle. "They are oak trees. Fig trees are smaller."

"Have you ever eaten a fig, Reverend?" said Margret.

"Yes."

"What did it taste like?"

We all leaned toward Reverend Barclay so the clickety-clack of the train would not drown out his words.

"Luxuriously sweet. You can eat it all. The skin is smooth and chewy while the reddish pulp is soft but not juicy. They are difficult to grow in England, but my mother grew a small one in a pot by a warm wall. You are not likely to see them in the fields here, but I believe they grow easily in New Zealand."

"*Tickle the dirt with a hoe and the land will laugh up fig trees*," I said, with a twinkle in my eye.

The Reverend laughed. "You're twisting my words, Robert, but that's the general idea."

'Luxuriously sweet.' The description lingered in my mind as the wheels kept rolling, rolling, rolling. By and by, our perky interest oozed into slumped postures. William and James were sleeping, Anderina was dozing, while the others (with bored faces propped on their hands) stared listlessly out the window.

W.E. Hamilton

I don't recall when my daydreams of land and fig trees slipped into sleep, but when I awoke, we were in Plymouth.

To Own a Fig Tree

The Ocean Mail

Once we were off the train, Reverend Barclay found porters for our luggage, and shepherded us from the station to the Plymouth dockyard. By now the children were very cross, and the adults little better. Only Robert sparkled with excitement as sandwiched between the Kelly and Moffatt family, we followed Reverend Barclay like a mob of sheep, past many tall ships until we came to the *Ocean Mail*.

"Our ship's a beauty," he said, scrutinizing the vessel. "Newer and better than I expected."

"Longer than I imagined," said Thomas Kelly.

"Iron ships are much bigger than the old wooden ones," said Robert. He pointed at the three tall masts. "She will fly along when the wind gets behind her sails."

"I like the sound of that," said Agnes Moffatt, lifting four-year-old Francis onto her hip. "If the last two days are a taste of travel, the less time on the sea the better."

Margret sat on her carpet bag beside the Kelly's daughter, Flora. "Florrie and I want to know when we can go on board," she whined, scuffing her toe on the ground?

"When the officials have sorted out our documents," Anderina snapped, "you'll have to be patient."

"It will be dark soon," I said, as a lamplighter leaned his ladder against a lamppost nearby. I see why they told us to get here a day before our ship sails. At this rate, I fear we will still be waiting by the time she pulls up the anchor."

It was a silly thing to say. Nevertheless, the lamplighter had been up and down his ladder so many times, a long row of lights twinkled before anything happened.

"What's going on?" said Anderina.

I leaned forward and craned my neck.

"An officer is separating people into groups."

"I hope this means we are going onboard," said Margret.

We waited expectantly, but when he came to us, all he said to me was:

"Name?"

"Robert Johnson."

He wrote it down before asking, "how many with you, Robert?"

"My wife and eight children."

"How many children under twelve?"

"Four."

He turned to Thomas Kelly.

"Name, Sir?"

"Thomas Kelly."

"How many travelling with you?"

"My wife and three children under twelve."

The official wrote the names down.

"Mr Johnson and Mr Kelly, your families will combine as a mess for the entire journey. You have your own plates and cutlery of course, however, once on board you will be given pots, jugs, a teapot and cooking utensils. Assign someone to collect your food each meal, and someone to wash the dishes afterwards. Keep your pots separate from other groups, and do not eat anywhere other than your assigned mess. For health reasons it is imperative you keep this rule." Then he turned to James Moffatt.

"Name, Sir?"

On and on it went. Lights were twinkling everywhere and the ship was lit up, before we started filing onboard.

"I shall leave you now," said Reverend Barclay as an officer motioned us forward. "Farewell, may God's favour be with you as you travel."

"Goodbye, God bless you," we called back as we stumbled up the gangplank.

Once on board, we milled about uncertain what to do until we heard the shout:

"Form a queue for inspection."

After a great deal of commotion, we shuffled into a wobbly line. When we had quietened, two men, a constable, and a woman stood before us. The captain stepped forward and spoke:

"I am Captain James Watson. Welcome aboard the *Ocean Mail*. We hope you have a pleasant journey." He pointed to the man on his right. "This is the ship's medical attendant, Surgeon Superintendent Doctor Frood. He'll say a few words, and then you will slowly file past him. After the inspection, single women follow Mrs Butt." He pointed to the woman. "She is the matron in charge. Single men follow the constable, and families follow the first mate, my brother John." John Watson nodded while we shuffled and a baby cried. "Over to you, Doctor Frood," the captain finished, stepping back as the doctor moved forward.

"Welcome everyone. It is my job to keep you all healthy and safe. To help accomplish this, there are sanitary rules between decks. This means steerage, cabin class, single men, and single women are kept strictly apart to stop the spread of disease. I will do my best to ease any discomfort you have while travelling. I look forward to getting to know you better over our journey; which hopefully will not take too long, as our esteemed captain is noted for running a fast and efficient ship. Now, please pass before me one by one."

Obediently, we shuffled forward, and the good Doctor cast his eye over each person. Occasionally he asked a question, pulled down a bottom eyelid, and inspected tongues. And sometimes we came to a halt as a man or woman was pulled from the line and told to stand aside.

"What do you think is going to happen to those people?" Anderina whispered.

"I expect they will not be allowed to sail."

Anderina swapped James to her other hip and bit her lip. "What if James doesn't pass the test? We have no money to get back home."

"No need to fret, a weak constitution is not the same as an infectious disease."

The doctor thought as I did, for our family passed under his scrutiny without comment. Once that ordeal was over, we separated into three groups. Mary and Elizabeth moved towards Matron, but she held up her hand.

"Stay with your parents, children."

"That's right, boys," said the constable, stopping Robert and John.

Robert's face flamed with anger and he drew up his stocky body. "I am not a child. I am a man of twenty-one, a qualified able seaman!"

To Own a Fig Tree

"And I am a woman of twenty," said Mary.

I stepped forward and looked up at the constable. "They are my children and what they say is true. Robert is twenty-one, Mary, twenty, John sixteen, and Elizabeth thirteen. They look far younger than they really are. Don't judge them by their height and fresh faces. We are like Shetland ponies, small but tough."

The constable ran his eye over me.

"Begging your pardon, Sir," he said to Robert. "Step this way."

Then Mary and Elizabeth went with Matron down the hatchway to the women's quarters in the stern, while Robert and John went to the men and crew's quarters in the bow. Anderina and I, along with the rest of the children, followed the second mate down the steep steps that led to the 'tween deck. There, we found ourselves in a large area made smaller by the low ceiling. In the dim lantern light, I saw what looked like stables running along the port and starboard walls, and in the aisle between them, a line of tables flanked with wooden benches. Behind us in a revolving stream, sailors carried trunks and kegs down a ladder to the hold below.

"I'm glad I am only five-foot," I said, reaching up and touching the steel beam above me. I wonder how fast the ship can go?"

"There is time enough to find out during the journey," said Anderina, as James and William started grizzling. "Come and find our berth." She glanced towards the carpenters busily sawing and hammering at the end of the room. "I hope we are not down there, it's very late to be installing the beds."

"It is indeed." I pushed through the throng and my family

followed closely as we jostled our way along the space between the benches and the berths. At last, I came to a berth with 'Robert Johnson, wife and four children,' written on it, and opened the stable door.

"Do yourself a favour and pack your bags under the beds," said Thomas Kelly from the next berth, "otherwise, there will not be enough room to get inside."

Looking in, I saw his advice was sensible, for the space was so tight I could touch the opposite walls, and the aisle between the skimpy bunks was narrow.

"It's better than I expected," I said, as I stowed the bags and cases under the bottom beds.

"Not unlike our box beds," agreed Anderina. She leaned in and sniffed the bedding. "Fresh straw in the mattresses and clean blankets." She rubbed the corner of a blanket between her fingers. "Rough but thick. I'm glad I brought extra blankets; one a bed might not be enough when we hit the cold."

"You are lucky to have four children with you, Anderina," said Eleanor, "because we only have three, we have to share our berth with strangers."

This was a mixed blessing, for by now the older children were grumpy and James and William were howling. Unfortunately, they were not the only ones. The din of crying children, shouting men, and raucous laughter was horrible.

"Margret and Laurie, sit on the top bunk and hold the boys," said Anderina, pulling a carpet bag from under the bed. "And keep your feet out of the way."

Lawrence and Margret scrambled up, and I lifted the younger children onto the bed, while Anderina (bending awkwardly in the tiny space) pulled out a blanket, a tin of biscuits, and James' lamb.

"Here you go, love," she said, handing the toy to him. Then she opened the tin and gave the children a biscuit each. "Help me rig this up, Robert," she said, pushing the bag under the bed with her foot. She tucked the edge of the blanket under the mattress of the top bunk. "The boys will settle better if we cut the chaos down."

I did as she said, and sure enough, once the boys were in bed behind the knitted curtain, they stopped grizzling. The rest of the evening passed in a blur. I think we had some kind of soup, and I know there was tea, but other than that I don't recall, for my senses were overloaded by the time I went to bed. On the whole, however, I fared better than most, for Anderina and I had a top-bunk each, while the four children slept below. This was particularly good, because after eight pregnancies my wife was stout, and sharing a bed with her like the other married couples was impractical, for there was no room for me. We were not long settled when a man shouted:

"I'm Mr Orgar, the storekeeper and the man in charge of the lamps. Lights out in another ten minutes."

Then there was a rumpus of scuffling and shouting as all those who were still up hastened to get into bed. And just as well, for it was pitch black once he snuffed the lanterns out. The noise, smells, and strange surroundings were not conducive to sleep, but after three days of travelling, we were all exhausted. Despite thinking I would not sleep, I must have dozed off, for the whistle of a steam tug awoke me at two in the morning, and when the fog of confusion cleared, I realized we were moving.

W.E. Hamilton

A Great Start

I lay on my bunk until curiosity drove me from my bed, and slipping my shirt and trousers over my long-Johns, quietly let myself out of the door. When I got on deck, I found other passengers were up there, including Robert.

"What's happening?" I shouted over the noise of the tug's engine.

"They are towing us to Gravesend," Robert shouted from the single men's area.

"I thought we would sail there ourselves," I shouted, looking at the furled sails.

"You must still be half asleep, Dad, we are not going anywhere without wind."

I nodded, feeling foolish.

"She is a grand ship," said Robert. "So much bigger than the sixerns, and newer than Shetland's merchant fleet. She's fully rigged, 1039 ton, and belongs to the New Zealand Shipping Company."

"How do you know?"

"I've been talking to the sailors."

"Of course you have," I said with a snort of laughter. "What else did they tell you?"

"She was built by Robert Thompson junior of Sunderland, and the captain says her behaviour, both as regards her sailing powers and as a sea boat, is beyond praise."

To Own a Fig Tree

"A fine recommendation. By God's grace, she will live up to it. Who's steering the ship?" I said, as I spotted the captain a distance away.

"The Thames pilot, he stays with us until we get to Gravesend, where another tug and pilot take over. I expect we wait at Gravesend until the tide is right."

I nodded, and we fell silent for it was difficult conversing at such a distance. It was lovely watching the silhouette of the land lighten into colour as the sun rose over the horizon. I stayed on deck until the breakfast gong clanged, and then I went below.

William and James sat on the bench by our berth, swinging their legs, their eyes scarcely higher than the tabletop. Opposite them sat the Kelly family, and in the centre of the table was a steaming cauldron, a jar of molasses, a teapot, and a jug of milk.

"This is a good start," said Anderina, taking tin plates from a canvass bag. "The porridge smells good and there is plenty of it."

"Where did you go, Dad?" said Margret, clambering into the gap between William and James.

"On deck. Robert and I saw the sunrise."

"I wish I'd seen it," said Laurence, taking the cup his mother handed him before sitting down.

"There will be plenty more, love," said Eleanor, ladling porridge into her family's plates.

"Have they got the sails up yet?" said Thomas Kelly, lifting two-year-old Thomas Junior onto his knee.

"No, not yet," I said, sliding in beside Laurence. "There is no wind so they are towing us."

Margret looked over at the Moffatts.

"Can Mary sit with Florrie and me?"

"No," said Anderina, setting down six plates. "You heard the man last night. We must stay at our own table."

"Why?"

"To stop disease spreading. Even the pots and pans are kept separate, so don't eat anybody else's food."

"That's right, mind you do as Mrs Johnson says, Flora," Eleanor agreed. She passed the ladle to Anderina before spooning a dollop of molasses onto her sons' porridge.

Thomas poured watery milk over their food as Anderina swiftly filled our plates. When she finished, she sat next to me.

"You can give thanks for the food now, Robert."

We bowed our heads, and I prayed:

"Dear Lord, thank you for this food. Keep us safe as we travel. Amen."

Then we picked up our spoons and started in on the porridge. While I ate, I looked around. Last night's chaos had settled into order and the din of shouting and crying was replaced with the hum of talking and laughter. Small groups of our friends were scattered at intervals along the line of tables. The mood was one of universal good temper and all seemed set on enjoying the voyage.

"Everyone looks happy," I said. "I can see the Henrys and the Williams."

"And the Stranges," said Thomas, pointing in one direction.

"I see the Jamiesons," said Eleanor, pointing the opposite way.

"Granddad and Grandma Coutts look bright and sparky," said Anderina. "I wonder how our girls are getting on?"

To Own a Fig Tree

"If the matron comes to the fence on the deck, you can ask her," I said.

Anderina smiled. "That's a good idea."

"It feels nice to be moving," said Margret, scraping her plate clean with her spoon. "Can I go up top?"

"Family devotions first," I said, opening my Bible at the book mark, "being at sea is no reason to stop our custom, we need God's protection and the comfort of his word more than ever."

Margret put her spoon down, and everyone at our table was quiet as I read a chapter. Then we sang a hymn and prayed.

"Now can I go," said Margret?

"You may leave the table," said Anderina, "but you must have a flannel wash and straighten your bed before the morning inspection."

Margret and Laurence bounced away.

"You got the food from the galley, Anderina, so I'll do the dishes," said Eleanor, as burly sailors carried tubs of steaming water down the stairs and placed them at the end of the row of tables.

Anderina looked at the rings of people forming around the tub and nodded gratefully. "We'll take it in turns, I'll do tomorrow's dishes."

When breakfast was over, Thomas and I left the women to deal with the domestic arrangements, and went on deck. Robert stood by the great coils of rope that hung from the *belaying pins* lining the *bulwarks*. He was grinning as the sailors showed him the ropes.

"Robert is happy," said Thomas.

"Yes, he's making the most of his opportunities to expand

his seafaring knowledge. I expect he will spend his time helping the sailors. We hardly saw him on the steamboat."

Thomas gave a short laugh. "Good on him. He is an ambitious man and I like that."

"There was no reward for ambition in the old country," I said in a bitter tone. "Hard work and improvements to our house and croft was always penalized by the rent rising." My tone lifted into hopefulness, "But in our new land everything will be different; ambition and toil will be rewarded with prosperity."

Thomas smiled. "I have heard the wages are good."

"Yes, and the land so fertile crops are easy to grow…"

We discussed our promising future until the woman and children came on deck. For the rest of the day, we milled about watching the changing landscape, until we arrived at Gravesend. There, we anchored, and the cabin class passengers boarded. That evening, the more frivolous English passengers danced on the deck to the music of fiddles and concertinas, while we Shetlanders, gathered with our brethren for prayers and hymn singing. We went to bed optimistic, and awoke once more to the sound of a steam tug. The weather was sunny and there was a light wind as it towed us down the Channel.

"We are finally on our way," I said, to Anderina, as the sails rose and the tug fell behind us.

"May God grant us travelling mercies," she said, staring up at the billowing canvas.

"May he indeed."

We watched England recede as Captain Watson set sail for New Zealand, and two days later, on August the twentieth, 1874, we lost sight of land.

To Own a Fig Tree

Misery

Captain Watson was a kind-hearted man with a suave manner. He and his brother, John, ran a fast and efficient ship. We got up at seven and the daily routine began with washing and dressing before breakfast at eight. After breakfast, we sent the children on deck, for the doctor had arranged for a clergyman (from the cabin passengers) to teach school during the morning. With the children out of the way, the rest of us pitched in with the chores. Berths were cleaned daily, decks scrubbed with vinegar and chloride of lime every Wednesday and Saturday, and bedding was regularly aired on deck. On the days they assigned our mess a washing day, Thomas Kelly and I, lay on our backs cradling our small children while our wives scrubbed our clothes clean, and hung them in the rigging to dry. We ate dinner at 1 pm and the afternoon was free. When the weather was nice, the single men helped the sailors mend sails and make nets. In this way, Robert and John's days flew by, but time hung heavily for those of us with children. Unfortunately, a sailor taught William to whistle, and his constant whistling (along with James' grizzling) added to the trial. The women kept busy with knitting, sewing, and mending, while we men whittled toys between rescuing our offspring from a watery death. Tea was at five and the storekeeper called: "lights out," at eight. Of Mary and Elizabeth, we saw only glimpses, for the single women were strictly chaperoned by the matron.

"And rightly so," said Anderina, looking at the wooden fence separating the girl's deck from the rest of us. "I don't trust the men in cabin class. Toffs consider lower-class women as fair game."

I whittled a slice off my wooden soldier's head.

"Yes, it is wise of the constable to insist they lock the girls in at night." I belched and shifted uncomfortably.

"Are you alright, Robert?"

"I don't feel so good."

"Neither do I," said Anderina. "I feel seasick."

I looked at the glassy water we glided over, and scratched my head.

"So do I, and yet we can't possibly be, for we are used to boats, and the sea is almost still."

It was a mystery. Despite light and favourable winds right up to *the line*[24], one by one, everyone from our group fell ill. The children wailed and the babies cried as they sweltered on their beds. I lay on the top bunk feeling more dead than alive, marvelling at my wife who (sick and nervous herself) patiently tended our fretful offspring.

"I did not expect to feel so dreadful," I groaned, as the doctor felt my stomach and looked at my tongue. "I'm usually very hardy and never ill."

"It's the diet, heat, and confinement," said the doctor. "All the Scots are debilitated. I shall recommend in future, they take more dried potatoes and oats if many passengers are Scottish."

I wiped the sweat off my brow.

"Aye, ship's biscuit and greasy pork sit in my gut like a brick."

---

24   equator

To Own a Fig Tree

"And those preserved carrots and onions are disgusting," whispered Anderina weakly. She pushed damp tendrils of hair off her red face. "I've never felt so hot. How long before the weather cools."

"I'm afraid it will get worse before it gets better," said the good doctor. "But take heart, they are bringing the trunks up so you can change into lighter garments."

"To shed these woollen clothes will be a blessing," said Anderina. "Have you got anything to help our stomachs? I've given the children everything I had for seasickness."

"Certainly."

Doctor Frood opened his black bag and brought out a bottle. "Try this," he said, uncorking it.

He gave us a dose of some foul-tasting liquid that made little difference.

"I know you feel bad, but move around as much as you can."

"Doctor Frood," came a loud urgent shout, "where is the doctor?"

"Here," he called, corking his bottle and putting it back in his bag.

A man with a face full of fear, appeared at the door of our booth. "My wife is going into labour."

The doctor shut his bag swiftly. "Where is she?"

"Follow me," said the man.

They disappeared and shortly after, we heard the commotion of a woman in distress coming from the small apartment set aside as a hospital.

"What a miserable time and place to have a baby," said Anderina, rallying herself and pulling her midwifery bag out from under the bed. "Just as well I kept my bag handy. Watch the children while I'm away, Robert. The doctor may need help."

She was gone for hours. By the time she got back, the sailors had all the trunks on deck.

"Mr and Mrs Barson have a little girl," said Anderina, smiling. "Both mother and baby are well."

I looked at my wife's glowing face.

"That is wonderful. It seems helping to deliver a baby was better medicine than the tonic."

"It was indeed," said Anderina. "Stay here while I go on deck to sort out our clothes."

"I was more than happy to stay put, for although the smell of the latrines and vomit below deck was horrible, I was too lethargic to move, moreover, my legs felt shaky and my head pounded.

Changing into lightweight clothing helped. Anderina packed the discarded clothes into our boxes, and the sailors stowed them away again. Now we were dressed more appropriately, we felt a little better. But it was short-lived relief, for the days got hotter and hotter, until the tar on the deck melted, and we felt we were in a bread oven.

"I'm sorry for the women, it must be dreadful wearing so many clothes." I said to Thomas, as we stood on the sticky boards and stripped off our shirts."

"Modesty extracts an enormous price in the tropics," said Thomas, throwing a bucket of seawater over me.

I returned the favour by throwing water over him. "It certainly does. The tropics is a hard place for women, and even harder for children."

To Own a Fig Tree

Thomas frowned and nodded. "When is the funeral?"

"At midday."

"So soon, the child has barely gone?"

"It is sensible in this heat. When the doctor finishes sewing the body into a canvas bag, the captain will hold a service."

"We should tidy up and put our shirts on," said Thomas.

It was a good idea because we had only just made ourselves respectable when the captain rang the midday bell, and everyone started gathering on the deck. I saw Anderina and the children come up through the hatch, so I hurried over to her.

"It was Emily Stanton who died," she whispered. "It's almost always the youngest children who die first. Oh, Robert," she shot a glance at James slumped on her hip, his head lolling lethargically, "I'm so afraid."

"She was very emaciated and dehydrated," I said. "James is still eating."

"Yes, but not much."

"What will be, will be, Anderina," I said with a sinking heart, "trust in God. He will do right; and if we are bereaved, he will help us through it."

"That is so," she said in a dull tone.

By now, everyone was assembled. Captain Watson stepped forward as the Stanton family and the doctor arrived with a small bundle tied to a piece of pig iron. Stephen Stanton put his arm around his wife as a sailor took the body, and lowered it onto a plank that projected over the side of the ship. The five remaining children huddled close to their parents, watching with wet eyes as an ensign was spread over their little sister. Then the captain conducted a brief funeral service and read from the Bible. As he finished with a prayer, two sailors gently removed the ensign, and lifting the end of the plank, slid the body over the side and into the water.

Sadly, the Stantons were not the only ones to lose a child. Over the next few weeks, the Solomon family lost Lilly, and the Cowelys lost Eva. Doctor Frood was unremitting in his attention to whoever required his help. Nevertheless, Anderina was regularly in and out of our medicine cabinet. She dosed us with quinine as we sailed through the tropics, rubbed ointment on heat rashes, and prepared tonics for James. I watched her as she sat at our mess table, grinding dried herbs with her mortar and pestle.

"Bless the captain for getting James an extra ration of milk," she said, dishing powder from her stone bowl onto a tiny set of scales. She added two miniature weights and removed a few grains before tipping the remaining powder into a cup. "I pray another cow will not die, for then where will we be?"

"It was a sad loss, but the cook assures me the rest are in good health. A wit wrote an obituary in the ship's newspaper."

"We have a paper?" said Anderina, pouring milk into the cup and stirring.

"Yes, some passengers started it and are passing it around for our amusement. It's called *The Champion of the Seas*."[25]

I held the article up to the lantern hanging off the beam above the table.

"Obituary," I read, *"On Thursday last, died at her residence on deck after a lingering illness, the cow. The doctor has not given any official report of the complaint under which the patient suffered. We believe, however, it was from general disabilities caused by the exhausting process carried on for*

---

25 Champion of the Seas No. 11 Monday, September 24, 1855

To Own a Fig Tree

some time, which while it made our tea more palatable, and the babies more chubby, tended to bring the generous creature to a rapid death. Rest in Peace."

Anderina chuckled. "You should write something, Robert, you are great at stories."

"Spoken stories, my love. Writing something for a newspaper is not the same as telling a yarn. I wouldn't want the toffs in cabin-class laughing at my spelling. Have a look at the funny pictures while I feed James his milk."

"You are clever to write at all," said my loyal wife, handing me the cup as she took the paper.

"Look on the second page," I said, as I coaxed James to drink.

Anderina turned the page, and grinned at the caricature of the captain. I was pleased to see her smiling, for concern over James churned our stomachs more than the greasy pork. Daily, we expected to get the fever, or awaken to find our youngest had joined the departed in the land of fig trees, but thanks be to God, neither of these terrible things happened.

W.E. Hamilton

Happier Times

Despite continual stomach troubles, there were wonderful moments on our voyage. Anderina was happy because Mrs Hawker's baby arrived safely.

"A healthy, lovely little girl," she said, sliding her midwifery bag under the bed. "Full-term and strong."

"A baby, that's nothing!" said Laurence. "We saw flying fish, whales and dolphins today."

"And seabirds with huge wings," said Florrie.

"And a shoal of porpoises came rolling after the ship like a lot of pigs," said Margret.

"That's nice," said Anderina vaguely. "Oh, Robert," she beamed with joy. "Matron let me talk to Mary and Elizabeth through the fence this morning."

"How are they?" I said eagerly.

"Like everyone else, they have the harmless sea rash but other than that they are well. A lot of the girls are moping about and crying with homesickness, but our girls are holding themselves together well. They have made many friends and Agnes Jamieson is part of their mess group."

"That is wonderful," I said, relieved to hear such good news.

"And Matron says we will cross *the line* tonight," continued Anderina, "and the captain has a special surprise planned to mark the occasion."

To Own a Fig Tree

"A special surprise! I wonder what that could be? squeaked Margret.

"You'll have to wait and see," said Anderina. "Mrs Butt would not tell me what it was. All she said was, 'make sure you go on deck tonight.'"

"Perhaps it is sweeties," said Margret.

"Maybe Cook has made a cake," said Laurence.

"I hope it's not rum," said Anderina, a frown crossing her face. "This is a good crew, but as soon as the demon drink gets into men, anything could happen."

But she had nothing to fear. The captain's surprise was quite different.

"Stand back," he said, as he made his way to the bow through the throng gathered on the deck. I lifted William onto my shoulders, and Anderina picked up James. Silence fell as he struck a match and a small flame flared brightly in the blackness. Then suddenly, a rocket shot up with a great whoosh. Several ladies let out shrieks of surprise which turned into a collective oo of wonder, as high in the air it exploded into starbursts of sparkling colour. The captain lit several more rockets, and when he had finished, we gave a great cheer as the bell rang. Then someone started singing, '*Should Auld Acquaintance be Forgot*,' and we all joined in with the curious mixture of happy/sad emotions that were our continuous companions. Mr Orgar, the storeman, was lenient with the lights that night, and just as well, for most of us stayed on deck talking and gazing at the unfamiliar stars until very late.

It was hard getting up in the morning, and even the weather was out of sorts, for the light wind that favoured us, now alternated between almost dead calm, and a head breeze.

W.E. Hamilton

Here James Watson justified his reputation as one of the ablest masters in the southern trade. Robert was particularly impressed.

"He is very skilful," he shouted, as we conversed at a distance. "A lesser captain would have got becalmed."

Anderina by my side shuddered. "It is still possible. I'm glad we are in a modern ship equipped with condensers. At least we don't have to worry about running out of drinking water like they did in the olden days."

"We will be alright," I said, "the captain can run this ship on a whisper of wind."

And indeed, he could, for he was flexible with the route he took southward. So flexible, we veered wide enough to see the coast of Brazil for a short distance.

"Make the most of the sight, folks," shouted the captain, as we peered at the land on our starboard side. "Few people see what you now see."

By now, the Southern Star was in the night sky, and the temperature steadily plummeting. We were glad to exchange our light apparel for winter clothing when the sailors brought up our boxes, for the weather was getting colder and colder, and ice burgs appeared in the distance. School finished, and no one ventured on deck without first wrapping up extensively. The captain held Sunday's religious services in the saloon for the cabin passengers, while the doctor read them below deck to the steerage passengers and crew. In keeping with our custom, we Shetlanders gathered after the service to pray and 'take the Book' from the leading brothers.

"I'm glad I thought to bring extra blankets," said Anderina, wrapping James in a fat bundle. "It's freezing."

To Own a Fig Tree

"I am sick of this ship," whined Margret, "it's so slow it feels like we will never get there."

And it wasn't only Margret who was sick of the slow pace.

"We won't make quick time like our last voyage," I overheard a sailor say to John, the first mate.

"Don't draw hasty conclusions, my friend," said John, "we haven't hit the *roaring forties*[26] yet."

I pondered on his words with apprehension, for the seas around Cape Horn were legendary. Although I brushed off sailor's tales as tall stories for Anderina's sake, I worried about their accounts of dreadful winds, fearful storms, and rogue waves ninety feet high. The Leading Brothers and I (keeping our fears from our wives) banded together in prayer. And our gracious God protected us, for we rounded Cape Horn without trouble, and set a straight course for New Zealand. Then our good ship showed her mettle and we flew along. The captain hung out a board each day to tell us the distance we had travelled in twenty-four hours, and for a clear fortnight, she cut through the water at an average speed of ten or eleven knots and hour, until one day someone shouted:

"LAND."

At that, we all rushed up onto the deck.

"It's not land, it's a long cloud," said Margret, with disappointment in her voice.

"No, lassie," said the second mate, "it's not just a cloud, New Zealand lies under it. The Maori people call it *Aotearoa*, the land of the long white cloud. Keep watching, and as we get closer you will see the land emerge."

26 Called the roaring forties because westerly winds in the southern hemisphere after forty-degree latitude are loud and stormy

W.E. Hamilton

And it was so. Little by little, three islands arose from the water, one small and two big ones. We continued sailing smoothly until we rounded the top of the South Island and entered Cook Strait. There, where the Tasman sea and the Pacific Ocean met, our good ship bucked about in a way that made our stomachs feel a great deal worse than usual. Things calmed down when we arrived in a wide bay on the morning of Saturday the seventh of November. We clustered on deck, and stared at our new land. The dots of a town nestled in a hollow, surrounded on three sides by hills. I squinted as I tried to see better. The hills immediately east and south were very rugged, and there seemed to be some flat land and little valleys running back into the hills (which looked like dark broccoli.) While I peered into the distance, our ship slowed and a steamer puffed purposefully towards us.

"Why are we stopping?" I shouted at Robert, as the sailors rolled up the sails and dropped the anchor.

"The captain won't risk landing at the port, for he has cargo to drop at Bluff."

"Is the harbour dangerous?" Anderina cried in alarm.

"It's not that. He is afraid he will lose his crew. Runaway sailors are common, and the police can't catch them all."

He had barely finished speaking when the captain rang the bell to gain our attention.

"Ladies and Gentlemen," he shouted, "we have reached our destination. A steamer will be here shortly, and once the officials give us clearance it will transport you to Nelson. Everyone is to tidy up for an inspection."

The doctor stepped forward and pointed to a spot on the deck. "Bring your mattresses up and stack them in a pile over

To Own a Fig Tree

there for destruction. Make sure you only touch your own mattress." He grinned. "We have a clean bill of health and I don't want it wrecked at the last moment."

"What about our trunks?" someone called out.

"Mr Orgar," said the captain, "would you care to comment?"

"The crew are bringing them out of the hold and will load them onto the steamer as soon as it arrives," responded the storekeeper. "They will be delivered to your accommodation."

"Once we have clearance," said the captain, "cabin passengers will board first, and then the rest of you will follow in groups. Be ready to move when you hear your name called. Doctor Frood and I will accompany you to the port where a tram will take you to the Immigration Hostel. On behalf of the crew and myself, we thank you for sailing with us, and hope your new life will be prosperous."

Then we clapped and someone shouted:

"Three cheers for Captain Watson, the ablest master in the Southern trade."

"Hip, hip, hooray,"

"Hip, hip, hooray,"

"Hip, hip, hooray."

Then we cheered the doctor, the families cheered the first mate, and the single women cheered Mrs Butt, the matron. The constable expected cheers too; for he had been very diligent in blocking the single men from the young ladies, but none of the young men bothered to toast him. After that, we went about our business. The bustle and confusion below as we scurried to pack up was awful. Adults shouted, children cried, and bodies and luggage got in everyone's way.

"Is this when we get to make a report?" said Anderina,

lifting the medicine chest into a suitcase.

"I suppose so."

"Then I'll complain about the food," said Anderina grimly.

"It wasn't terrible," I said, "it was the sudden change of diet, climate, and exercise, that has done us in. I feel half the man I was before the trip."

"You're all skin and bones," said Anderina. Her eye fell on James' emaciated body and her face softened. "But the main thing is we have all survived the journey."

"Praise God for that," I said, nodding. "What is a little loss of condition? In this land of milk and honey we will soon put it back on. Did you see all those trees covering the hills?"

"Is that what they are," said Margret, folding a blanket before stuffing it into a carpet bag?"

"Are they fig trees?" said Laurence, swinging off a top bunk.

"Too far away to tell," I said, "we shall know once we get on land."

"Stop swinging and make yourself useful, Laurie," said Anderina, "put the carpet bags on the mess table so we have more room, and then you and Margret, take James and William up top, but keep them out of everyone's way.

"That is a good idea," said Eleanor, coming out of her berth looking flustered. "Florrie, you go with the Johnsons and take your brothers with you."

Once the children were out of the way, things went more smoothly. By the time they called us for inspection, everything was packed and done. The, *Wallace*, steaming towards us, slowed as she got close, and reversing her engines bumped against us gently. Then her crew dropped a gangplank onto our ship and the officials boarded. One of the officials was a doctor. When it came to our turn, he ran his eye over each of us. "Do you have any complaints?" he asked.

"The food was awful," growled Anderina, folding her arms. "I have felt sick the entire time because of that greasy pork."

"The Scots have not thrived on the rations," agreed Doctor Frood. "I put in my report that the passengers did not like the pork, dried onions, or carrots, and in future, if a ship is transporting a large contingent of Scottish folk, they alter the diet to include more oats."

"And what do you think of Doctor Frood's services?" said the second official.

My wife unfolded her arms.

"He was kind yet firm in enforcing sanitary rules 'tween decks,' and unremitting in his attention to whatever his patients required"

"That is high praise indeed," said the official, "and doubtless, under Providence, this has contributed in no small degree to the pleasing result we now find." He turned to the doctor. "I understand the ship has enjoyed no sickness and there were only three deaths."

"That's right," said Doctor Frood, "all of them infants."

"But two babies arrived safely during the journey," said Anderina. "Both in good health."

The official smiled and wrote something in his book. "And what about the rest of the staff? How did you find them?"

"Marvellous," I said. "Captain Watson is very competent and runs a fast tight ship."

"He does indeed," the official agreed, "he accomplished his last voyage here in seventy-seven days, and this voyage is only one day later, despite, I am told, very light wind for much of the time."

Anderina nodded. "And so kind-hearted. He treated us royally."

"And the rest of the crew were also excellent," I added.

"I'm pleased to hear it," said the official, passing onto the next family.

Anderina took her knitting out of her bag. "This could take some time," she said, her fingers moving rapidly. "Ship life has made me soft; I wish I had something to sit on."

The children shuffled and talked among themselves while William whistled and James sat on the deck languidly, silent and taking little interest in anything. At length, the official part of the visit was over. The captain rang the bell to gain our attention and the official doctor said:

"Congratulations, Captain Watson and crew, for a job well done. Your passengers all speak highly of you. Also well done, Doctor Frood, the ship shows a clean bill of health, no sickness of any kind existing on board. I am happy to say I find everything in order, and all passengers are free to enter New Zealand."

At this, we clapped.

"Only one thing remains to be said," said the other official with a smile. "Welcome to New Zealand."

To Own a Fig Tree

Nelson

It took several trips to get the passengers of the *Ocean Mail* transported to land. While we waited to board the *Wallace*, the constable let the young men onto the main deck and the matron let the single women out. Then there was a great commotion of shouting, laughing, and hugging as separated families reunited.

"Elizabeth and John, I'm sure you have grown two inches at least," said Anderina, kissing them on the cheek.

"And so has William," said Robert, "swinging his little brother up onto his shoulders. His eyes lighted on James and he fell silent.

Mary took James from me carefully, and smoothed his hair gently.

"Dear James, what a good boy you are."

John and Elizabeth swapped troubled glances, and our collective mood plummeted.

"ROBERT JOHNSON AND FAMILY," came a shout.

The call could not have come at a better moment. We threw off anxiety, and boarded the *Wallace* thankfully.

"Goodbye *Ocean Mail*," Margret shouted as we chugged away. "I am not sad to leave you."

Her words were not funny, yet we all roared with laughter and felt better for the outburst of emotion.

The hills grew bigger as we moved closer, and a cluster of small dots enlarged into a town. Among the houses were big buildings and several churches with tall spires. We passed buoys and leading marks as we slid around the curved channel to the harbour entrance. To our left loomed a long spit of boulders on which stood a lighthouse surrounded by a huddle of keeper's cottages.

"Do you think that bolder bank is manmade or natural?" said John.

Robert squinted at it.

"Natural, I guess. It would take a huge effort to build something like that."

The door of a cottage opened and several children rushed out. They ran along the bank waving at us.

"They must live there," said Laurence, as he waved back.

By now, some of the distant houses were visible. They were simple rectangular buildings. Most had gabled ends, but a few sported hip-roofs and even the odd dormer window or two.

"Look how straight and sharp they are, said Anderina, "what are they made of?"

"Wood with shingle roofs," said Robert. "I've seen similar weatherboard ones in some of the coastal villages in England."

"I like their pretty colours," said Margret, staring at the buff-coloured buildings with dark trims and green or brown doors, "I've never seen a red roof before."

"What's the striped overhang?" said Mary.

"It's a veranda," said Robert, "they have them in places where there's a lot of sun and rain."

The steamer slowed and, reversing briefly, churned the water to a boil. Wharfies grabbed the thick ropes the sailors threw out as we drifted towards the wharf, and there was a small jolt when we bumped against the dock.

To Own a Fig Tree

"We are finally here," I said, as they made the boat fast and the gangplank jiggled into place.

"So many people," said Elizabeth, referring to the large crowd eagerly watching us disembark. "Most of the town must be here to welcome us."

Margret looked at the sea of hopeful males dressed in their Sunday best with their hair slicked down. "Reverend Barclay was not exaggerating when he said there were far more men than women."

"Look straight ahead as you walk past them, girls," said Anderina. "Remember the proverb, 'marry in haste repent at leisure.'"

"Elspeth and Clementina are making eyes at them," pouted Margret.

"That is entirely different," sniffed Anderina, picking up her carpetbag and inching into the crowd. "They are older than me, poor things. I don't blame them one bit for looking back. May the Lord grant them good husbands!"

I grabbed William before we funnelled into a line and tottered down the gangplank. As the captain had promised, a horse-drawn tram was waiting for us.

"Are you going to the Immigration Hostel?" I asked the driver.

He gave a shout of laughter. "Is that what they are calling it? Climb aboard, I'll take you to the…" he let out another burst of laughter, "Immigration Hostel."

"Why is he laughing?" said Anderina, squeezing into the crowded vehicle.

"Ignore it, the English are strange."

The driver flicked his whip and we moved smoothly

forward. The horse jogged along the middle of the tramway, and after two miles, we came to a relatively flat patch of land where the town and business area was located. Houses spilt up and over the low hills behind the town, and a handsome church stood on a knoll. I noticed a brickyard, a cloth-weaving factory, a jail and a cemetery. The town was well laid out and seemed prosperous.

"Such a handsome Post Office," Mary exclaimed, as we passed a classical revival building.

I pointed to a large building nearby. "Look, Anderina, a school for girls."

"A school," Anderina exclaimed, "bigger than a laird's house, and entirely for girls! Are you sure, Robert?"

"I'm sure. New Zealand is more established than I expected. Aren't you glad we came?"

"Humph, it's too early to say."

We rolled along until we came to an impressive cluster of six buildings set well back on large grounds. There we stopped.

"WAIMEA ROAD, *Immigration Barracks*," called the driver with another laugh. "You have to be mad to stay there." He chuckled as if he had made a hilarious joke.

"The man is not right in the head," said Anderina, grabbing her carpet bag and lifting James onto her hip.

I thought so too, until we walked down the path leading to the front entrance, and read the notice in the ornamental garden.

"Nelson *Lunatic Asylum!*"

I turned to run back to the tram, but it had gone.

A couple aged about forty and wearing a black-armbands stepped out of the front door.

To Own a Fig Tree

"Don't be alarmed," the man called, "you are in the right place. The Immigration Barracks are currently housing the mental patients while they finish building their new quarters. I suppose they have swapped our accommodation for security reasons. My name is Daniel Scarlett, and this is my wife, Harriet."

I stepped forward and shook Daniel's hand.

"I'm Robert Johnson, and this is my wife, Anderina, and our children, Robert, Mary, John, Elizabeth, Margret, Laurence, William and James. We have just got off the *Ocean Mail*."

"What security reasons?" said Anderina.

"They have to erect fences and the cells for the dirty and violent patients."

"Oh."

"Your children look about the same age as ours," said Harriet.

Anderina put down her carpet bag. "What are their names?"

"Our eldest is Rose, who's nineteen, then there is Charles, who's seventeen, Elizabeth, and Daniel, fifteen and fourteen, James is twelve, Sarah ten and William seven." Her voice faltered and she glanced down at her black armband. "We lost Harriet, our youngest, on the way here."

"I'm so sorry," said Anderina. There was an awkward pause, and I heard the crunch of gravel as fellow immigrants passed us.

"We arrived on the *Adamant* and have been here since August the thirteenth," said Daniel hurriedly. "I was hoping to find work before this, but Nelson has called for more people than it has need of. The first assisted immigrants have absorbed all the household servants and farm hand jobs, and two more ships are due any day." He paused, "are you handy with a theodolite?"

"A what-o-light?"

"Obviously not. Pity, the province needs surveyors. Some men have picked up work on the new railway line, but many of us have not." He wiped a hand over his face, "I am afraid the pioneering idyll has passed."

This was bad news indeed. My heart plummeted and Anderina's face turned the colour of clotted cheese. Harriet interrupted her husband.

"It is not as bad as Daniel makes out," she said with brittle brightness. "Don't let us keep you standing out here, the little ones look exhausted."

I turned to Daniel. "What do we do?"

"Go to the front desk, and the officer in charge will sign you in and give you a room. We will talk again later."

I nodded my thanks and we parted.

To Own a Fig Tree

The Hostel and Hope of Land.

We stepped through the front door of the Immigration Hostel into a corridor so lofty and spacious, it had the appearance of a long room lined with doors. A crowd was gathered around the officer sitting at a desk with a large book open in front of him. Behind him, a row of keys (with tags bearing numbers) dangled from hooks. We waited patiently and when it was my turn the man (without glancing at me) said in a clipped tone:

"Name?"

"Robert Johnson."

"From the *Ocean Mail*?"

"Aye."

He flicked to the J section in the book and ran his finger down a list of names. "Here we are, Robert Johnson, five dependants, plus two single men and two single women."

"That's right."

"Where are you from, Robert?"

"Shetland."

"Shetland!" The officer's head jerked up and his eyes honed in on me. "What are your skills, and are you accustomed to hard work?"

"I'm a crofter and fisherman, used to severe labour."

The man tapped his fingers together. "Good, good. What is the weather like where you come from?"

W.E. Hamilton

"Winter is freezing and summer is three months of dirty weather."

"Excellent. How do you cope with isolation?"

"Don't know another way of living."

"Nice. Tell me, Robert, do you want land?"

"Land is my greatest desire."

The official took a document from the drawer in his desk and beckoned me closer. "The Government is giving Crown grants of land in the Special Settlement of Karamea, and you are the type of man they are looking for. Read this prospectus and if you are interested, go to the Provincial Secretary's Office, and ask for an application form. You'll find it here…" he wrote 'Government Building on Hardy and Tasman street,' on the back of the prospectus and handed it to me.

"Thank you very much," I said.

"Oh, and be sure when you fill out your application, to stress you are used to isolation, severe labour and dreadful weather." He turned and picked three keys off the hooks.

"You and your family are in room three, halfway down the hall on the right-hand side," he said, giving me the key. "There are six buildings here. Four of them containing ten to twelve bedrooms, and a common sitting room. The fifth building is the kitchen and dining hall, and washhouse. You will find a recreation hall situated in the centre of the buildings." He handed a key to Robert and another key to Mary. "Single men's quarters outside to the left, and single women's quarters is the building on the right. You will find an additional laundry and washhouse located off the woman's barracks. There are two baths in each department with hot and cold water, and gas lighting throughout. If you feel unwell, the smallest building is set aside as a temporary hospital."

"Thank you," I said, turning to leave.

"Good luck with the land," said the officer, "don't leave it too long to apply. The land is limited and there's keen interest in it."

He turned to the next in line:

"Name?"

I thrust the key into Anderina's hand. "You find the room and get settled. I must go at once. A chance of land is too good to miss."

She nodded, "go, don't wait."

So, clutching the paper, I strode out the door. I had not got many steps down the driveway when I met the Scarletts coming back from their walk.

"Did you know they are opening up a special settlement in some place called Karamea?"

"No," said Daniel, his eyes brightening.

"When the officer heard I came from the Shetland Isles, he quizzed me closely as to my occupation and the weather. Then he suggested I should apply for land."

I showed Daniel the paper he had given me.

Daniel ran his eyes over it and let out a long whistle. "This could be the answer to our prayers," he said to his wife. "A chance to own land for little more than the labour of our hands."

"Go there now," Harriet urged.

"Yes, come," I said, "then we will be neighbours. We must be quick for the officer stressed the interest is high."

"Alright," said Daniel. He turned, and I followed him as we hurried off. It was not far to our destination. I looked at the Government Building in awe.

W.E. Hamilton

NELSON SPECIAL SETTLEMENTS

- That about 3,000 acres of land on the left bank of the Karamea be set aside in the first instance for a special settlement.

- That a person be placed in charge, to whom be intrusted all stores and Government property, who will superintend all public works, and from whom the new immigrants may obtain advice and tuition in bush and road work, and in cultivating the land etc.

- That thirty families be the first settlers; the head of each family to be employed on public works for one month, at 6s. per day, full time, and for three days in each week for six months certain; afterwards at a wage of 8s per working day, if required.

- That rations be served out to those requiring them for the seven months they are engaged on public works at cost price; payment of same to be a first charge on wages earned.

- That an allotment of fifty acres of land, also an allotment of about five acres, be leased to each head of a family for fourteen years, at an annual rental of 2s. per acre, and at the end of fourteen years a Crown grant to be given to each leaseholder without further payment.

- That the land so allocated be chosen by lot.

- That one of the settlers be appointed storekeeper, under the control of the overseer, on terms to be agreed upon.

- That 5cwt. of seed potatoes and 1 bushel of oats or rye seed be given to each family, to make provision for winter use.

- That a tent-cover or tarpaulin be furnished to each family if required, the cost of which to be deducted in equal monthly instalments from the wages due to such family.

To Own a Fig Tree

> • That tools be furnished to the settlers at cost prices, and payment be taken in equal amounts monthly.
>
> • That a boat be placed under the control of the overseer for the use of the settlement. The Waste Lands Board will be recommended NOT to grant leases to any persons of lands selected under these regulations, unless the persons selecting or applying to lease such lands shall personally occupy the same, and give sufficient evidence of their intentions to become bona fide setters thereon, by clearing and cultivating or otherwise improving a fair proportion of the land allotted to them. A fee of 1 pound will be payable to the Waste Lands Board upon every application for each separate block of land applied for, and also a deposit of 6d. per acre towards the expense of the survey for every acre of land applied for; but the amount so deposited for the survey will be placed to the credit of the applicant towards the payment of his rent.
>
> Nelson, 20th November, 1874   WM. Rout.
>   For Provincial Secretary.

It was two storied, spanned an entire block, and was a conglomeration of wings with square turrets and tall bay windows under elaborate gables.

"I have never seen such a grand place," I said.

"It's an interesting construction," said Daniel, "broadly Jacobean in style, but novel for being built in wood rather than brick or stone."

I had no idea what he meant, but I nodded as if I did.

"I'm from Shetland where do you come from?" I said,

changing the subject.

"Great Tew, Oxfordshire in England where I was an agricultural labourer."

He strode up the steps of the entrance and I followed him, glad to have company in this intimidating place. Daniel waylaid a passing man.

"Where is the Provincial Secretary's Office?"

"Over there," he replied, pointing the way.

We followed his direction to the room with the words, 'Provincial Secretary,' on a brass plaque, and passed through the door.

"Karamea Special Settlement?" queried the man behind the desk in a bored tone.

"Yes."

He handed us a set of forms each and pointed to the tables around the wall. "Fill these out. Successful applicants will be announced at a meeting at the Immigration Depot, on Thursday the nineteenth of November."

I took the papers and spread them on the table, then picking up a pen on the desk, I dipped it into the inkwell and scratched 'Robert Johnson' in the first box.

Slowly and methodically, I plodded my way through the questions. I answered truthfully, and (taking the officer's advice) inserted the words 'isolation, severe labour, and dirty weather,' wherever possible. I was only half done when Daniel handed his papers in. We exchanged nods as he left the room. By now, the tables were lined with men intently filling out forms. Many of them were Shetlanders. Among them were Peter Coutts, Robert Henry, and James Moffatt.

I bent my head over my paper once more and stared at the

To Own a Fig Tree

next question. The first part: 'was your weekly wage under thirteen shillings per week,' I answered easily enough. 'No,' I wrote in the box. It was the following bit that stumped me: 'If yes, specify the amount you received?' Men came and went as I sat pondering. I couldn't write 'nothing.' In the end, I sent a silent prayer up to God, and wrote '*truck* and barter.'

The rest of the questions were not so hard, and the last one, 'why do you want to go to Karamea?' was simple.

My hand trembled as I wrote, 'because my greatest dream is to own land, a fig tree, and be in bondage to no man.'

That being done, I passed my papers in, paid the fee from the residue of my expense money, and went back to the Immigration Hostel.

W.E. Hamilton

An Odd Place

I knocked on the door labelled, three, and Anderina opened it with a scowl.

"What's wrong?"

"It's the women here. Those toffee-nosed-English think more highly of themselves than they ought. I asked where the kitchen was, but instead of answering, they mimicked my accent and laughed. And I overheard others complaining that paupers pouring off the ships are ruining the province."

"Never mind," I soothed, "we will be out of here soon. We have a strong chance of getting land, something I never dreamed could happen in this life."

"I suppose so," said Anderina, sitting on the almost-pirate chest.

"I see our luggage has come."

"Yes, and just as well, for without it we'd have nothing to sit on."

I looked around the room. Like the hallway, it was spacious with a lofty ceiling. A tall window set high on the wall opposite the door, was fitted with iron bars but no shutters or curtains.

"A big room for one person but a squeeze for six," I said. "Where are the beds?"

Margret and Laurence giggled.

"It's no laughing matter," said Anderina, with a frown. She pointed at five taut wires running through the walls at the end of the room. "Those fiddle strings are it." She picked a straw tick off a pile in a corner, and threw it on top of the wires. "See?"

Laurence clambered up on it and bounced.

"If you do this," he said gleefully, "you can make all the beds on this side of the building jiggle."

"I've never seen anything like it before," I said. "Is this the way the English sleep?"

"No, Harriet Scarlett was as shocked as me when she saw the odd arrangement. She says everyone lies on the floor."

"Robert reckons the lunatics designed them," giggled Margret.

"Did you find the kitchen?"

"In the end, but no thanks to those women. It is large and they serve meals in the dining room three times a day." Anderina wrinkled her nose. "The food smells awful. Boiled cabbage and starchy puddings."

"What about the sitting room?"

My wife sniffed and tossed her head. "I'm not going back in there. It's a tiny room made smaller by the big mouths of those mean women."

"Today is November the seventh, we will know if we have land by the nineteenth. That's..." I counted on my fingers, "twelve days. Just think, Anderina, in less than two weeks we might have our own land."

Anderina heaved a sigh. "It will be hard waiting, especially without our cosy box beds."

She was right, it was hard. It was not the boring waiting of life at sea, for in Nelson there was plenty to see and do, it was the nervous seesawing between hope and fear-of-missing-out, that stretched the time.

I and the other men explored the town while our wives washed and mended every stitch of clothing our families owned. During this time, the Johnson and Scarlett children became firm friends, and Anderina and I got to see a lot of Daniel and Harriet. They'd had a much tougher voyage than us. A group of children (including our youngsters) were playing on the front lawn when we compared trips.

"It was not as bad as I expected," I said, as we walked to the seats by the garden. "No storms, and only two deaths. In fact, Old Benjamin Coutts, who is seventy-nine, has finished the journey more robust than he started."

"Remarkable," said Daniel.

"The crowd of eligible young men flocking around his daughters are rejuvenating him," said Anderina, smiling. "I noticed even their dutiful son, Peter, has started walking out with Jemima Jamieson. I expect Peter can finally see his way to supporting a wife and children."

"I hope so," I said, "elderly parents and four unmarried sisters are a heavy load for him to carry."

I switched back to the former topic as I sat on the grass. "The worst part of the trip was the food. It gave us more stomach troubles than the waves."

"You are blessed. Ours was a nightmare," said Harriet, settling down on the slatted bench next to Anderina.

"We sailed from Plymouth on the seventh of May, in the Adamant, an 815 ton iron Barque, built in 1858," said Daniel.

"Twelve days after leaving port, measles broke out," said Harriet, "and twelve children…" Her voice faltered, "including our little Harriet, died. The surgeon tried hard to save them but there was nothing he could do." She stopped and there was a silence before Daniel picked up the thread of the story.

"Then we hit severe storms, one off Trinidad, where we lost the light for three days, and the bowsprit was carried away by heavy seas."

"It was awful," said Harriet. "We were tossed about and anything not tied down flew about the place."

"The second heavy storm happened in the Tasman Sea," said Daniel. "It lasted thirty-six hours, with the seas running tremendously high from the north-east, while the wind blew in hurricane force from the south-east."

Harriet shuddered. "I did not think we would live through it, but it calmed down, and after ninety-eight days at sea, we limped into Nelson on August the thirteenth."

Daniel chuckled. "We caused an even bigger stir than you did, because we were the first ship of immigrants to arrive."

Harriet sighed sadly and dabbed her eyes. "Was coming here worth losing our youngest? Sometimes I wish we had not gone to that tent meeting in Milton-under-Wychwood."

"But, Harriet, we may get the chance to own land," said Daniel, "something I never thought could happen."

"Maybe, maybe not. You're not accepted for the Special Settlement yet. Perhaps it will be like all the lucrative jobs you were certain to get the moment we arrived."

"We couldn't stay, my love. Conditions for agricultural workers in England are terrible. At least we have hope here. Back home there is almost no employment, especially in winter, and when there is work, children as young as eight spend long hours weeding and picking potatoes. Our cottage was small and damp and there was nothing other than bread, skim milk, and cheese to eat. Remember the old folks they threw into the poorhouse when they were past working. Is that the life you want for our children?"

"Perhaps the Union will change things for the better," Harriet said in a small voice.

Daniel shook his head.

"The strikes only resulted in lock-outs. If we could have stopped the harvest, we might have had a chance, but there are too many new machines and unskilled labourers desperate for work. Even the chairman, Joseph Arch, is for emigration now."

"But he was strongly against it," I broke in. "I've read his views in the Labourer's Union Chronicle. He believes the only solution to the suffering of the agricultural workers is to band together to demand better conditions."

"Not anymore. He says emigration is the speediest way to improve the English labourer's conditions, and it is better to go to New Zealand than Brazil, where the language and customs are so different."

I could see by her restlessness, Anderina was growing impatient as we talked.

"There is no point wasting emotion on regrets or what could have been," she said. "For better or worse we are here."

There was an awkward pause. While scrabbling to break the uncomfortable silence, my eyes alighted on a man skulking about the circular garden a little distance away.

"Who's that?" I said, in a low voice.

Daniel gave a snort of relieved laughter. "Oh, that's Edwin King. He's an odd bird."

"What's he doing? He looks like he is about to pinch something."

To Own a Fig Tree

"He's not taking anything," said Daniel, as the man furtively pulled a small packet from his pocket. "He's sneaking seeds into the dirt."

"Why," said Anderina?

"He used to work for Sutton's Seed Farm of London. He always carries seeds and whenever he spots an opportunity, he plants flowers."

"He would have planted them on the ship if he could have found a little patch of soil," laughed Harriet. "He's come out with his brother."

I nodded at a nearby youth, who (judging from the motley fuzz on his chin) was about eighteen. "Is that his brother?"

"No, that is Harry Lineham." Daniel lifted his voice: "Harry, come and meet Robert and Anderina Johnson. They arrived on the *Ocean Mail* the other day."

"Hello," the young man said, swinging in our direction.

"This is Harry Lineham," said Daniel, "the Linehams came with us on the Adamant."

"How do you do?" I said, shaking his hand.

"Johnson? Robert and John Johnson are in the single men's quarters with me. Are they relations?"

"Yes," Anderina smiled, "they are our sons."

"Splendid fellows," said Harry.

"How's your brother, Harry?" said Harriet.

"Good," he swivelled and pointed to a man throwing a small child in the air. "He's over there playing with his children."

"Not Alfred, how is Thomas? What happened after the officials removed him and his family from the depot?"

Harry sighed. "He's only middling I'm afraid, Mam. They took him off to the hospital on account of his troublesome leg.

W.E. Hamilton

When he got there, the surgeon told the immigration officer his case was likely to be tedious as diseased bone had to be removed." We sucked in our breath and Harriet's hand flew to her mouth. "Mr Elliot was not pleased," continued Harry, "he made a full investigation of the matter, and sent a report to Featherston in London, asking why a man with a chronic bone problem was recommended for emigration by a Baptist minister, and has a medical certificate signed by a physician in Cranfield."

"Oh dear," said Daniel, "are they going to deport him?"

Harry's face lit into a smile. "Far from it, Mr Eliot badgered the Immigration Department until they approved an allowance of fifteen shillings a week to the family, and Thomas has had the disease cut out. He's in a lot of pain, of course, but the worst is over. I sent him an application form for the Special Settlement, for I am hoping God will be gracious and grant him a full recovery."

"We shall add him to our prayers," said Daniel.

"Please do! I'm going to Thursday's Special Settlement meeting to stand in for him."

"Uncle Harry, uncle Harry, why won't it fly," shouted a boy, running towards us dragging a kite along the ground?

"Coming Charles," Harry shouted. He turned back to us. "Excuse me, I have an emergency to attend to," he said with a grin. "Yes, a flightless kite is a crisis," I said, grinning back.

"See you at the meeting if not before," Daniel said.

Harry nodded. "Nice to meet you, Mr and Mrs Johnson."

"Nice to meet you too."

And with that, Harry tipped his hat, and ran off to fix the kite.

The Meeting

The nineteenth of November finally arrived. The room where the Special Settlement meeting was held, buzzed with anticipation as Daniel and I, accompanied by our two eldest sons, Robert and Charles, walked in. At the appointed time, Mr Elliot, the Immigration Officer, stood up.

"Thank you for coming today. I know the question uppermost in your mind is, who is accepted for the Karamea Special Settlement? So, without further ado, I will read out the names of the successful candidates."

I held my breath as he said:
Peter Coutts
James Coutts
Alfred Lineham
Edwin King
James Moffatt
Daniel Scarlett
Robert Johnson…

The list went on, but I scarcely heard a thing beyond my name. I drew in a deep breath as I exchanged delighted glances with Robert, Daniel and Charles. When Mr Elliot had finished reading the names, he said:

"This ends this part of the meeting. I wish those of you not selected all the best in finding more suitable employment. The men whose names I called, please stay behind."

There was a reshuffle as men left.

"Benjamin Coutts will be pleased Peter got land," I said to Daniel in the general hubbub. "I expect he and Barbara will stay in Nelson for a bit to marry off their daughters."

"Thomas Lineham got land too," said Daniel.

"Did he? I confess I didn't hear much after my name was called."

"I didn't hear much myself," said Daniel. "I only noticed because I was listening for his name. I hope the fact he is not here will not disqualify him."

"Quieten down, quieten down," called Mr Elliot. Once we had settled, he gestured towards a dark-haired man with a bushy beard.

"This is, Eugene O'Connor. He represents the Buller electorate in the New Zealand House of Representatives, and is a member of the Nelson Provincial Council. I'll hand over to him, for he is the man in charge of this project."

Mr Elliot sat down amid clapping, and Eugene O'Connor stepped forward.

"They call me the Buller Lion," he said, in a lilting Irish accent, "I like to think it's because I'm the king of the beasts, and make things happen."

We laughed.

"You have read the prospectus, and now I will flesh it out a little. There are fifty-thousand acres of forested land in the Karamea district, thus providing two means of livelihood, agriculture and timber-milling. In addition, fish, gold and coal are in the area."

At this, murmurs of excitement broke out.

"Currently, there is no overland access to Karamea,"

To Own a Fig Tree

continued O'Connor, "but there is a fine harbour, and steamers capable of taking produce to markets in Nelson and Westport, pass almost daily. The Government has set aside three thousand acres on the South side of the river for a Special Settlement. This is not an impulsive decision, and you were not randomly selected."

We looked at each other in surprise.

"No. We specifically requested agricultural labourers, of sobriety and fortitude from the Midland and Western counties of England, who are raising families on seven to thirteen shillings a week. Also, unemployed Cornish miners, Manxmen and Shetland Islanders (accustomed to a harsh climate.) We believe your rugged way of life, and the severe manual labour you are accustomed to, will enable you to thrive where less hardy immigrants will not survive."

That last statement was cause for worry, but as we linked it to gold and land, we missed its significance.

"Ten years ago, the area was surveyed, and blocks of land laid out. We will allot each head of family fifty acres by ballot when you arrive."

Clapping broke out.

"With a further five acres at a later time."

Another burst of clapping.

"We have appointed a superintendent to take charge of the stores and Government property, and to oversee all public works. Stand up, Hyland."

A man hesitantly arose, and we clapped.

"This is Agent Richard Hyland from Moutere. Take a good look at him. He is the man to go to for advice about work or your new way of life. He will give you tuition in bushcraft,

W.E. Hamilton

roadmaking and cultivation of land. If you are unsure how to fell a tree or build a house, ask him." He nodded to Hyland. "You can sit down now."

Hyland sat down quickly, and Mr Elliot stepped forward with a covered board, which he sat on a chair before us.

"Not all of you will proceed to Karamea at once. The Immigration Officer has chosen thirty families as the first settlers. If your name is on the board, you will depart for Karamea tomorrow. If not, you will go a little later. You can reveal the names now, Charles."

Mr Elliot whipped off the covering.

First Settlers of Karamea

Charles Martin, Frederick Liley,
Samuel Friend, Daniel and Charles Scarlett, William Andrews, Edwin King,
Robert and Peter Henry, Thomas Edward Charles, Robert Johnsons (senior and junior)
Thomas Edward Kelly,
James and William Moffatt, James Strange, Paul Pike, Peter and James Coutts,
Eli Merchant, John Sinclair, William Rule, Daniel Hawker, John Skirton, Alfred Burton, Stephen and Henry Stanton, William Houghton, Newton Bungay, W.S. Williams, Laurence Laurenson, Thomas Jamison,
John Naylor, James and Charles Penny, Thomas and George Corlett.

To Own a Fig Tree

Silence fell as we eagerly scanned for our names, followed by a rumbling of excited talk.

"We are in, Son," I said in delight.

Robert nodded, his face beaming, "and so are the Scarletts."

O'Connor waited a few moments before quietening us with his hand.

"Each head of family will receive a tent, tools, a waterproof coat, sturdy boots, five-hundred-weight of seed potatoes, and one bushel of oats (or rye) seed to provide for winter use. To avoid any suspicion of Government-self-interest, you will appoint a settler as storekeeper under the control of the overseer, who will also be in charge of the boat we supply for the settlement."

"We haven't any money, how will we pay?" a voice called out.

"The head of each family receives full employment for the first month, at six shillings a day. Thereafter, you receive eight shillings a day, three days of the week, for six months. During that time, we supply provisions at cost, and expenses are deducted from your wages."

O'Connor looked around. "Are there any more questions?"

"What about our wives and children?"

"Until the land is clearer and you have built shelters, the women and children continue staying at the Immigration Hostel. Your wives get part of your wages as a living allowance, which they verify they have received by signing for it each week."

"Are there any more questions?"

I put up my hand. "Are there fig trees on the land?"

"No, Sir, you'll have to plant fruit trees yourself. There are, however, rata, black, red, and white pine, and totara. All excellent timbers."

"What public works will we be employed on?" said Daniel.

"Initially, Government land needs clearing and a store built. After that, we plan to find the best route overland to Westport, and make a bridle track into the area."

"Is there currently any way out of Karamea other than the sea?"

"Only a treacherous track around the coastline. It is passable in an emergency, but not advisable as big boulders have to be crossed and landfalls are common. But the Karamea harbour is second only to Westport's harbour.[27]

"What time do we leave?"

"First settlers depart on the *Wallace*, at nine in the morning. Be at the dock early to receive your coats and boots."

There was a silence, so O'Connor finished by saying:

"Gentlemen, I wish you well in this undertaking. I believe in the future prosperity of the settlement, to the point I and fifty-six other men have invested in property on the north bank of the river. Have a safe trip tomorrow, and I look forward to seeing you at Karamea. Good luck neighbours."

O'Connor sat down amid cheers and clapping, and shortly after, we rushed off to tell our wives the good news.

---

27   Opinion of the 1870s

To Own a Fig Tree

High Hopes Are Dampened

I awoke early on Friday, excited at the prospect of seeing my land. But the lovely blue sky and warm days had changed into dirty weather. The *Wallace* tugged at her moorings while we waited impatiently for the storm to pass. The harbour master from Westport, Captain Leech, who arrived aboard the *Charles Edward* on Saturday, was unfazed by the setback. He took a pipe and a tin from his pocket, and settling into a chair at the immigration depot, watched us lazily as we chose supplies.

"No point adding trouble to that treacherous old bar at Karamea," he said, opening the tin and squashing tobacco into the bowl of his pipe with his thumb. "What sort of pilot would I be, if I grounded the *Wallace* on her maidan voyage into the harbour?"

"A bad one," laughed Robert, trying on a pair of stout boots from a pile in the corner of the room.

"Exactly," the captain tamped his tobacco down as he added, "besides, it will give McNairn more time to get a couple of temporary signals up. It's a devil of a job to get around the coast by foot."

"Who is McNarin?" I said as I sorted through the waterproof coats.

Captain Leech lit a match, and sucked the stem of his pipe for a couple of puffs before answering, "A Westport Official.

W.E. Hamilton

He's got the unenviable job of erecting signals at the entrance to the Karamea River." He pulled a face. "And I have to replace them with permanent beacons. Oh well, Mr Tizard can make himself useful and help me."

I found a coat marked SM and pulled it on.

"Who's Mr Tizzard?"

"The Westport Customs Collector. He's coming to familiarize himself with the route." Smoke trickled out of the captain's nose as he tucked his tin away in his pocket. "Though why he needs to be familiar with the route to a new port of call is a mystery! If you ask me, he's just coming for the fun of it."

"I don't blame him," said Robert. "I have my able seaman's certificate. Is there any chance I could come along with you sometimes to increase my experience? I'm a hard worker."

The captain pulled his pipe from his mouth, and ran an appraising eye over him. After a long pause he said:

"Maybe. I like a good keen man. Ask me again once you are settled, young fella." He returned his pipe to his mouth, and stretched back in his chair.

I shrugged on the waterproof coat, and when I found it fitted nicely, went over to the table where Agent Hyland sat.

"This one will do for me," I said, "and I will have another one for my son, and two pairs of boots." Hyland looked down at the big ledger before him, and headed up a page with my name. 'Two coats at thirty-four shillings each, two pairs of boots, thirty shillings each,' he wrote in the column. "Do you want to hold on to them now, or put them with the potatoes and other stuff for the *Wallace*?"

"I'll hold onto them," I said.

"Good idea," said Captain Leech, "that rain's not going

To Own a Fig Tree

away in a hurry."

I picked out some more things which Hyland entered in the book, and then I went back to my room at the Immigration Hostel.

"I wonder what Karamea is like?" said Anderina, when I showed her my coat and boots.

"Similar to here, I imagine, only rougher and undeveloped. Poor Alfred Lineham's downcast he's not going on the first trip to Karamea."

My wife said nothing, so I continued:

"John must be the man of the family while Robert and I are away. Get him to send a letter to the folks back home, telling them of our safe arrival."

Anderina's mind was on other matters. She dismissed Alfred's disappointment and John's new responsibility with a wave of her hand. "It will do John good, and Alfred will go with the next intake of settlers."

"Don't forget the letter."

"I won't."

She looked into the air thoughtfully. "Fifty-seven families plus thirty new families will make quite a large [28]*toon*."

"I'm not sure the other families are there yet," I said uncertainly. "O'Connor said we are the first settlers."

"But you told me he and fifty-six others have already bought land there, and we will be neighbours," said Anderina.

"Well, yes, he said, he and the others have land on the North Bank and we have land on the South Bank."

"He must mean first settlers of the South Bank," said Anderina, with satisfaction. She looked at the rain slashing

---

28 Town

W.E. Hamilton

against the windowpane and sighed. "What a pity about the weather. The sooner we get to Karamea, the better."

"It seems to be easing," I said, squinting at the clouds, "I think it may be possible to leave tomorrow."

And so it was. Despite drizzling rain, the weather next morning was calm enough for us to get away. We were in high spirits as we boarded the steamer at 7 am Sunday, the twenty-second of November, 1874. Our families and several others, including, A. Pritt and W. Rout, from the Provincial Council, gathered to witness our departure. We stood on the deck of the *Wallace* in our new coats and boots, staring at Mr Elliot on the dock as he waxed eloquent.

"My dear fellows," he said, gazing up at us, "*I have no doubt that by hard and incessant work, temperance, and prudence, you will bring your land into profitable cultivation, thus gaining comfort and independence in the future. You will succeed, for colonizing is the special mission of the Anglo-Saxon race, and the same blood flows in your veins as in the men who gave language and laws to the whole continent of North America, to vast territories in Africa, to the huge continent of Australia, and numerous lesser countries.*"[29]

He stopped, overcome with emotion. It was a rousing farewell speech, and we responded with rousing cheers. Then A. Pritt called:

"*Three hearty cheers for the brave little body of pioneers.*[30]"
"Hip, hip, hooray,"
"Hip, hip, hooray,"
"Hip, hip, hooray."

---

29   The Colonist 24 Nov, 1874
30   Nelson Evening Mail 23 Nov 1874

To Own a Fig Tree

Then we, the little body of brave pioneers, hip-hoorayed the Immigration Officer, and after him, the New Zealand Government. The cheers would have continued longer, but for the steamer's whistle - one loud blast, and that was the end of that.

"Goodbye, goodbye, God be with you," we shouted to our loved ones.

None of us wondered as the *Wallace* pulled away from the dock, why Mr Pritt called us brave. We were preoccupied with the marvellous future before us.

"No more unemployment in the Cornish mines," said a nearby man.

"No more sterile soil," I said.

"Fifty acres of our very own," said Daniel.

We discussed our hopes and dreams as we chugged up and around the top of the South Island. But as we started down the West Coast, Captain Leech, looking at the waves with a worried frown, said:

"The seas are getting up."

And now he mentioned it, we saw it was true. The waves got higher and higher and by the time our vessel approached the Karamea entrance, she met heavy seas and slanting rain.

"Captain Leech," shouted Captain Heffer, over the noise of the wind, "time to take over the wheel."

"I daren't risk taking her in," Captain Leech shouted back. "There are five rivers all disgorging silt from the mountains in this sort of weather. There is no telling where the bar has shifted. Our boat will break up if she hits it. Keep heading for Westport."

Captain Heffer nodded. "You're right. I feel the barometric

W.E. Hamilton

pressure dropping. There is a storm coming, we'd best shelter in Westport until it passes."

It was disappointing, but a wise decision as the land was shrouded in mist, and there was no sign of the temporary signals. Fortunately, we had two captains, for by now we were making little headway and progress was slow. The rest of the day, the whole night, and all Monday morning we battled the sea, until we finally crept into Westport's entrance.

Once we moored, the captains and Mr Tizard went home, for there was no point us all staying cooped up on the boat.

"We will be back as soon as it is safe to set out again," said Captain Heffer.

We made ourselves as comfortable as possible among the potatoes and tarpaulins. At least we had something to eat because there were enough supplies to last a month.

"Not that flour and salt are much good on its own," said Daniel. "Once we have eaten all the bread and ship's biscuits we will be in problems."

But we didn't have to wait more than two days, and those days were not a waste of time, for we got to know each other a little better. I knew all the Shetlanders, and had much in common with the rest of the men, for most of them were agricultural workers. Alfred and William Williams, however, were Cornish miners, David Hawker, a stonemason, and Fredrick Liley, a painter.

"Why would a painter want land?" I said. "Wouldn't you do better in town where there are lots of houses?"

Before Liley could answer, the man beside him spoke.

"I'm Samuel Friend, an agricultural worker, and Liley and I emigrated together. I want land and persuaded him to come.

To Own a Fig Tree

What he didn't tell you is besides being a painter, he is a pit sawyer."

Liley nodded. "I'm not much into farming but when I heard there is good timber, I decided to give it a go."

One of the two Manxmen in our number spoke up:

"I'm not a farmer either, but anything is better than staying on an island thirty miles long by ten miles broad, where the chance of a foot of land is as remote as flying in a balloon over the Pacific."

This was bad indeed. Camaraderie engulfed us as we agreed the Manxmen had it hard. Then we swapped yarns of the old country until the weather eased on Wednesday. That night, shortly before twelve, the captains and Mr Tizard returned, for the tide was right. Robert helped loose the boat from her moorings, and finally we were off. The propeller churned the water behind us as we chugged along making good time.

"I hope McNairn got the temporary signals up," said Captain Leech, peering along the coastline as the dawn broke.

But he had nothing to worry about. The markings showed up clearly against the blue sky and quiet sea. We slipped into the Karamea entrance with ease and the river was smooth, as with soundings of fourteen feet, we crossed the bar two hours before full tide.

"Lower the lighter," shouted Captain Heffer. "You have two hours to get the supplies and everyone onto the shore. Captain Leech is leaving on high tide whether or not you are ready, for we have a rendezvous to make, and I won't linger in unknown waters."

We rushed to lower the lighter, and forming a chain gang, passed stores quickly into it.

W.E. Hamilton

"Take these and erect them yourself, Hyland," said Captain Leech, throwing the permanent signals into the bow.

Agent Hyland's shoulders sagged and his posture slumped. "How am I going to do that?"

"You'll figure it out," said Captain Leech dismissively. "Just make sure they're up before we come back next month."

By now, the lighter was fully loaded.

"Where do we land, Hyland?" said Daniel.

Hyland looked up and down the shoreline.

"Um, ah, somewhere." He pointed to a spot on the beach. "Maybe there…ah no, over there."

We were men's men, used to tough conditions and decisive actions. Even our women were gutsy.

"Make up your mind," Peter Coutts said, contempt skulking at the edge of his tone.

"There," said Hyland, pointing randomly.

The place seemed as good as any, so Robert and I and a couple of other men leapt into the boat, and taking up the oars, pulled hard. We ferried load after load of goods and men to the beach and within the allotted time, we had all the stores and everyone safely landed. Then with a whistle blast, the *Wallace* churned up the water and steamed away. Shortly after, the *Charles Edward* came into view.

"There go Captain Leech and Mr Tizzard back to Westport," said Robert, as tiny figures leapt from one boat to the other.

Desolation descended upon us as we watched the two steamers part, before disappearing in opposite directions. But shrugging depression off, we turned impassive faces towards the land.

To Own a Fig Tree

Difficulties

It was a beautiful summer's day, and we found ourselves on a beach scattered with bits of timber. We knew Karamea was surrounded by steep hills and mountains because we had seen them from the sea, but other than that it was hard to tell what the land was like, for beyond a thin rim of sand, enormous trees towered into the sky blocking everything else from sight. The significance of Mr Pritt's toast to the '*brave* little body of pioneers,' dawned on me with sickening clarity.

"I've never seen anything like it," I said, tilting my head back and staring up. "I had no idea trees grew as tall as this! How do you Englanders deal with them?"

"They are not like English trees," said Daniel, picking up a short plank and poking it at the wall of undergrowth between the enormous trunks. "You can walk through an English wood without trouble." He pushed harder but the matted mass of ferns and bushes refused to yield. "We'll have to cut our way through this."

"Now I know why we need slashers," said Hawker.

"There is no point wasting energy hacking into the wrong area," said Peter. He turned to Richard Hyland. "Where is our land?"

Hyland waved his hand vaguely towards the trees.

"I don't know, somewhere in there. Elliot assured me the land is surveyed and the boundaries laid out. You'll have to hunt for the pegs."

Alfred Williams bent down and examined some of the boards lying about.

"It looks like there are gold miners in the area," he said. "These were once part of a water flume. If we scout around, we might find their track. Perhaps they know where the surveyed land is."

This seemed sensible, so we divided into two groups and set off in opposite directions. Hyland, showing little enthusiasm, trailed lethargically at the end of the line. We didn't find tracks or miners as we walked steadily onward. We did, however, make an important discovery when a short time later, both parties met up again.

"We are on an island!"

Agent Hyland suddenly awoke from his stupor. "Oh, now I know where we are."

All eyes bored into him.

"We are on the Government Reserve where the town will be. We have to clear this island and build the store here. Your land must be over there, for it is on the south side of the river."

Every head whipped around with renewed hope. By now, the tide was going out, and we saw it was possible to wade across a shallow part. Without saying another word, we took off our boots, rolled up our trousers and strode into the water, while Hyland, getting in the boat rowed after us. The trees were no smaller on the south side, neither was the undergrowth less dense. We spread along the beach hunting for survey pegs. Alas, the few we found leaned drunkenly in the ground like rotten teeth, and there were no signs of boundaries slashed through the bush.

To Own a Fig Tree

"The good news is, this is fertile land," said Edwin King, throwing a rotten peg on the ground. "The bad news is, ten years of rain forest growth has destroyed the surveyor's work. It will have to be redone before we can claim our land."

"All this exercise is making me thirsty," said Hawker. He turned to Hyland. "Where did you put the water container?"

"I didn't bring any. Rivers surround us, we don't need water," said Hyland.

"You fool," exploded Hawker, "it's tidal." He scooped a handful of water from the river and thrust it at Hyland. "Here, taste it!"

Hyland backed away without trying it and threw up his hands. *"Well, how was I meant to know, they didn't tell me anything,"* he shouted, before slinking down the beach a distance.

We ignored his sulking for we had bigger problems. I slapped the sandflies settling on my legs, rolled down my trousers and pulled on my boots. "If some of us follow the folds in the land, we are sure to find fresh water."

"That's a good idea," said Peter, "the rest of us will stay here to hack out a place to camp, and get our stores above the high tide mark." He got an axe out of the boat. "Come over here, Hyland," he shouted, "we need your help."

Richard drifted towards him reluctantly. "What do you want?"

Peter thrust the axe at him. "You're supposed to instruct us in bushcraft. How do we chop down these gigantic trees?"

Hyland took the axe gingerly and waved it around ineffectively. "You just hit a tree until it falls down."

"Here, give that to me before you cut yourself," said

Frederick Liley, striding over and taking it from him. "I am a pit sawyer, not a tree feller, but I've seen trees dropped." He marched over to a cluster of slender trunks. "Start with the smaller trees, and chop out a V like this…"

I wanted to stay and watch, but finding fresh water before nightfall was a priority. I took a slasher and a bucket from the boat and set off with twenty other men. Searching for a valley was good in theory, but in reality, the trees hid the terrain. In the end, we marched towards the bush and attacked the foliage between the trunks. At first, my blade just bounced off the vines that wound like fat ropes between the trees and gigantic ferns, but after a few more swipes, I started making headway. Gnarled roots tripped my feet as I pushed through bracken, bushes, and long stringy stuff, and soon my hands were bleeding from cutty-grass, while leaves bristling with sharp hooks scratched my face and clung to my hair. Despite the sunny day, it was wet and dark in the bush, for the leafy canopy high above us hid the sky. We hunted for hours but did not find water. The first stars were out when we trailed back to the camp, thirsty and disheartened. The men left with the supplies had cleared pockets of space, and rigged up tarpaulins and pitched the tents.

"No luck," we said, shaking our heads.

"I've been shipwrecked more than once and lived to tell the tale," an older man said. "We have more chance of finding water here than at sea."

None of us wanted to eat the dry ship's biscuits without water.

"Put a pebble under your tongue," said the old sailor, "it will help keep your mouth moist."

To Own a Fig Tree

So, sucking on pebbles, we went to bed hungry and thirsty.

The next morning, I and the Shetland brethren, along with Daniel and the rest of the believers among us, read the Bible and prayed fervently that the Lord would lead us to water. Then all thirty-seven of us began our urgent search. Robert and I walked to the end of the track I cut the day before, and started slashing through the foliage. I had not yet regained the strength I lost during the voyage. My throat was parched, and my arms and legs ached from the previous day's activity, but I ignored the discomfort. While we worked, warbling and trilling sounds like bells and flutes, rose over the noise of the men whacking bushes, and small birds followed us, flicking out their tails like little fans. After hours and hours of fruitless searching, we found nothing. None of us got much sleep that night. Instead, we lay in the dark listening to the unfamiliar sounds of the nightbirds. The next morning, we said our prayers before dawn, and hacked paths through the bush with the energy of desperation.

Finally, I heard shouting close by.

"It's Daniel and Charles," said Robert, stopping to listen. "They must have found water."

"I pray so," I said, changing direction and cutting my way towards the commotion.

"Hello Johnsons," rasped Daniel, as we broke into a small clearing amid the thick bush.

"Have you found water?" I croaked.

"No," he pointed to four derelict buildings almost hidden by creepers. "But miners have lived here at some time."

I walked over and pulled at a door.

"Not recently," I said, as the door fell off its rusted hinges.

"True, but there must be water near here," said Charles through cracked lips. "Perhaps there is a well or spring."

With renewed vigour, we hauled away creepers, and finding a dip in the ground, followed it to a creek about a mile-and-a-half from our camp.

"WATER, WATER, WE'VE FOUND WATER," we shouted, as falling on our knees, we dipped our cupped hands into the burbling liquid rushing over rocks between the ferny banks. Never before or after has a drink tasted so good. We quenched our thirst, and then filled our containers to the brim. The others, hearing our shouts, soon found their way to our oasis. That afternoon we blazed a trail to the water, and by dinnertime, we had chopped a wide track to the creek.

Despite finding water, that evening we were silent as we ate ship's biscuits and drank black tea by the campfire. Any expectations of acquiring land easily had perished during the last two days, and we were overwhelmed by the mammoth task before us.

To Own a Fig Tree

Black Sunday

The day after we found water was Sunday. In keeping with our custom, we had breakfast, read a chapter of the Bible, sang a hymn, and prayed. Edwin King waited patiently until we chorused: "Amen." Then he and several other infidels picked up slashers and set off towards the track. During the drama of the last two days, Agent Hyland had so slipped into the background we ceased to notice him. Now as we opened our Bibles to 'Take the Good Book,' he arose and cleared his throat.

"Why are you all still sitting around, there is work to be done?"

Poor man, he's so muddled he doesn't even know what day of the week it is, I thought.

"It is Sunday," I said, to jog his memory.

"I know that," said Hyland, "get up and start work."

I folded my arms. "Sunday is a day of rest."

"I'm in charge," spluttered Hyland, going red in the face. "Get to work."

I drew myself up to my full height, and looked him square in the eye with my shoulders back. "The Sabbath belongs to the Lord, not you, Richard Hyland."

The other men also arose and faced him defiantly.

"That's right," they said. "The Lord has commanded us to

rest on the Sabbath and we will obey him here, just as we did in the old country."

"But the job is too big to only work six days a week," said Hyland, "start work at once. When you have cleared the land, you can go back to resting on Sundays."

"No," I said, "the job is too big to disobey the Lord's commandments. We cannot do this in our own strength. The only way to conquer this land is through him empowering us. My hand shall not touch a tool on the Sabbath," I said, sitting down and picking up my Bible once more.

"That's right, we will not be working on the Lord's Day," chorused the others, also sitting down. "Come join us, Richard," I said, opening my Bible to '*Joshua*.'

Hyland clenched his jaw, and stared at us indecisively for several minutes before stamping his foot and stalking off.

Then I and several of the leading elders read portions of scripture and expounded on them, and after that, we sang hymns and prayed at length. Then we *broke bread*[31]. After the meeting, I slipped under a tarpaulin stretched like a tent roof between trees.

"I need this," I said to Daniel, as I lay on my blanket. "The last few days have been exhausting."

"They certainly have."

"We are in a bad way," said Lawrence Lawrenson, his head sticking out of the open flap of a nearby tent. "We have a formidable job before us."

I nodded. "It is not anything like the watercolour pictures Reverend Barclay showed us." My tone turned bitter. "He never told us we had to clear giants from the land before we

---

31   a religious ceremony

To Own a Fig Tree

could 'tickle it with a hoe.'"

"No smoking joints of mutton either," said John Sinclair.

"Don't worry, John," said Robert, pulling a face. "Hyland will show you how to get one."

John rolled his eyes and Hawker spat on the ground.

"That Government agent is useless," said Alfred Williams, hanging a billy of water over a small fire. "Richard Hyland is not a leader and has no idea what he is doing. I wonder why they picked him?"

"Rumour has it he knows influential people, and named-dropped in his application," said Daniel.

Hawker snorted disdainfully, "that would explain it."

"To think I felt sorry for Alfred Lineham missing out," I said, "now I think he was the lucky one."

Peter Coutts nodded as he aimlessly threw a stick. "I can't bring my sisters and elderly parents to this bleak wilderness."

"My wife is expecting a township of eighty-nine families," I said, rubbing my hand over my face. "I don't know how I will tell her the toon is an island of jungle."

"It's been a huge mistake," said Alfred Williams. "I should have stuck with mining." He struck his palm with his fist. "We should walk out."

"How?" said Peter. "The steamer won't be back for a month and you saw the coast, high hills meet the sea in rugged bluffs. Tizard said many lives have been lost trying to get around the cliffs."

"We could try to find a way overland," said David.

"And go round and round in circles, lost forever," said Peter.

"And even if we got out," I chipped in, "we owe money for

our coats, boots and equipment."

"And the allowance they pay our wives each week is not a gift," said Daniel.

"We could get work and pay our debts off," said Liley.

"Maybe you could, for sawyers are in big demand," said Daniel, "but I tried for months to get a job. The Nelson farmers have all the workers they need."

"Let's face it," I said grimly, "we are trapped. There is no way out of our predicament. We have travelled halfway around the world to swap one master for another."

The water boiled over and hit the fire with a hiss. Alfred did not lift the billy from the flames and neither did anyone else. We were too disheartened to care. We did not dare voice our sense of betrayal, and nothing stopped afternoon prayers and hymn singing, but I doubt I was the only one who felt God had forsaken us.

To Own a Fig Tree

Karamea Jack

We were in black moods when we awoke on Monday morning. Breakfast, prayers and a hymn did little to improve our tempers. Edwin King, who had not had a day of rest, was particularly crabby.

"Blasted mosquitoes," he said, touching the welts covering his face.

Charles crossed his eyes as a sandfly landed on the end of his nose. "If the cannibals take too long to find us, the mosquitoes and sandflies will have beaten them to it," he said, slapping his face.

And indeed, it appeared that way, for day and night we were constantly slapping and scratching.

"I hope you lazy blokes will work today," said Edwin, in a sulky tone, "instead of leaving it up to a few of us."

"Of course," James Moffatt growled, "the Sabbath only comes once a week."

"Things may be bad here, but at least we get paid six shillings a day," I said, picking up my slasher with a sigh.

Hyland spoke for the first time since we defied him. "Only for Government work, Monday to Thursday. Don't think the Government will pay you for clearing anything on the South Bank. Clear your land in your own time, and…" he smirked, "the Government doesn't pay for days of rest. If you want to squander one of your days with a sabbath, that's your business."

"Alright," said Daniel, "how do we earn money?"

"Clear the Government Reserve, I suppose."

"You suppose!"

Turning our back on him with the contempt he deserved, we, who were leading elders, huddled together in discussion.

"No point wearing ourselves out clearing land that may not be ours," said James Moffatt.

"We'd best wait until it's properly surveyed," I said.

Daniel stared at the island across the river. "Seeing as we are stuck here, we might as well work on the town-site. That will benefit everyone even if they don't pay us."

This was sensible, so leaving the pitiful agent at the camp with our supplies, we picked up our tools and waded across the river.

The trees loomed thirty yards above our heads as we stood on the sand trying to work out the best way to get rid of them.

"We can't even chop them down," said Liley, "for the undergrowth is too dense to swing an axe."

"What about burning the little stuff out?" said Daniel. "It's an island. If the fire gets out of control, it can't go far."

Liley rubbed his chin thoughtfully.

"Hmm, that might work. It's pretty damp," he said, looking at the dark streaks running up the tree trunks. "But we could give it a go. Scout around for kindling while I find a spot for the fire."

He wandered off a little way and started cutting a pathway between two giants. We did as he said and soon had armfuls of sticks and leaves, which we mounded into a large pile by a dead bush. Then Liley, pulling waterproof matches from his pocket, lit the fire. A small flame wavered and spluttered under

To Own a Fig Tree

a rising line of smoke, and I fanned it with my hat.

"We needn't fear it turning into a raging forest fire," said Liley, pulling a wry face. "Stay here, Johnson, and keep the fire going. The rest of us will spread out around the island. With a bit of luck, we can burn our way in like spokes of a cartwheel."

"Alright."

They moved away as I crouched down and blew the flame bigger. Birds, disturbed by our noise and the smoke, squawked and flew over my head as they fled from the island. Apart from a few showers of rain that slowed the fires into smouldering heaps of black smoke, the idea worked. By midday, many pockets of fire meandered through the trees and several days later, we could walk through the blackened tree trunks. Then the really tough work started. With blistered hands and aching backs, we chopped, and chopped, and chopped. I grumbled to myself between each swing of the axe as I chipped away at the big trunks.

"In my life…" chop,

"I've fished the *haf'* in a small boat…" chop,

"Grubbed rocks from hard ground…" chop,

"Climbed sheer cliffs for gulls' eggs…" chop,

"Dug, and raked, and hoed…" chop, chop, chop,

"But never have I done anything as difficult as this!"

I paused and wiped the sweat off my brow. "Lord," I said, looking upward, "figs better taste amazing, for trees are vastly overrated."

I did not expect an audible reply, so I nearly dropped my axe when a voice answered:

"Oh, they are good alright. I plan to buy a pound of dried figs when I trade in my gold."

W.E. Hamilton

Turning, I saw a stranger. He had a long beard and wore tattered clothes. A swag was slung over his shoulder and he carried a basket in one hand, and a billy in the other.

"Hello," he said, tipping his battered hat, "Jack Black's the name, but folks call me Karamea Jack. I'm on my way to Westport, and I heard a commotion on the island so I've come to see what's happening."

"Hello, I'm Robert Johnson. I and a group of other men have come to settle in the land."

Karamea Jack's eyes twinkled. "Doesn't sound like you are enjoying it much."

I pulled a face. "You weren't supposed to hear my grumbles."

"Where are you from, Robert? I don't recognize your accent."

"Shetland."

"Ah, that explains it."

"What about you, where do you come from?"

"I've been so long in these parts I don't rightly remember. Me and my two buddies have spent the last ten years seeking gold up the Karamea river and on the black sands of the beach."

I looked around for two other men.

"Oh, my buddies are not with me," said Jack, "they are back at the camp. Only starvation or a full pouch of gold is worth trekking all the way into town."

My heart started beating fast. "So, you know how to get overland to Westport?"

"I reckon I do. I've gone up and down the river tributaries and through the hinterland more times than I can count. Sometimes I go to Westport over the mountains, sometimes

To Own a Fig Tree

I take the Heaphy track through Collingwood to Nelson. It depends which is the shortest way once my pouch is heavy."

By now the shadows were lengthening and the dull thuds and plinks of chopping were tapering off, as it was getting time to eat.

"Come back for dinner with me, Jack," I said, thinking how excited the others would be to see him. "It's not much, just potatoes and damper, but you are welcome to share it."

"Now, that is right kind," said Jack, grinning. "I'd like that very much. But I can't come empty-handed. Follow me and we'll get something to add to the pot."

I was not sure what Jack meant, but I was keen to call it a day. He led me out of the bush, and we waded over to the mainland. I could see Hyland lounging about on the beach by the supplies. Jack flicked his eyes over him but said nothing. Instead, he turned and followed the river inland until we found a quiet spot.

"Here," he said, thrusting his basket at me, "hold the tucker bag."

I took it curiously as he whipped out a knife from a sheath at his hip. It was not like any bag I had seen before.

"It's called a kete," said Jack, noticing the way I turned it around in my hands. "The Maoris make them from flax."

"What's flax?"

Jack pointed his knife at a large plant with long stringy leaves that splayed from the ground like a fountain. "Jolly useful stuff, flax. You can make almost anything from it." He reached up into a tall tree fern and cut a giant hairy spiral from it. "These young ponga fronds are tasteless but fill a gap when you are hungry."

"How do you eat them?"

"Skin and boil them."

I watched as he expertly stripped the black hair away. When he finished, he handed me the pale green curl, and I put it in the bag as he cut another frond. "How many men in the camp?"

"Thirty-seven."

Karamea Jack let out a long whistle. "That is quite a few. I had no idea there were so many of you. Have you got a knife, Robert?"

I pulled my pocket knife out. "Yes."

"Give me the bag then, and help me collect more. Take only one frond from each ponga, for the fronds make food for the plant."

I nodded, and pushing my way over to a tall fern, reached up and cut my first fond. It was difficult to peel. Jack had the basket almost full by the time I had the hair stripped from my frond.

"Now we want a rotten old stump," said Jack, as I popped the frond in his bag. I followed as he eased his way into the undergrowth. As if led by a sixth sense, he walked straight to a dead tree. "Perfect. Put your knife under the loose bark like this, Robert." He slid his blade under a flaky part of the trunk and flicked it off. Underneath were several white worms as fat as my thumb. "Ever had a huhu grub before?"

I shook my head. Karamea Jack popped one into his mouth and munched it up.

"Here, try one. When they are raw, they taste like honey."

"What are they like cooked?" I said, keeping my face impassive.

"Peanut butter."

To Own a Fig Tree

I had no idea what peanut butter was, but I said, "I like peanut butter better than honey. I'll wait until they're cooked."

"Suit yourself," said Karamea Jack, digging grubs from the tree rapidly.

When he had all the grubs, he made a small clearing, and taking a handkerchief from his pocket, stretched it out on the ground. Then he cut a stick from a branch, and rapidly whittled it into a whistle. "I'd rather have a mountain duck or a pigeon, but a weka will have to do. The smarter birds keep away from strange activity. Wekas are not great eating, but they make a tolerable soup. Hide and keep still, this shouldn't take long."

He picked up a big stick, and we hid within striking distance of the handkerchief. When we had stopped rustling about, Jack stared intently at the hanky as he blew squawks and squeaks from his whistle, his arm poised to strike, and within minutes a brown henlike bird stepped out of the bushes. Jack's hand tightened around his stick, but he waited until the weka pecked curiously at the strange object in its path. Then:

WHOOSH, THUD, it was dead.

"Now we can go," said Jack, handing me the bird. "Take me to your friends."

W.E. Hamilton

A Way of Escape for Some

Dinner preparations were underway when I walked into camp with my new friend.

"This is Jack Black, but folks call him Karamea Jack," I called out.

Every man stopped work and there was a stunned silence.

"Gidday folks, I was passing through on the way to Westport and thought I would drop in on you."

At this, everyone started babbling with wonder and shouted excited questions.

Jack stepped back a pace. "Whoa, first things first. I'll answer you all in good time." He lifted his tucker bag, "I brought a little something for your pot."

"We haven't got one big enough to hold food for thirty-seven," I said, "that is why we cook in many small pots."

Karamea Jack looked at the long line of little fireplaces stretching down the shore and shook his head.

"This won't do, won't do at all; with this arrangement the mosquitoes will have a feast. If you place your fires in a circle, rather than a line, and sit in the centre of the ring, the smoke will keep them away."

"I'll try anything to get rid of them," said Edwin, drawing a large circle in the sand with a stick.

"So will I," said Daniel, shifting stones onto Edwin's line.

To Own a Fig Tree

"I'm glad I haven't lit my fire yet."

Karamea Jack took the weka from me, and sitting on a rock, plucked it while I found the biggest pot in the camp, and the others rearranged the fires. When the fires were lit and the food bubbling nicely, we took rocks and some of the boards lying about, and made seats within the ring of fires. For the first time since we arrived, the mosquitoes left us alone.

"That's quite a trick," said Alfred. "Where did you learn it?"

"From the Maoris."

"The natives didn't eat you?"

Karamea Jack gave a shout of laughter. "They don't do that anymore, most of them are friendly. They are very smart and know all sorts of useful things. Here is another tip. Keep a fire smoking at the door of your tent and you won't get bitten at night." He slapped the board he sat on. "I see you are making good use of the Black-Sander's flumes."

"Black-Sanders?"

"Flumes?"

"That's what they call men who work the black sands for gold." He patted the board again. "This here comes from four diggers who toiled for a year, working between tides to erect three miles of flumes at Kongahu, across Granite and Blackwater creeks to the beach. At the end of the time, they thought they were about to make it rich, but…"

All eyes were on Karamea Jack as he leaned forward and swept a piercing glance around our group.

"On the night the flume was completed, heavy seas broke onto the shore, ruining not only the flume but the beach they intended to find gold in!"

We let out a collective gasp, and Jack leaned back, pleased by our reaction to his story.

"Poor blokes, they chucked it in after that. Now there is only me and my two buddies working the beaches and the rivers."

"Is there still gold in the area?" said Alfred Williams.

"Gold!" Jack's eyebrows shot up at the question. "Does an apple tree bear apples? This is gold-bearing country. Twenty years ago, there were lots of Chinese and European gold miners in the mountains; four of their old huts are not far from here."

I nodded. "Yes, we found them. Why did the miners leave?"

"Hunger. Not everyone likes grubs, ponga fronds and tea-tree tea. Getting provisions into the area killed the rush, not lack of gold."

"You said you were on your way to Westport," said one of the Manxmen.

Jack looked in his pot and stirred the contents. "Yup, it's a pain, but every so often I have to go into town."

"Do you know your way out of here?

"I should say I do. After ten years of trekking up and down rivers and mountains, I know lots of ways in and out."

"Can some of us come with you?" said Alfred Williams.

"Well, that depends…" said Karamea Jack, ladling chunks of ponga, grubs and weka onto a tin plate.

"On what?"

Jack's eyes twinkled as he handed Alfred the food. "On whether or not you like my soup."

To Own a Fig Tree

O'Connor Saves the Day

Despite its appearance, the soup was good, and early the next day seven men[32] departed for Westport with Karamea Jack. Those of us remaining were in low spirits. Miserably, we chopped at the trees, hour after hour, and that evening as we huddled inside the ring of fires, we felt like shipwreck survivors on a desert island. Daniel's shoulders slumped as he peeled potatoes, Peter hung a billy over a fire lethargically, and Edwin hummed '*Ten Green Bottles*,' until someone threw a peel at him and Liley yelled:

"Shut up, King!"

"It's amazing how a man we met for a few hours can make such a difference," I said. "Things seemed much better when Karamea Jack was here, and much worse now he and the others have gone."

"I'm glad he's going to drop in on the way back to show us how to build raupo huts."

"He's like, Squanto, who helped the Pilgrims in 1621," said Naylor.

"Who," I said puzzled, "I don't remember reading about him in the Bible?"

"He's not in the Bible."

I thought of the other book in my library. "Who killed him,

---

[32] Departing men were the Manxmen, two of the Cornish miners, a carpenter from Middlesex and two stone masons from Gloucestershire

the church or the King?"

"Nobody killed him, he was an Indian who taught the American Pilgrims how to fish and plant corn, and where to find nuts and berries."

"You are a man of book learning," said Daniel, dropping potatoes into a pot.

Naylor nodded. "I like reading and history."

"I wonder how the others are getting on?" said Daniel, sighing. "I wish I could have gone with them."

"The steamer will be here next month," said Peter, "you could catch it back to Nelson."

"Not possible. I have a big family to support. I have to see this through."

"That's right," said Hyland, from the outer edge of the group, "you can't leave because you owe money to the Government store."

"Who asked your opinion?" growled Peter. "We don't even know if you are keeping accurate records?"

"I'm honest," said Hyland, his voice turning squeaky with umbrage. "You can look at my books anytime. You're the ones who haven't bothered to appoint a storekeeper. I'm not stopping you."

"He has a point," said Daniel. "We do need a storekeeper. Who wants the job?"

There was a long silence.

"I'm not much good at spelling," I said.

"I never was one for figures," said John Sinclair.

There was another silence.

"What about Naylor?" said James Moffatt. "He's a man of book learning. What is your figuring like?"

To Own a Fig Tree

"Alright," admitted Naylor.

"And your handwriting?"

"Not bad, I am a teacher."

James grinned like a man who has solved a difficult riddle. "I think it is obvious who the right man for the job is," he said. "I nominate Naylor as the storekeeper. All in agreement, raise your hand."

A forest of hands flew up.

Naylor smiled. "I didn't like to push myself forward, but as you have chosen me, I would be honoured to serve as the storekeeper until my services as a schoolmaster are required."

"That was easy," said Peter. "I wish we could solve the problem of the trees so swiftly. I fear we will have little accomplished by the time the steamer calls with fresh supplies in a few weeks."

He was right about us doing little, but he was wrong about the timing. Four days before Christmas the *Charles Edward* puffed into the river, two weeks before she was due. By now, we were too downhearted to express surprise over either the boat's early arrival or the unexpected guest on board. We stood watching as Hyland rowed him to shore. When the lighter scuffed onto the beach, the guest leapt out of the boat with great energy. He had long legs, was wearing a rusty velvet coat and a felt hat. The face under the broad brim suggested a man of decisive character, a real goer, and not a man I would like to cross.

"I feel I have seen that chap before," I said.

"Of course you have," said Daniel, with a chuckle. "Picture him in a black suit in the Government Building."

"O'Connor!" I said with a start of recognition.

"Got it in one," said Daniel.

"Good morning men," said O'Connor, "I am Eugene O'Connor, the Provincial Secretary. You may remember me from the Special Settlement meeting."

We nodded and murmured, "yes."

"Yesterday, rumours reached me of a revolt. Seven men near exhaustion put in a dishevelled appearance at Westport. They claim all is not well in Karamea. As soon as I heard the report, I booked a fast passage on the first vessel leaving Nelson, and I am here to investigate." He pulled a pencil and notepad from his pocket. "What's going on?"

A babble broke out.

O'Connor held up his hand.

"One at a time." He looked at me. "I'll start with you. What have you to say?"

I took my cap off. "We don't know where our land is, Sir, the rain forest has grown over the survey lines."

"Hmm. Needs resurveying," O'Connor muttered as he wrote. When his pencil stopped moving, he looked at Daniel.

"We are completely isolated and the Government agent is not a fit leader, he doesn't know what he is doing."

"It's not my fault," Hyland cut in, "the men won't listen to me."

"There is no point," sneered Liley. "You know nothing about bush craft, or building or tree felling."

"I could do a lot better," whined Hyland, "if my son was here to cook my dinner."

O'Connor gave Hyland a withering look, and wrote something down before asking:

"Have you got any land cleared?"

To Own a Fig Tree

Once again, a babble broke out as we escorted him down the beach to a patch of ground.

"We thought we would start on the Government Reserve because we don't know where our land is," I said.

Hyland puffed himself up importantly. "And I told them they wouldn't be paid for anything else."

O'Connor, ignoring him, muttered under his breath: "I can see I have to take a more active part in this settlement if it is to succeed." He straightened, and raising his voice, said, "We have got off to a bad beginning but it doesn't have to stay that way. For starters, I am increasing your wages from six to ten shillings a day."

This was an instant morale booster. We cheered and clapped.

"As soon as I get back to town, I will arrange for two competent sawyers and a surveyor to come here."

His eye fell on my son and three other men.

"You four, I want you to search for survey pegs. When you find a rotten one, cut a clearing around it and replace it with a large stick that is easily seen."

He swivelled around and his piercing gaze fell on his agent. "Hyland, where are the seed potatoes and turnips?"

"They are on the mainland with the supplies."

O'Connor pointed to two men. "You and you, go with him and bring them over here. Ten men dig up this ground, and help Hyland plant potatoes and turnips. We need to get them in quickly, so there is food for winter."

"We could do with a pig," said Edwin. "If you handle them right, pigs are great for digging up the ground and grubbing out boulders."

O'Connor nodded, as he scribbled, 'pig,' on his pad.

W.E. Hamilton

"What about a cow? A bit of milk for our tea would be nice," said Peter.

"Alright. One cow." He looked up. "Of course, it is too early for packhorses and cattle, but these will be supplied on easy terms once there is pasture to support them. As to the isolation, I will organize with the owners of the *Charles Edward & Co*, for a ship to call early each month, and, Hyland…"

"Yes Sir."

"There is a rough track around the coast to Mokihinui. In the middle of each month, appoint a man to act as a mail carrier. That way we will have continuous communication."

"What about our wives and children?" called a voice from the back of the crowd. "When can they come?"

"I will make sure they arrive as soon as possible. But before then, we need a storehouse and shelters." O'Connor put his pad and pencil in his pocket as his eyes swept over the debris lying about the shore. "Those of you not planting or surveying, collect all the timber you can find. Have you chosen a storeman yet?"

"Yes, John Naylor, the schoolmaster."

"Good choice. He can assist Hyland until the school is built." He tapped his tooth with his pencil. "Do you have any other concerns?"

We shuffled our feet and shook our heads.

"Good. I'll see you are well looked after. By the time I come back in January, I want to see a store and a jetty at the mouth of the river." He paused and stared at us fiercely.

"Do you think you can do it?"

"Yes," we responded.

O'Connor cupped his hand behind one ear. "I can't hear

To Own a Fig Tree

you. I'll ask again. Do you think you can do it?"

"Yes," we shouted, our energy and hope rising.

"I still can't hear you. DO YOU THINK YOU CAN DO IT?"

"YES, WE CAN DO IT," we shouted with gusto.

"OF COURSE YOU CAN," shouted O'Connor. *"Colonizing is the special mission of the Anglo-Saxon race!"*

We clapped and stomped our feet. O'Connor smiled at our response, and when we quietened, said:

"I have fresh supplies for you in the boat. Before you do anything else, I want them unloaded so the *Charley* can leave on high tide."

We set to work with a will, and soon all the sacks and boxes were on the beach. Then it was time for O'Connor to go.

"I'll be back in January to see how you are getting on," he shouted over the water as he boarded the *Charley*. "Have a Merry Christmas."

"Merry Christmas," we called back.

O'Connor tipped his hat, and moving to the stern, stood waving as the steamer pulled away. Then someone shouted:

"THREE CHEERS FOR THE FATHER OF KARAMEA."

And everyone cheered long and loud for the man who saved the day.

W.E. Hamilton

A Big Surprise

Things were a little better after Eugene O'Connor's visit; for hope energised us. I felt my strength returning as each day I dug in the garden or helped build the store. Christmas came and went with nothing more than an extra day of rest to mark the event. The steamer arriving early on January the thirteenth, was far more exciting. The men working on the jetty were the first to see her.

"The *Charley* is here, the *Charley's* here," Charles shouted, running towards the garden waving his hat.

"Where?"

"By the entrance."

We threw down our spades and ran to the beach.

"It looks like there are women on deck," said Daniel, squinting into the distance.

"You must be mistaken," I said, "there is no way O'Connor would bring the women and children. He knows we are not ready for them."

"You must be right," said Daniel, "my eyes are playing tricks on me. There is no way it can be them."

"We might as well go back to work," I said, "the tide is still low, and the bar so unpredictable, it will be several hours before the steamer can safely venture over it. Come back and tell us when the *Charley* is in, Charles."

Charles nodded and sped off.

To Own a Fig Tree

It was midday before Charles alerted us. Then we rushed onto the beach and watched in excitement as the steamer slowly slid to a halt a few yards from the bank where we stood.

"You were right, Daniel," I said, torn between joy and consternation, "you *did* see women and children. I can't wait to greet them, but where are we going to house them?"

"Where indeed?" said Daniel, his face fluctuating between smiles and frowns.

Hyland rowed the lighter out, and O'Connor assisted the women and children to the thin ribbon of sand. Then there was a commotion of laughing and shouting as families and friends reunited.

"Daddy, Daddy," shouted Margret, Laurence, and William, running towards Robert and me.

I caught William and swung him into the air as John strode up. "Hello, everyone, where is your mother?"

"Mr O'Connor has gone back for her, and Mary and James," said John, "they will land with the next group."

"Alfred and Harry, you're here," said Daniel, slapping the Lineham brothers on the back.

"Not only us," said Alfred, Thomas was well enough to come. He lifted his voice and shouted, "Come and meet the Johnsons, Thomas." A man with a cheerful face and a boy at his side limped over. "Thomas, this is Robert Johnson and his family."

"Hello, nice to meet you," he said, as we shook hands.

"Where's Mary and the children?" said Daniel, looking around.

"It's just me and George," said Thomas. "I left the family in Nelson. They'll come out sometime around Easter, once the baby is born."

"Good idea," I said, "this is no place for a pregnant woman."

"I'm nine, how old are you, George?" said Margret.

"I'm ten and I'm going to help Dad build our house," said George, standing tall with importance.

"Yes, you are," said Thomas, "you are my right-hand man."

"How is your leg?" said Daniel.

"Good. For a while l endured a fiery trial, but the Lord saw me through the hard time, and now the diseased bone is gone, I get stronger every day and..."

"Excuse me," I said, cutting across his words, "I've seen my wife and daughter."

I hurried over to the lighter and wading into the water, swung Mary out and onto the sand. Then I handed her James, and scooping up Anderina, staggered the short distance to dry ground.

"What are you doing here so early?" I said, setting her down.

"All I want is to be with you, helping to build our new life. I could not bear to spend another day at the Immigration Hostel. The food was full of refined flour and overcooked, and I can't stand those toffee-nosed women. They laughed at the way I talked and sneered because I couldn't read."

"They don't know you can't read," I said.

"Oh yes, they do. Every week we had to sign for the remittance our husbands assigned us. Those awful women wrote their names and hung around to watch me make my mark. I put up with it until the officer in charge of the hostel said the *Michelangelo* was due to arrive, and we must expect to share our rooms. Then I and the rest of the Special Settlement

To Own a Fig Tree

women, marched down to the Parliament Buildings, found Mr Elliot and demanded he send us to Karamea *at once*. He wasn't going to let us go, but when he heard another hundred-and-fifty people were about to arrive, and the hostel was full, he promised to send us on the first ship leaving for the Westcoast, with Mr O'Connor as guardian. So, we left yesterday at two pm and here we are." She looked around with bright eyes. "Where is the *toon*?"

"There is no town yet."

"Well then, where is our land?"

I waved my hand at the bush across the river. "Somewhere over there. You shouldn't have come. We are not prepared for you."

Anderina (still not realizing the difficulty of the situation) frowned. "Aren't you pleased to see me, Robert?"

"Of course I'm glad to see you. But we are working sixteen hours a day and sleeping under tarpaulins. I don't know where you and the children will stay."

By now, the luggage was being unloaded. Robert and John dumped the almost-pirate chest beside us, and Anderina slumped down on it as my words sank in.

"No *toon*, no houses, no shelter?"

I nodded. "No town, no houses, no shelter." I waved my hands at the thick bush. "We have to carve it out of the rain forest."

Anderina stared at the blackened tree trunks, standing like bristles in a hairbrush. Then my stoic wife, who never cried, did something shocking. She threw her apron over her head, and wept loudly.

W.E. Hamilton

A Temporary Solution

I stood by my weeping wife, unsure what to do. The other men were also at a loss, for by now all the women were sobbing. O'Connor, ignoring the wailing, called the men away for a meeting.

"Good afternoon, gentlemen. As promised, I have brought sawyers. This is James Black and David Grayney," he said pointing to the men. "They are pit sawyers and I have instructed them to give each family three days of free labour."

"What is the point of having timber for a house if we don't know where to build it?" said Edwin King.

O'Connor's eyes fell on my son.

"Robert, did you find any survey pegs?"

"Yes, quite a few, and we marked them just as you told us to."

"Very good." O'Connor pointed to a third stranger. "This is Mr Rawson, the surveyor I promised to bring. He will resurvey the land. Robert, you and your team take Rawson with you and show him the pegs you found. Then you can help him with the survey lines. Now let's see how the garden is progressing," he said, as the five men strode off.

We led him down the beach towards a clearing a little distance away.

"I see you have made a start on the jetty," said O'Connor, jerking his head backwards. "How did you get on with the store and garden?"

"Two acres cleared and planted in potatoes and turnips," said Edwin King.

"And the store is almost built," said Hyland. He pointed to a huge pile of fallen trunks and branches. "It's behind there."

"Did you strike any problems?"

"We had a bit of trouble getting the timber across the mud flats because a lot of the men are unaccustomed to boats," I said, as we skirted around the logs and debris, "but we managed in the end."

O'Connor picked his way through the maze of stumps to our garden, and scrutinized it. "Very good," he said. Then he went over to the store and tried unsuccessfully to shake the wall. "Rough but solid, it will do temporarily."

"Our priority is to get some sort of shelter for the women and children," said Daniel, with a worried frown. "Fortunately, it is summer but the warm weather won't last, and it rains a lot."

O'Connor nodded. "Stop all other work until you have sorted something out."

"What about those four abandoned huts?" Daniel said. "They are not much, but they are better than nothing. Surely we could pull them together."

"There is little room in them for thirteen women and all the children. That is four or five families per hut," said James Moffatt doubtfully. "We might get them in at a pinch, but what about the luggage?"

O'Connor went into the shed. "Store it in here until you have shelters built."

"But I sleep in here," Hyland protested.

"Even with twice the luggage, you'd have more room than the women and children," growled Fredrich Liley, with disgust.

O'Connor turned to Daniel. "How many men do you need to fix those huts?"

Daniel looked into the air as he calculated. "Maybe four men per hut."

"Alright," said O'Connor, striding towards the beach. "I've got twelve hours before high tide. Fifteen men go with Daniel to fix up the huts. Ten of you go back to the *Charley*, there is still stuff to be unloaded. Edwin King, you're the one who wanted a pig. Take charge of the livestock. When the others have finished unloading, they can help you build fences. Johnson, tell the women to take cooking equipment and necessities out of their luggage. When they have done that, you can all stack everything in the store. Hyland, keep a record of everything that goes into storage. John Naylor, you can help him. Those of you without a job, come with me, I'm going to teach you how to fish without hooks."

I hesitated. "What about the problem of the women and children all crying?"

"Don't worry." O'Connor, pointed to two men talking earnestly with the weeping women. "The reporter from the *Nelson Colonist*, and Mr McLean, a member of the Provincial Council, will keep them entertained until their stuff is unloaded."

"Why did McLean and the reporter come?" said Liley, as we separated into groups.

"To disprove the rumours circulating in Nelson and Westport that the settlement is about to collapse." O'Connor sighed and his words faded as the groups moved in opposite

To Own a Fig Tree

directions. "At least, that was my original plan. I wish I had not brought them along…"

A bird warbled, and I missed his last words.

"Did you catch what O'Connor just said?" I asked Edwin.

Edwin nodded. "He said, I hate to think what they will write about Karamea and me when they get back."

W.E. Hamilton

Only Bare Necessities Please

As a member of the Provincial Council, Mr McLeon was an important man, yet he was upstaged by livestock. The women and children stopped crying, and watched with interest as we herded the swimming animals out of the water.

"Does anyone wish to comment?" said the reporter, bustling over with his pencil and pad.

"That is a fine sow," said Edwin, as we herded a pig out of the water. "With a bit of luck, she is expecting piglets."

"Two cows," I said, "twice as many as we asked for."

"And sheep," said Peter Coutts. "We weren't expecting sheep."

"Lambies," said James, clutching his woollen toy.

"Perhaps they are the smoking joints of mutton Reverend Barclay's pictures promised us," I joked.

Margret rushed over to the dripping sheep protectively. "No, Daddy, don't eat them!"

Anderina glared at me with red-rimmed eyes. "Nobody is going to eat them, Margret. We need their wool."

"Dispute over sheep," muttered the reporter, scribbling on his pad. "Who is for and who is against eating the sheep? I need numbers."

Ignoring him, I turned to the women. "Shortly, the men will have finished unloading the luggage. You will be pleased

To Own a Fig Tree

to hear we have found temporary accommodation for you…"

Sighs of relief and happy murmuring greeted this statement.

"The men will continue to live in the camp on the beach until we get the land surveyed. We have four huts in the bush which we are currently fixing up. Space, however, is very limited. Four or five families will have to share each hut, so there is no room for anything other than bare necessities."

Muttering and a few tears flowed at this news.

"In a minute, I want you to sort through your belongings and take out essentials like cooking equipment, blankets and a change of clothing. We will store everything else in the Government Store until you have your own shelter. Are there any questions?"

"How will we know it will be there when we go to claim it?"

"Agent Hyland and John Naylor will keep a record of everything stored, and who it belongs to."

I looked around. "If there are no more questions, we need to get going."

There was a tiny pause, and then a flurry of noise and activity. Anderina got off the almost-pirate chest, opened it briefly and banged it shut again. "I don't need the clock or Robert's certificate yet," she said. She opened the lid of the large suitcase beside the chest, and was about to take out her midwifery bag, but I stopped her.

"There is no point taking that," I said. "Look around, none of the women are pregnant."

"They may be," said Anderina, with a mulish expression.

"If they are, we will be housed and settled by the time you need your bag."

At the mention of our own home, Anderina smiled and put the bag back in the case.

"We won't need the squeeze-box or hymnbook either."

My wife sucked in her breath, and her tone was sharp as she said:

"Shame on you, Robert! Do you mean to tell me you are breaking the Sabbath?"

"No, dear, nothing like that, only the infidels work on the Lord's Day. All the believers rest and 'take the Book'. We sing without, 'The Little Flock Hymns,' or music because we don't want books or instruments ruined by frequent rain."

"That makes sense."

James gave several little coughs, and Anderina's attention instantly switched to him. "I'm glad I got the medicine chest restocked in Nelson," she said, placing a hand on the frail child's forehead. "I definitely need it. I don't like this cough James has developed."

"You can't take the entire cabinet to the hut, there is not enough room for it. Just take the bottle of cough syrup."

Anderina glanced around to make sure our children were not listening, and leaning forward, whispered, "I fear it is the same type of cough that ailed our poor Elizabeth-the-first."

"*Consumption?*"

Anderina's face went white, and she placed her hand over my mouth.

"Shh, don't speak the word, I can't bear to hear it."

"Perhaps it is just an ordinary cough," I said, my voice wobbling slightly.

"Perhaps, I pray it is."

We were quiet for a few moments.

To Own a Fig Tree

"Even if it is as you say," I said, breaking the silence, "there is no point taking quinine and smelling salts. We'll ask Hyland to store the cabinet where it's easy to get, in case of an emergency."

Anderina nodded, took a large bottle of orange liquid from the cabinet, and placed it in her carpetbag.

"Mary," I called. "Take this to the store." I handed her the medicine box. "It's not far and you will find it easily. Give it to Agent Hyland and tell him it belongs to Robert Johnson, and ask him to keep it handy."

"Will he want your name on it?" said Mary, chewing her lip. "Yes, and Mr Naylor will record it in a ledger."

"Please don't send me," she said, pushing the cabinet back at me. "Remember what happened when you sent me to the Post Office in Shetland to register William when he was born? Mr Naylor might ask me to spell Johnson." Her mouth drooped. "It's my fault William's last name is spelt with a T and E."

"It's not your fault he's 'Johnstone'. I blame myself entirely," I said. "I thought if the Registrar wrote all the different ways to spell Johnson, you could pick the right one." I handed the cabinet back to her. "Besides it is quite unimportant how they spell 'Johnson' in the ledger."

"Be a good girl, Mary," said Anderina, "I'm busy, and Elizabeth is watching William and James."

"Oh, all right."

After she left, my wife and I switched our attention back to the boxes.

"What about this?" said Anderina, opening another chest and holding up a lantern.

"Yes, the lantern would be good, and take the plates and

cutlery we used on the ship. Also, the camp oven."

Anderina put the plates and utensils in the camp oven, and the oven beside her carpet bag.

Harriet Scarlett nodded with approval. "That's a good idea, Anderina," she said, copying. "Are you taking many blankets?"

Anderina looked uncertain.

"I'm not," said Agnes Moffatt, "the weather is so hot we'll swelter under blankets. For the same reason, there is no point taking petticoats either."

I looked around and felt pleased; the women had perked up now they were busy. They chatted as they bustled about sorting through boxes, while the children dug in the sand and paddled at the edge of the water. Realizing I was unnecessary, I left them to get on with the job and went to help unload the last of the supplies.

To Own a Fig Tree

A Wonderful Discovery

It was late afternoon by the time we had packed the luggage in the store, and ferried the women and children across to the mainland. There, the women chatted and the children ran about laughing and shouting, as they milled around the men's camp, unsure what to do.

"Leave your cooking gear here," I shouted above the hubbub, "then come with me."

There was a rattle of metal as camp ovens, tin-plates and utensils hit the sand, followed by mothers calling their offspring to heel.

"This way," I shouted, waving my hand towards the pathway slashed through the bush. The pungent smell of dying fern filled the air, and cicadas pulsed noisily, as men with suitcases on their shoulders, women with bags in their hands, and children carrying lanterns, blankets or chamber pots, followed me down the track. It got darker and darker as we went deeper and deeper into the bush. As we neared the huts, we heard the banging of many hammers, and when we reached the clearing, I saw the men had fixed the walls and roofs, and were now hanging the doors. Although the huts were much improved, they were still very makeshift and rough. After the women's reaction to their new land, I was not keen to show them their new homes. But I had nothing to fear. They rallied their wits and looked at the huts with their usual stoicism.

W.E. Hamilton

"Could be worse," said Anderina.

"At least it's shelter," said Harriet.

Agnes Moffatt stuck her head in the door and looked at the rough bunks her husband had just finished making. "The beds are better than those foolish wires at the Immigration Hostel."

Edwin, pulling a seed packet from his pocket, pointed to a patch of brown bracken and said, "Karamea Jack reckons dead pig-fern is almost as good as a straw ticking." Then he stepped aside quickly to avoid the rush of swirling skirts. When all that remained of the pig-fern was a few tough stalks, he scattered seeds over the ground between them. I frowned and shot him a piercing look.

"Edwin King, did you speak the truth, or did you just want somewhere to plant your seeds?"

"Both," he chuckled, "thanks to me, the ladies will have soft beds and lovely flowers."

I was about to ask him what type of flowers they were, but my wife called me.

"Bring the suitcase, Robert. Agnes, Harriet, and I will stay in this hut."

I hurried over to where Anderina stood, her arms full of pig-fern. She jerked her head towards a small gap on the end wall between the bunks.

"Put it over there, and take everything out of it."

"There are supposed to be at least four families in each hut," I said.

"Yes, but we three have the most children. The women with smaller families are only too glad to avoid all our children," said Anderina, as I put the suitcase where she wanted it.

When the case was empty, Anderina dumped pig-fern in it

and covered it with a knitted blanket.

"There!" she said, arranging a stick so the lid could not fall shut. "That will make a nice bed for James." She turned to Laurence and Margret, who were swinging off the bunks. "You children go outside, let Mrs Scarlett, Mrs Moffatt, and I work in peace. You too, Robert, this is women's work. I'll manage better by myself."

I nodded. "As I'm of no use here, I'm going back to the camp. When you are settled, follow the track to the camp for dinner," I said, passing out the door, "and don't forget to bring the lantern."

"Alright," said Anderina, spreading the rest of her fern over a narrow bunk.

When I arrived at the camp, I found the fishing party was back, the ring of fires was extended, and O'Connor was instructing his fishermen on the art of skinning and cooking eels.

"Once the skin is off, wrap it in flax and roast it over embers," he said, picking up a long green leaf and demonstrating. "You got that?"

There was a chorus of yeses. O'Connor saw me as the men scattered, each to a pile of eels.

"Hello, Johnson. Did you get everything unloaded and the women taken care of?"

"Yes. Once they have organized themselves, they're coming back here for dinner."

"Good, good." O'Connor pointed to a sack of potatoes. "Peel those and get them cooking."

I nodded and got on with the job. And just as well, for the food was barely cooked before everyone swarmed into the camp. Then there was a huge commotion; tin plates and utensils clattered, adults talked, and children giggled, shouted, or cried. Now we had the women settled, we all agreed our families coming early was a nice surprise. And that was not the only surprise of the day, for Mr Rawson and his helpers arrived with momentous news. Robert was bouncing with excitement as he shouted:

"We've found a plateau almost clear of trees!"

O'Connor put his cup of tea down, and looked at the surveyor. "Is that right, Rawson?"

"Yes, Sir. A mile south of the river the land rises sharply, and at the top of this is a long flat terrace in the lee of lofty mountains. This will speed up surveying, for there is nothing on it."

"And we can start planting almost as soon as we get our land," said Robert, his eyes shining.

"Hold fire on the celebrations," said O'Connor, rubbing his nose thoughtfully. "There must be something wrong with the soil if nothing grows on it."

"Oh, it's thickly covered with toetoe, ferns, moss, and little manuka trees," said Rawson. "When I said 'nothing was on it,' I meant nothing huge and difficult to remove. Once the land is surveyed, it will be a small job to clear."

"It seems we have cause to celebrate, after all," said O'Connor, as we cheered. "Draw lots for the land as soon as you get some blocks laid out, Rawson. And, Hyland, while the men are waiting for the surveyors to finish, they can continue clearing the Government Reserve, and build a permanent store to replace the makeshift one."

He turned to Mr McLean and the reporter from the Colonist,

To Own a Fig Tree

and smiled triumphantly. "I hope you chaps were not hoping to muckrake. For if you were, you must be greatly disappointed. Don't forget to include this latest discovery when you write up your reports."

W.E. Hamilton

Land at Last

O'Connor, the reporter, and Mr McLean left at midnight on the high tide. In keeping with O'Connor's instructions, we cleared the Government land, and the sawyers made lumber from the timber we cut down. Meanwhile, Rawson, with the help of Robert and three others, spent long hours dividing the South Terrace into fifty-acre blocks. Within a short time, the first ballot was held, and I drew a section about a mile from the jetty and Government store. As soon as I heard, I gathered my family and climbing the steep hill, slashed a track onto our land.

"Can you believe it? *We own this*!" I said, as we stood on the plateau surrounded by scrubby trees and fluffy toetoe. "I never thought I would own land this side of the grave. Now all we need is a house and fig tree."

"It doesn't belong to us yet, Robert," said Anderina, shifting James from one hip to the other. "It is only leased."

"True. But it is as good as ours, for the yearly fee is small and in fourteen years the Government will give us the title deeds to it."

"You're right," said Anderina, smiling.

"It will be a pretty view once we have the scrub cleared away," said Mary, leaning on the spade she carried, "the way the river twists and bends is interesting, and the glimpse of sea reminds me of home."

To Own a Fig Tree

Elizabeth, remembering a small island in the river below, asked:

"Who owns the little island?"

"I don't know, maybe it's the Government's or perhaps it belongs to some of the absentee owners on the other bank."

John pulled a face. "It's unfair that the people who don't live here have the best land, and can walk to the store at low tide without wading."

I was about to answer, but Daniel Scarlett cut my words short, as he and his family stumbled towards us.

"It's a bit of luck you and the Linehams are our neighbours," he said, beaming. "I'm glad we are not next to Samuel Friend, that chap is not like the others. He never exerts himself or puts his back into work."

"It's God's blessing we are together," I agreed.

"The children get along so well," said Anderina, looking at Sarah and Margret riding stalks of toetoe like hobby horses. "But two Williams and Elizabeths is confusing, we'll have to add an S or J to them."

Harriet, still puffing from the climb, nodded. She put her thumbs in the small of her spine, and her corset creaked as she leaned back for a moment.

"You men need to cut a better track up that hill, it's terribly steep," she said, pushing sweaty wisps of hair off her red face. "I dread the idea of carrying our boxes and supplies up it."

"There is no point worrying about boxes, my dear, until we have some sort of shelter built," said Daniel. He turned to me. "Where are you going to put your house, Robert?"

"Anywhere, the land is flat. The real question is, how long before the sawyers get around to cutting lumber for us?"

"Could be months," said Daniel, slapping at mosquitoes.

"Months!" Anderina and Harriet echoed his words with dismay.

"I don't want to stay cooped up in a little hut for months," said Anderina, waving away buzzing insects.

"I don't want to have to climb that hill every day to work in my garden," said Harriet.

"If there were lots of loose rocks around, I would begin making a house immediately," I said, looking in vain, "but there is nothing other than a few stony outcrops scattered between the toetoe."

"Karamea Jack said he would call in on his way back from Westport and show us how to build raupo huts the way the Maoris do," said Daniel.

"But when will that be?"

"Sooner than you think," said Daniel, "for here he comes."

"Naylor was right about him being our 'Squanto,'" I said, as Daniel and I walked towards him. "This is the second time he has shown up at just the right moment."

"Gidday folks," said Karamea Jack, lifting his hat.

"Hello," we replied, shaking his hand. "How did the trip go?" "I enjoyed it, but the other blokes were pretty banged up by the time we got to town."

"We heard they arrived dishevelled and exhausted," Daniel said. "So much so, Eugene O'Connor booked a fast passage on the first boat to check up on us."

"It worked out well," I said, "O'Connor brought a surveyor and two sawyers with him which has hurried things up."

"I see womenfolk and children," said Jack.

"Yes, our wives insisted on coming with O'Connor. It

caused a bit of concern at first, but we have fixed up the miners' old huts and put them and the children in there temporarily."

"Ladies," I called, "come and meet Karamea Jack. This is my wife, Anderina," I said, as she came close, "and Harriet is Daniel's wife."

Jack was a friendly man, but there was a frown on his face as he raised his hat and greeted the women. "Summer is galloping by," he said, eyeing James with concern. "You need better shelters for the women and children before Easter. When do you think you will have land?"

"That's the best part," I said, beaming. "Surveying is much faster now we found this plateau. You're standing on my farm."

Daniel pointed west towards the sea. "And mine's somewhere over there."

Jack smiled and put down his swag. "Where do you want your hut, Robert?"

"Anywhere," I said.

Anderina laid a hand on my arm. "No, Robert, it must face the road that runs along the middle of the settlement."

"That's right," Harriet agreed. "Houses must always face the road."

"There isn't a road."

"Not yet, there isn't, but Robert says the surveyors have slashed out its position. We can ask him where Rawson has put it when he gets back with the surveying team tonight."

"I know where it is," said Daniel, leading the way south, "it runs along our back boundaries."

We picked our way around bushes and trees until we came to a straight line gouged through the scrub.

"The house can go somewhere around here," said Anderina.

"I don't mind a long driveway."

"Now we have the position we can get started," said Jack, dropping his swag on the ground. "First things first, clear all the foliage away."

I slashed at a stunted manuka tree, and Daniel was about to help, but Harriet plucked at his sleeve.

"I'll leave you to it, Robert," he said, "Harriet is anxious to choose our house site."

We waved goodbye and they disappeared down the 'road.' When they were gone, Jack reached into his coat pocket and took out a hip flask and a tobacco pouch.

"Drink, Robert?" he said, offering me the flask.

I smiled, but shook my head. "Not for me, thanks, Jack. I don't drink."

Jack took a swig before putting the flask back in his pocket. "I suppose you don't smoke either."

"That's right."

Jack grunted and sprinkled tobacco onto a cigarette paper. "If you clear a section today, tomorrow I will show you how to build a hut," he said, rolling it into a cigarette. He licked the edge of the paper to seal it, then he pointed to the billhook and spade. "You'll need those, some sharp knives, and a tarpaulin. Can you get them?"

I nodded.

"Bring the family, there are jobs for everyone." Jack lit up, sucked in and puffed out a couple of times leisurely. Then slinging his swag onto his shoulder, he said, "See you bright and early in the morning."

"Bright and early," we echoed, as our 'Squanto' picked up his tucker-bag and ambled off.

To Own a Fig Tree

Building Our First House

There was no time to waste. Anderina chose the place for our home and we got busy preparing the house site. Oddly, in a land where everything was difficult, clearing this ground was easy. The toetoe and even the stunted little manuka trees, popped out after a couple of thrusts of the spade and several good tugs.

"It's very shallow-rooted," said Anderina, examining a clump of toetoe. "And the topsoil is spongy and damp."

I was pleased.

"That will save us from having to water the garden constantly."

Elizabeth took hold of a long toetoe stalk. It was stiff and ended in a creamy 'horse's mane' high above her head. "Where's John," she said, snapping it? "He should be helping."

"He is helping. He's working on the Government Reserve so your father can build our house," said Anderina. "We couldn't manage without your brothers taking over your father's obligations."

"Laurence, Margret, and William, stop playing and drag all the loose tussock into a pile over there," I said, pointing to a spot by the billy and lunch basket.

"How big an area do we have to clear?" said Mary.

"As long as there is daylight, just keep going. The whole twenty-five acres has to be cleared eventually. We need ground for a garden and pasture for cattle."

"And an orchard of fig trees," Laurence piped up.

I laughed. "I'd settle for a mixed orchard with just one fig tree."

William stopped dragging toetoe stalks. "When do we get it, Dad?"

"I don't know, son." I ruffled his hair. "But God's timing is perfect, so the tree will come at the right moment." I nudged him. "Until then, there is work to be done, so get a move on."

Despite needing the occasional reminder not to play, our children were hard workers; with the family pulling together we had a large patch of ground stripped bare when Karamea Jack arrived early the next morning, carrying a bundle of reeds and leaves. After the usual greetings he said:

"I see you've got your tools." He handed my wife a bundle of reeds. "Anderina, this is raupo. It grows in swampy areas and around the edges of lakes." He pointed. "There's a patch over there. I want you and the children to cut lots of it, load it on the tarpaulin and drag it back here." He showed her portions of nikau palm and bark from the lacebark tree. "When you have the reeds, go into the bush and collect stuff like this. While you are getting it, Robert and I will collect ponga trunks. Have you got that?"

Anderina picked up three knives and nodded.

"Come on children," she said, handing Mary and Elizabeth a knife each, "follow me."

"Robert," said Jack, "come with me."

"Where are we going?"

To the patch of bush at the end of this plateau."

"Do you know what a ponga is?" he asked, as we walked

towards the mountains.

"Those big tree ferns with the hairy spirals you made soup with?"

"That's right. We need lots of them, but they must be eight-foot in length."

"What do we do with them once we've got them?'

"Stack them in a pile at the house site until we have enough.

We kept walking until the scrubby vegetation thickened into dense bush. Jack found a patch of pongas, and felling a big one with a few slashes of his machete, chopped the splay of leafy fronds off the top end.

"That's how we want them," he said, "about eight-foot-long with the diameter of a bread-n-butter plate."

"How many?"

"Start chopping and keep going until I tell you to stop. Then we will drag them to your section."

I nodded, and swinging my billhook, slashed into the bottom of the nearest ponga. Felling pongas was easy, for they were not like trees; their trunks were black and rough and the fibre inside was much less dense. Within minutes, I had my first ponga down and the crown off.

"They are light," I said, surprised by my log's weight.

"Yup, there're good reasons why the Maoris use them extensively."

I puffed a little as I worked, but by now my muscles were hard and my strength restored, and at the end of two days we had a stack of ponga logs and a large pile of raupo, nikau leaves, and lacebark beside the house site. On the third day, Jack paced out an oblong.

"Two pongas for the back," he said, lying them on the ground end to end. "Now, Robert, a ponga on each side." I nodded and grabbing two logs, dropped them in place. Meanwhile, Jack slashed another log in half. "Which side do you want your door, Mrs Johnson?"

"On the right."

"Half on the right," said Jack, dropping the short log in the right corner. He walked a few paces and dropped a full log opposite it. "Now we have the base laid out. Put a log at each corner, Robert, then dig them in so they stand upright, while I get Anderina and the children started on the weaving."

He turned to the large pile of raupo. I got on with my job and by the time I had finished, Anderina and the children were industriously making thatch.

"Next job, Robert," said Jack, "is to make the walls. Place the trunks as close as you can."

"How do you stop them from falling over?" I said, lying a ponga on top of the base.

Jack laughed as my ponga rolled onto the ground.

"Vertical, not horizontal," he said, lifting it and demonstrating. "Keep them upright and dig the base of them into the ground. For a window, stand a few shorter logs together. We'll glaze it with calico, but keep it small and high so you can sit below the draft."

"Where do you want it, Anderina?" I said.

Anderina stopped braiding lacebark momentarily.

"At the front by the door."

"Good idea," said Jack, "that way you can drop a tarpaulin over both openings when the weather gets bad."

We worked solidly and by evening, the walls were up. The next day Jack and I built the roof with the gables over the

To Own a Fig Tree

side walls, and thatched it with Anderina and the children's weaving, while they packed the draughty cracks between the pongas with mud. Then we drew soil up and around the bottom of the structure, and tamped the dirt floor even.

"Thank you so much, Jack," said Anderina, as Margret and William twirled around the room. "I don't know how we would have managed without your help. What can we give you in return?"

Jack finished lashing oiled calico to the window frame. "Knowing you and your little ones are sheltered is thanks enough," he said, cutting the end of the twine with his knife.

"That is very kind. Children say thank you to Mr Black."

The younger children obediently chorused, "Thank you Mr Black," but Elizabeth (indignant at being called a child) kept silent, and Mary, gazing around the walls, burst out:

"You forgot the chimney!"

"I didn't forget," Jack smiled. "These huts are very flammable, so it's best to cook outside."

"Where do you suggest we put it?" I said, fastening a canvas sheet over the doorway.

Jack pointed a short distance away. "In front of the door, it will keep the mosquitoes out of the house." He turned and eyed our new home thoughtfully. "It's rather small for a family of ten."

"Robert, John, and I will sleep under a tarpaulin," I said.

Karamea Jack sucked his lip, and rubbed his chin doubtfully. "You'll need more protection than that when winter kicks in. If you want to make a quick shelter, make an A-frame hut."

"How?"

"Build a roof on the ground without walls. Do you think

you can do it without my help?"

I nodded. "I'm good with my hands, and once I've made something, I never forget how I did it."

"Almost afternoon smoko time," said Jack, removing his hat and fanning his hot face with it. "I'll get you started and then leave you to it."

Anderina, taking the hint, collected the lunch basket, scratched a hollow in the ground and made a fire, while Jack and I decided on a spot for the men's quarters and paced out the oblong.

"Did you bring paper and pencils, love?" I said, as Jack sat on a log near the fire and rolled a cigarette?

"Of course," said Anderina. She fished about in the basket and handed me a pad and pencil.

I ripped off a page, and over a cup of tea, Jack calculated how many pongas I would need while the children danced in and out of the house.

Elizabeth, meanwhile, took the pad and withdrawing a small distance, sat sketching.

At length, Jack's smoke was finished, and the tea drunk.

"Stay and have dinner with us," said Anderina.

"Thank you for that kind offer, but I'd best be off," said Jack, putting on his hat. "If I stay any longer my buddies will think I have fallen off a cliff."

He rolled up his swag and was about to hoist it onto his shoulder when Elizabeth, seeing he was leaving, rushed over.

"I drew a picture of our house to thank you," she said, handing him a sketch of the hut.

Jack whistled with admiration. "That is pretty good, Missy. It looks just like the real thing. Are you the artist of the family?"

To Own a Fig Tree

"Well, no," said Elizabeth modestly, "most of us draw."

"I'll keep this as a reminder of you all," said Jack, folding the picture carefully and tucking it into his roll. "Next time I'm passing, I'll drop in to see how you are going. Then, swinging his swag onto his shoulder, Karamea Jack picked up his billy and tucker-bag, and with a farewell wave, disappeared into the scrub.

W.E. Hamilton

Shifting In

Now we had a house, Anderina wanted to shift immediately.
"Can't we wait until the A-frame is built, dear?" I said.

Anderina folded her arms and gave me a steely look. "I'm not spending another night cooped up in that hovel, Robert. It's low tide, and there is time to collect our luggage from the store before it rises."

I could have withstood her, but I also was keen to move in.
"Alright, the A-frame won't take long to build, let's go."

Leaving Mary in charge of James and William, we stumbled across our land, skittered down the steep hillside, and trudged seaward. When we got to the bank opposite the Government Reserve, we found a crowd gathered there.

"It seems everyone has the same idea as us," I said to Daniel, as we looked at the lighter coming across the river filled with boxes and bags.

Anderina sat on a rock next to Harriet, and fanned her face with her hat. "I'll look after your boots, Robert, while you wade over and arrange for our luggage to be ferried across."

I nodded, and taking off my boots, rolled up the hems of my trousers, and pushed the legs of my knitted underwear up over my knees.

Edwin King, catching sight of my woollen undergarments, pulled a face.

"Why on earth are you wearing long-johns in this heat,

To Own a Fig Tree

Johnson? Don't you realize February is summer down here?"

I shrugged.

"Makes no difference to me; summer, winter, and in-between-seasons, you'll not catch me without woollen underwear. More than once, wool saved my life when a freak storm soaked me to the skin."

"You're mad," said Edwin, sprinkling flower seeds in a patch of dirt at the edge of the sand.

"No madder than you, Johnny Flowerseed," said Daniel, also taking off his boots and rolling up his trousers.

"My name is Edwin, not Johnny."

"I know. I call you Johnny Flowerseed because you are Karamea's Johnny Appleseed."

"Johnny who?"

We looked at Daniel blankly.

"Oh, never mind. Forget it. Naylor would get the joke," he said, following me into the water.

"The new store is coming along well," I said, as we waded.

"Yes, O'Connor will be pleased when he next visits. We have cleared the land, and the store is almost finished."

"When is the *Charley* due?"

Daniel threw up his hands and shrugged. "Maybe tomorrow, maybe next week. Who knows?"

I nodded. "Depends on the weather and tides, I guess."

"That, and a politician's whim."

I chuckled, and stepping out of the river, shook the water off my legs before joining the queue stretching from the door of the old store.

"How is your house getting on?" said Daniel, lining up behind me.

"Finished. Now all I have to do is build an A-frame hut. Karamea Jack was very helpful. How are you getting on?"

"We have got about an acre cleared, but no house of course."

"Where are you going to store your stuff if you haven't got a shelter?"

"I bought a couple of tents. They will do until we get something more permanent."

I nodded. "Tomorrow I want to build the A-frame, but how about I come over the next day to show you everything Jack taught me?"

"Sounds great," said Daniel, as we shuffled forward, "and I'll help you with the A-frame tomorrow."

"That will speed things up. With the two of us working together, we could start on your hut after lunch."

There was a lull in our conversation, and as I stood quietly, I heard Ezra Hall say to James Moffatt:

"I don't trust Hyland. I'm sure I've not had as many potatoes as he has written down."

"He's charged me for ten pounds of flour," said James, "but my wife only got five," he wagged his finger in the air. "And I can prove it, because she made the flour-bag into a shirt for my youngest son, and it says, 'weight five-pounds,' on the back as clear as clear."

And they were not the only ones suspicious. I heard many grumbles and accusations as I waited to get to the head of the line. I listened, growing more and more alarmed until at last, the counter was directly in front of me.

John Naylor found 'Robert Johnson' in the ledger and ticked off the items one by one as Hyland found our boxes and bags.

To Own a Fig Tree

"John, can I have a look at my account," I said, as Hyland searched for the last bag?

"Alright, but be quick, there are a lot of men waiting."

He opened another book, and flicking through the Js, found my name before swivelling the book around. I scanned the numbers swiftly and they seemed in order, so I thanked him and left.

Now I had our luggage, I joined a second queue to go back. Men were still grumbling about the Government store, but I forgot their complaints once I'd crossed the water, and everything was on the South Bank. Then I hoisted the almost-pirate chest onto my shoulder, while Anderina and Elizabeth took the handles of another chest, and Margret and Laurence took two carpet bags each, and we joggled our luggage over the rough terrain.

"I knew this would be the worst part," Anderina puffed, as she struggled up the hill.

"Can I sit down?" Margret whined.

My calves were on fire, but I did not stop.

"Not much further, you can rest at the top."

We kept plodding up, up, up, and collapsed in a puffing heap on the edge of the plateau. After a breather, there was more stumbling over the uneven ground before we got to the hut.

"Only three more trips," I said.

"First, let me have a drink," said Laurence.

"You can have one when we go back down," said Anderina hard heartedly, "I'm not carrying more water up that hill than I have to."

Anderina had a point. We stopped at the creek on our way

back and drank our fill.

Then we collected more luggage and trailed home. Back and forth we went until all our bags and boxes were taken off the bank by the river. The shadows were getting long by the time we finished.

"I don't think I can walk another step," said Anderina, sinking onto the ground beside the fire. "Good girl, Mary, for cooking dinner."

"Willie and James helped collect the pongas and huhu grubs," said Mary, ladling lumpy soup into a plate.

"Good boys," I said, ruffling their hair.

William puffed out his chest with importance. "I sat on Mary's shoulders and cut the pongas with a big knife."

"I carried the huhu tin," said James, finishing his words with a coughing fit.

Anderina, reaching for the bottle of cough medicine in the lunch basket, paused as a dreadful thought hit her.

"Robert, we forgot the medicine cabinet!"

I slapped my hand on my head.

"So we did."

Anderina poured medicine into a spoon and dosed James. "After dinner, you must get it when you collect my things from the miner's hut."

"I can't get it, the tide is up."

"Well, first thing tomorrow you must go back for it."

"Tomorrow won't work either. Daniel is coming to help with the A-frame, and then I am helping him with his house," I said in dismay. "It will be alright where it is. You've got the cough medicine James needs, and I promise to get it quickly if anyone gets sick."

To Own a Fig Tree

Anderina put the medicine back in the basket with a resigned sigh.

"I suppose a few days won't matter. Friday will have to do."

"Friday it is."

But Friday it wasn't. For between Anderina setting up the house, and me building the A-frame and helping Daniel, Friday came and went without any of us giving a thought to the medicine cabinet. And after that, the heavy rain came, and in the wake of the trouble the bad weather brought, the cabinet was forgotten again.

———

W.E. Hamilton

A Damp Home and Castles in the Air

A thick curtain of rain fell and the water rushing off the mountains roared down the hills and rapidly spread over The South Terrace. Our roof worked well. Nevertheless, the floor inside our hut was little better than the sodden ground outside, for the spongy soil sucked up water like ink on blotting paper. James sat in his suitcase like a sailor in a boat as the water rose.

"We have to get everything out of the wet," said Anderina, putting the clock and our three books on top of the almost-pirate chest.

"Come on, Robert and John," I said, pulling on my raincoat. "We need to do something about this."

The boys quickly donned their coats and followed me outside to a pile of ponga logs.

"Good thing you had some left over from the A-frame," said John, picking one up.

"It certainly is. John, take these back to the hut and help your mother and the girls make a platform for the boxes and bedding."

He nodded, and carried his log into the house as I picked up two spades and gave one to Robert.

"Come on, Son, we need to dig a ditch around the house."

"Where shall we drain the water away, Dad? Our hut is in a small hollow."

To Own a Fig Tree

"Away from the mountains," I said, "that's where the real problem is coming from."

But I was only partly right as I eventually found out; for under the spongy top soil and the gritty subsoil was a rock pan. Robert, I, and our neighbours dug deep ditches around our houses, yet still, the water rose.

Once the rain stopped, the men gathered to discuss the problem while the women hung the bedding out to dry, and cleaned the grime off boxes and bags.

"We have got to sort out this water problem," I said.

"The sawyers have a stack of planks cut," said Daniel, "I suggest we divide them between us and use them as floorboards, for we cannot go through winter like this."

"Aye," said Ezra Hall, "it was bad enough without adding freezing cold to it."

"I've seen the way they build houses in Nelson; the floors are often a foot or more above the ground," said Naylor, "we should do the same."

"And maybe a series of deep ditches to channel the excess water into the river," said Peter Coutts.

This course of action seemed good to us, and soon every man (other than Hyland) was diligently building floors or digging ditches. I built my floor before I dug the ditches, for getting James out of the damp was imperative. After that was done, Robert and John were free to help me with the digging as they had finished surveying the South Terrace, and the Government land was cleared. Digging gave us plenty of time to think. After several hours of silence, Robert burst out:

"We need a boat. The river is a highway into the land. The store is so far away we lose one day a month carrying our supplies up to the Terrace." He threw a spadeful of dirt out of the ditch. "At ten shillings a day in lost wages, between the three of us our supplies are costing an additional thirty shillings, or twenty-four hours labouring on the farm." His eyes narrowed. "Half a mile upstream from the store is a fall which a boat could cross at half-tide, and a quarter of a mile upstream where the river bends, is a perfect landing place. If we had a boat, I could bring supplies up the river."

"There is the Government's lighter," said John, putting a foot on his spade and driving it deep into the soil.

"Huh," snorted Robert, "Hyland's boat, you mean. He won't lend it to anyone. He says he needs it constantly for Government business."

"What business?" said John, levering dirt up. "The *Charley* only arrives once a month."

Robert dug his spade into the ground savagely. "There is no Government business, he's just stingy."

"Don't fret, there is nothing you can do about it, Son."

Robert stopped digging and wiped his perspiring face. "Actually, there is. I've seen a giant white pine at least eighty-foot tall. I reckon we could get two large canoes out of it."

I also stopped digging and leaned against the side of the trench. "That would be a lot of work for one man."

"Oh, I wouldn't have to do it alone, Peter Coutts is keen to help."

I took off my hat momentarily, and scratched my head. "How would you do it?"

Robert looked into the air with unseeing eyes as he visualized his boat.

"We'd have to drop the tree first, of course, then cut it in

To Own a Fig Tree

two, and gouge out the middle."

"Hmm," I said, staring at a canoe-shaped cloud. "You'd have to strip the bark off and shape the ends."

"Could I help paddle?" said John, his face flushed with excitement.

"Yes, so long as you do what I say, brother, because I'm the captain."

"Aye, aye, Captain Johnson," said John saluting.

Robert beamed.

"Captain Johnson, that's much better than Robert junior. We could start a delivery business, and one day I could buy a steamer."

Owning a steamer was impossible, and I opened my mouth to say so. But before I got my first word out, my eyes fell on our house, and I felt the land under my feet.

I patted my son on the shoulder and pointed heavenward.

"With God, anything is possible, Robert," I said, "even a steamer and a fig tree."

W.E. Hamilton

O'Connor Has Doubts

On February the twenty-fourth, 1875, we were so preoccupied with digging, nobody noticed the Charles Edward slipping over the bar until we heard her whistle blow.

"It's the *Charley*," shouted Robert, throwing his spade down and climbing hastily out of the ditch.

John scrambled after him while I (picking up their fallen spades) followed more slowly.

"Is the steamer in?" said Anderina, coming out of our hut.

"I guess so." I pointed at our running sons. "The boys have gone to see, and I think I'll go too. Do you want to come?"

Anderina took off her apron and tucked stray wisps of hair into the bun at the back of her head.

"Run along, don't wait for me, I'll come soon."

I leaned the spades against the wall and set off at a brisk pace.

When I got to the Government Reserve, it was like watching a re-enactment of the previous month; twenty-three women and their children sat on their luggage crying, while the husbands hung around uncertainly. Once again, visitors accompanied O'Connor; not the reporter from the Colonist or Mr McLean this time, but Mr Elliot (the immigration officer) and two other men. They were talking to Robert while O'Connor was busy with Hyland replenishing the store.

"Mr Elliot, Mr Prit, and Mr Baigent, this is my father,

To Own a Fig Tree

Robert Johnson," said Robert, introducing me.

"A fine son you have," said Mr Elliot. "He's been telling me of his idea for a landing further up the river." He flicked his head towards O'Connor. "When Eugene is not so busy, I will suggest he has a shed built at the site your son proposes, and that Hyland ferries goods to the shed for distribution." He waved his hand towards the men fording the river. "Then all this wading and carrying supplies can end."

"How will we get the materials and heavy building equipment down there?" I said. "The track along the river is narrow, and getting planks for our floors was difficult."

"Hmm, that's a good point," said Elliot. "The track must be made wide enough for a bullock team. Nine feet ought to do it."

"Tell me, Mr Johnson," said Mr Baigent cutting in, "what's the timber like here? Have you seen any good big trees?"

"Apart from the South Terrace where we are, the land is covered with gigantic trees," I said. "Karamea Jack says they are kahikateas, totaras, and ratas."

"Excellent," said Mr Baigent, rocking back and forth on his toes. "I'm in the lumber business in Nelson, and I hope to set up a sawmill here."

This was good news. I turned to Mr Prit. "Are you also into milling?"

"No, I'm the Provincial Solicitor; I'm here on legal matters. The Government has recently requisitioned Karamea's North Bank."

I wanted to hear more, but O'Connor bustled over, and the subject was dropped.

"Men," he addressed the husbands hovering around their

weeping wives. "Your families will stay in four huts over the river while you live in the camp. There is not much room in the huts so only take bare essentials, and move the rest of your luggage to the old store. Then John Naylor will show you where to go. I've much to do and only three days to do it in. You and you," he pointed at Robert and me, "round up the First-Footers; I must meet with them."

We looked at him enquiringly. "First-Footers?"

"The first men to set foot in Karamea."

"Oh!" We chuckled at the name, and were about to move off, when O'Connor (staring at Robert) said:

"Aren't you one of the survey gang?"

"That's right."

"Find Rawson, and tell him we've got the North Bank. I want to see him about laying out the boundary lines for the March intake."

Robert nodded and sped off.

As the arrival of the steamer had drawn the entire community to the mouth of the river, it did not take long to gather the First-Footers together. When we were assembled by the store, O'Connor addressed us.

"Gentlemen, we are about to begin the land-ballot for the new arrivals, but I am concerned that the South Terrace may be unsuitable for settlement."

At this murmuring broke out and someone shouted:

"I don't want to lose my land."

"I've already cleared an acre," came another shout.

"And I have built a hut," I called.

"Are you going back on your promise?" shouted Alfred Lineham.

To Own a Fig Tree

O'Connor held up his hands to quieten us.

When we were silent, he said:

"Nobody is going to take away your land. I just want to know how you are getting on? Have you had any problems?"

"When it rained, we had a lot of trouble with water flooding the ground," said Thomas Lineham, "but we are digging ditches to drain the land, and installing wooden floors in our huts."

"Hmm," said O'Connor, rubbing his long nose thoughtfully. "The pit sawyers will continue producing lumber, but I advise you to put most of your efforts into clearing the land rather than building your houses. It's best to see what the soil is really like before you waste lumber and effort on more substantial buildings."

"There is nothing wrong with our land," said Liley, folding his arms and sticking out his chin, "I don't want a steep piece covered with gigantic trees."

"I hope you are right," said O'Connor. "Just to make sure, Mr Elliot has been ordered to make an official investigation of the matter and report back to Central Government."

We shuffled and looked uneasy.

"Mr Elliot has your best interests at heart, and as such, I trust you will help him with his investigations."

We nodded and mumbled assent.

"Now for other matters; I hear rumours there is a problem with the bookkeeping at the store."

At that, excited shouting broke out.

Once again, O'Connor quietened us with his hands.

"One at a time, gentlemen."

Then he listened to all our grievances carefully. At length, he turned to our useless overseer.

"It seems to me, Hyland, your bookkeeping is not as meticulous as it should be. You are to display a list of goods and prices in a prominent place, and send a copy to Nelson, together with reports showing stock in hand and requirements of the settlement."

Hyland's pride was pricked.

"Is Mr Naylor under my orders or not?" he said crossly. "Nobody listens to me. And how can I do a good job when you ignore my requests to send my son to cook for me, and won't give me the piece of land I want?"

O'Connor drew himself up and his eyes bored into the whining Hyland. "How dare you snivel about your dinner, and expect to be exempt from the ballot box? Is there any area you have shown competence? Get a backbone, and straighten up this mess before I return next month if you want to remain overseer!"

"We need to use the boat sometimes," Robert piped up.

O'Connor nodded. "And, Hyland, share the boat."

"But…"

"No buts, SHARE THE BOAT AND THAT IS AN ORDER."

He turned back to us.

"I see that you have cleared the Government Reserve. Well done. Your wages will be credited to you in the store's ledger. For the wellbeing of this settlement, we must have overland access to Westport."

We clapped and cheered at this.

O'Connor raised his hand, and we quietened.

"So, the next Government project is a track over the mountains. As winter is approaching, however, we will delay work on it until you are more settled in."

"How will we pay for our supplies if there are no wages," called Daniel?

"Don't worry, the store will extend credit and you can pay your debts off once the work begins."

"Are there any other issues?"

We stood silent.

"Well, then gentlemen, I and Mr Prit, and Mr Baigent will explore the north bank and into the interior during the next few days. While we are gone, Mr Elliott will investigate the South Terrace and the problems you are experiencing. I will meet you again before I leave." His eyes twinkled. "Only one announcement remains; I've saved the best till last." He waited until he had our full attention. "The Nelson Post Office has sent a mailbag for you."

Then he dismissed the meeting, and we rushed over to the store.

W.E. Hamilton

A Letter and a New House

The new women were on the South Bank mingling with the First-Women when I got across the river with my letter. As I shook the water from my legs and put on my boots, Anderina detached herself from the group and hurried towards me.

"Huh, I know just how they feel," she said, watching the sad mothers gathering their children and luggage together for the trek to the miner's huts. "At least they won't have to wait weeks for their land. Take the children home with you, Robert. I'm going with Harriet and Agnes to help the newcomers settle in."

"Don't take too long," I said, waving the letter. "I have news from home."

Anderina's face lit up. "Who's it from?"

"Arthur."

"Read it to me now, Robert."

"Without waiting for the others!" I said, pretending to be shocked.

Anderina glanced at the women muddling about with bags. "Go on, we have a few minutes."

"Oh, alright."

I slit the envelope, opened the folded page and read aloud:

To Own a Fig Tree

Dear Brother and family,
We are pleased to hear you have arrived in New Zealand safely. John wrote of your wonderful opportunity and I expect you have your land by now. You certainly have done the right thing. Since you left, twenty-seven families (from Corston, Quam, and Neeflans, on the Quendale estate in Dunrossness) were thrown into the world to find themselves new homes as best they could. May God have mercy on them. They were crofters, not fishermen, of course. It is a sinful thing to throw families out in December with winter knocking at the door. They wander about homeless with babies in straw baskets, while the sheltering walls of their homes are torn down to build fences for the sheep that have replaced them. Many who were previously afraid to leave are now seriously considering emigration, for we fear it will be the start of another round of clearances like Lamb Hoga in 1822. We pray we will not be like the poor folks of Fetlar, who lost a third of their population back then.
If the clearances continue, who knows, maybe we will follow you out, brother. All the family are well, but miss you sadly.
God bless you, from,
Arthur.

Anderina and I were silent for a moment.
"Makes the voyage and hardship seem worthwhile," said Anderina with a shudder. "Imagine James with only a basket for protection!"
I sighed. Hardy men cannot last a Shetland winter without shelter, let alone women and children. They are likely to be

dead by now, I thought. I could see by her face Anderina was thinking the same thing. To distract her, I tucked the letter into my pocket and said:

"The pit sawyers have a stack of lumber ready for houses, but O'Connor advises us to concentrate on clearing away the scrub instead of upgrading our house. He thinks there's something wrong with our land."

"Fiddlesticks," said Anderina, "our priority is to get James out of the damp. The hut won't do for winter. If there is lumber to be had, we must start building as soon as possible." Anderina flicked her head towards the Government Store, "go back and see if you can get your three-days-worth of lumber now."

The idea seemed good to me, so I took off my boots once more, and waded back across the river.

James Black and David Grayney were pleased to see me.

"I'm glad someone wants their lumber now," said James. "If the others follow O'Connor's advice, we'll end up with a big stockpile."

"Why aren't you waiting?" said David.

"I've eight children, the youngest a frail two-year-old," I said, shaking my head. "If I don't get him in better housing, we will lose him this winter."

James rubbed his chin and raised his eyebrows at David in an enquiring manner.

David nodded at him before turning to me.

"That is a big family," he said. "If you build your house before the others start, we will give you six day's free labour instead of three."

"Gentlemen, I can't thank you enough," I said, shaking their hands fervently.

To Own a Fig Tree

"Have you ever built a house before, Robert?"

"Only stone ones."

"Ask John for advice if you get stuck."

My eyebrows shot up.

"John Naylor, the schoolteacher?"

"That's right. He's a man of many talents. He's done a bit of building and enjoys doing roofs."

"Fancy that! I never would have guessed."

"Remember," warned James, "be quick if you want extra lumber."

"I won't forget. I'll get started today," I said, waving as I waded into the river.

As soon as I got home, I told Anderina of the sawyer's generous offer.

"Oh Robert, how wonderful. Where shall we build the new house?"

"Not here, this is a hollow," I said, picking up a spade and four rocks. "I know of a spot that is slightly raised. It means a bigger trek to the store, but at least the house won't end up sitting in a pool of water when it rains."

"I don't care how far we have to walk, Robert, so long as we are not in a squelching quagmire."

I led the way down the 'road' until I came to a hump.

"I thought here perhaps," I said, "what do you think?"

Anderina stomped around the land speculatively.

"Yes, it's a good position." She moved her arm in a swooping movement. "Instead of a short and straight driveway, we could sweep it around in a long graceful curve."

I narrowed my eyes and (visualizing a sweeping driveway) saw that her suggestion was good.

"Alright, now what kind of house do you want?"

"In Nelson, I saw a square house with a window on either side of the door and a roof like a pyramid. I wouldn't mind one like that."

"Square, that's easy enough." I dug a toetoe bush out of the way and dropped a rock on the ground. "This will be our left front corner," I strode eight paces to the east and dropped another rock, "and this is the right corner."

"It doesn't look very big," said Anderina, pulling a face as I marked out the back corners.

"The floor plan of a house always looks tiny before the walls go up, my love, trust me, this will be a bigger house than our old one in *Zetland*."

Anderina chewed on her lip.

"Do you think we will need the floor raised like the one in the hut?"

"Too right. I'm not taking risks. This house will have legs like a big box-bed so the water can run underneath."

"Are you sure we'll get it finished before winter?"

"We have to. John will help and in the evenings, Robert will pitch in after his surveying work."

Anderina nodded.

"And the children and I can lend a hand with the lifting when you need us."

"Now that is settled, we must act immediately," I said. "Leave Mary to look after James and William, and we will start hauling lumber here right away."

Anderina agreed, so that is what we did. Hyland reluctantly loaned us the lighter, and we ferried lumber onto the South Bank, then we carried or dragged it along the edge of the river, up the face of the escarpment, and over the rough ground to the site of our new house.

"You're taking a risk building a house here, you only get one lot of free lumber," said Mr Elliot with a frown when he came poking about our land with a spade. He dug a hole and pulled out a handful of subsoil. "I don't like the look of this gritty subsoil. It looks like infertile pakihi land[33]."

I brushed his concerns aside, for compared to barren Shetland, this land was lush with vegetation.

"Sheltering in a hut over winter is a bigger risk," I said.

"There is that," Elliot agreed. "Hopefully, I am wrong. If anyone can fix the problems, it is you blokes. Your drains are deep and extensive. I shall say in my report you are all extremely industrious and conscientious."

"All - even Hyland?"

Elliot snorted disdainfully. "O'Connor is doing a good job, but his overseer is truly incompetent. I shall recommend Richard Hyland is replaced as soon as possible."

"That would be a relief," I said, "for we need someone who really knows about bushcraft. Someone like Karamea Jack would be invaluable."

"I'll see what I can do," said Elliot. "In the meantime, you will be pleased to know that the Government has bent the rules and is allowing a few experienced colonists to settle here for the good of the community. The sawyers James Black and David Graynay wish to stay, and Mr Baigent is hoping to establish a timber mill. I'm sure you will find their experience invaluable."

"I have already," I said.

---

33   Flat land with infertile waterlogged soil

W.E. Hamilton

Mr Elliot filled a leather pouch with soil. "I'll take a sample to Nelson with me for further investigation. The *Charley* leaves on high tide so I must head back. All the best with your endeavours, Mr Johnson." He shook my hand and left me to get on with my work.

―――――――――

To Own a Fig Tree

Progress

The crickets were chirping, and winds blew softly by mid-March. The settlers made the most of the daylight as summer neared its end, and the settlement spread. My children were hard workers and they toiled beside their mother and me to build our house and clear the land. Despite this, Willie and Laurie still had the energy to scamper through the maze of tracks linking the small clearings dotted about the scrub. They kept us informed of our neighbour's progress.

"Since William Liley turned eighteen, he thinks he is a man and treats us like little kids," complained Laurie, as Anderina handed him his dinner. "But his house is not as good as the Friend's house, and Samuel is only eleven."

"Yeah," said Willie, swallowing a bite of potato. "Samuel and his dad have a slab and thatch house but William and his father only have a grass and thatch one."

"Frederick Liley is taking 'Connor's advice, and is concentrating on land clearance rather than house building," I said, putting down my empty plate before taking the pad and pencil from the lunch basket.

"How are the other settlers getting on?" said Anderina, putting the kettle on embers.

"George Lineham and his dad have two houses, one of them is a ponga hut they use as a shed. The new one is slabbed but not yet thatched, with a chimney big enough to take five-foot logs. It also has the two windows that a kind lady sent them."

"I suppose that was someone Thomas met when he was in the hospital," said Anderina.

"The windows are this long," said Willie, stretching his arms out. "Three feet wide and four feet six inches high. George says it's much better than their old house in Lidlington."

A look of longing came into my wife's eyes. "Oh, Robert, do you think you could order us some windows?"

"Not this month," I said, writing 'two cows in milk' on my order form. "Cattle are our priority."

"Of course," said Anderina, "nourishing milk for James is essential. I was thinking we might have windows as well as the cows."

"We don't have the roof on yet, so it's a bit early, maybe next month."

Anderina gave a wistful sigh.

"Do any of the other neighbours have windows, boys?"

"No, most of them just have huts of calico, grass and saplings; or slabbed like the Lineham's house with thatched kiekie roofs."

"The huts on the swampy ground are so rickety they shake when we jump on the road," giggled Willie.

Anderina frowned. "I hope you boys are not making a nuisance of yourselves."

"Oh no, the kids who live in the huts showed us how to wobble them."

Anderina's face relaxed. "I wish I had time to visit and see the houses myself."

"How are our neighbours getting on with clearing their land?" I said.

To Own a Fig Tree

"George and his dad have a whole acre felled and the sun can get all around the house," said Willie. "You can even see the ocean from the edge of their land."

"George says the view here is much wilder and more dramatic than the Vale of Bedford and the Chiltern Hills where they come from," said Laurie.

"What about Mr Lineham's brother, how is he going?" I said.

"Mr Alfred Lineham is doing alright and so is Mr Allen on the section next to George and his dad."

The kettle whistled, so Anderina lifted it off and filled the teapot.

"What about the Scarletts?"

"They've got two acres ready to be sown with grass seed."

"Two acres," exclaimed Mary.

"That's not as much as Ezra Hall, he's got two-and-a-half acres ready for seed."

"We've only half an acre cleared," Anderina frowned.

"That is because we put our energy into the house, my dear," I said, writing 'turnip seeds' under 'cows in milk.'

"We are the only ones with a wooden house," said Willie.

Anderina looked gratified by this news.

"Both Mr Brown and Mr Line have only half an acre cleared," said Laurie.

"And are jointly ordering from Nelson a pit saw, a half-inch auger, an inch auger, and half a dozen fowls," said Willie.

"Is there anything you kids don't know?" said Robert, ruffling his younger brothers' hair.

"Nope," said Willie beaming. "We know George's dad killed a sheep last Saturday night, and they and another man ate it."

"They must have brought one of the sheep that came on the *Charley* last month," I said.

"George said it was a fine fat sheep, and they have as much suet as they would have had in six months in England, but it will only last them about a fortnight here."

"And sometimes they have two hogsheads[34] of sugar" said Willie, his eyes growing wide with wonder, "and flour of any amount, and butter and tea in any quantity."

"Why can't we have meat, and sugar, and butter, like the Linehams?" said Margret.

"George says it's because the store gives it to them for free," said Willie.

"It's not free," I said, adding potatoes to my list. "Not free at all. We will have to pay for it with sweat and toil, and until we can grow our own meat and churn our own butter, we'll have to make do with potatoes, eels, and bread."

"I bet you kids don't know who owns that little piece of land at the bend of the river," said Robert slyly.

"We do too," said Laurie, throwing his shoulders back.

"All this side of the river belongs to the crown," I cut in.

"I thought so too," said Robert, "but oddly, that small block is privately owned, and not even Rawson knows who it belongs to."

By now Laurie and Willie were almost bursting with pride.

"We do," they chorused.

"It belongs to a man called George Jabez Cooper, and he lives in Westport."

"Are you sure?"

---

34   about fifty or sixty pounds

To Own a Fig Tree

They nodded vehemently.

"How do you know?"

Laurie and Willie looked at each other with puzzled expressions.

"I forget," said Laurie, "do you remember who told us, Will?"

"Nope, but I know it is true."

"Who is doing the mail run this month?" said Robert, changing the subject abruptly.

"I dunno," I said. "We may have to pull straws."

"I'll go."

"Are you mad, brother?" said John, pulling a face. "That is a four-day-round trip. You have to cross the Otumahana mudflat to get to the beach, and then it's miles of dodging waves as you walk around the rocks to Mokihinui!"

"I know." Robert smiled and turned to me. "Have you finished your list, Dad? I'll take it with me when I tell Hyland I'll go tomorrow."

"Almost," I said, writing, 'fig tree,' under the last word.

"Why do you want to go, Bob?" said Laurie."

"It's a long way," said Willie.

"Finally, something my nosey little brothers don't know!" said Robert, with a twinkle in his eye. "It's a surprise. You'll have to wait until I get back before I tell you."

W.E. Hamilton

Robert Surprises Us

Robert was away on the mail trip longer than we expected.

"Perhaps he is lost or injured," said Anderina anxiously on the fifth day, "he should have been back yesterday."

"He's not lost," I said, hiding my fears. "He is surefooted and strong. He'll be back when he is ready."

And he was, for the very next day, he turned up looking very pleased with himself.

"Good, you're finally here. You can help your father and Elizabeth with the nailing," said Anderina, hitching her end of the weatherboard into place. "Did you strike trouble on the way?"

Robert picked up a hammer and shoved a fistful of nails into his pocket. "No, quite the opposite. I decided to carry on to Westport."

"Why?" said Elizabeth between bangs.

"I visited Captain Leech and talked to him about getting my Foreign Trade Mate's Certificate. He says to settle in first and then he will see what he can do about it."

"Good, good," I nodded.

"That's not much of a surprise," said Laurie, standing on tiptoes as he held the other end of the board. "I thought it would be something more exciting."

Robert took another nail and held it in position. "Oh, that's not the surprise," he said, belting the nail home. "I'm not

To Own a Fig Tree

telling you what it is until it is finished."

"You can let go of the board now," I cut in.

Relief crossed their faces as Anderina and Laurence dropped their arms.

"Can you spare me for a couple of weeks, Dad?" Robert asked. "There is something I want to do after work."

"I think so," I said, banging the last nail in. "John will help in the evenings, and Elizabeth and I can manage without you during the day. If we get stuck, Mary can help with the nailing."

Laurie rolled a rock to the corner of the house (and taking the end of the next weatherboard) stood on it.

"Swap jobs with Margret after this one, Laurie," said Anderina, lapping the board over the one below.

"Aw, do I have to? I like this job better than digging the garden."

"Don't backchat, and, yes, you do. Margret is taller and can reach higher."

"Please tell us what the surprise is," said William, dragging a board behind him.

"No."

"Aw come on."

"Don't bother your brother," I said, as I made sure the end of the board was flush with the stud.

"Aren't you curious, Dad?" said Laurie.

I was, but I curbed it, and after two weeks of tight-lipped silence, Robert asked the family to follow him down to the bend in the river, for he was about to reveal the secret surprise. When we got there, we found Peter Coutts standing beside two thirty-foot canoes.

"You are looking at the beginning of the Johnson and Coutts

Ferry Service," said Robert, folding his arms and putting a foot on one of the canoes.

William let out a whistle of admiration.

"You should have asked me to help," said John.

"Dad needed you for the house."

Anderina's eyes were wide with wonder. "Did you make them yourselves?"

"From the eighty-foot white pine?" I added.

"Yup, Peter and I dropped it and cut it in half."

"Then we stripped off the bark, shaped them, and dug out the middles," said Peter.

"*Eighty-foot tall!* It's a wonder you weren't killed!"

Robert ignored his mother's outburst.

"When I went to Westport, I did more than contact Captain Leech. I also tracked down George Jabez Cooper." He took his foot off the canoe and stamped on the ground. "You are standing on my property. I own the lease on this block until Cooper's death."

"I told you Laurie and I knew who owned it," said William proudly.

"I can hardly believe it," I said. "Our son has land, Anderina!"

"God is good," she nodded.

"The wharf and shed will be built here," said Robert, pointing to a clearing slashed in the bush. "Steamers can unload their goods into the shed, then Peter and I can ferry them up and down the river." He waved towards the hill behind us; and I shall build my house over there. But not until I've finished helping you, Dad," he added hastily.

"What are you going to call this place?" said Mary. "It must

To Own a Fig Tree

have a name."

"I don't know."

"Call it Robert's Wharf," said Elizabeth.

"No, it won't be my wharf or shed, only the landing spot is mine."

"Robert Junior's Landing, then," said Margret.

"Yuck," Robert pulled a face, "Junior sounds so childish."

"I know," said Anderina, "Johnson's Landing."

"Johnson's Landing? Hmm."

We turned the idea around in our minds and nodded our approval.

"Johnson's Landing, it is," said Robert.

Now the name was settled, we turned our attention back to the canoes.

"You boys have done a wonderful job," I said. "Have you tried them?"

"Not yet, we were waiting for you."

"Your parents and sisters will be proud of all you have done, Peter," said Anderina. "When do you think they will get here?"

"Not for a while, because Mum and Dad are too old to come before my house is finished. Besides," he grinned, "every week the possibilities of my sisters getting married in Nelson increase."

Laurie jiggled impatiently, bored by the chitchat. "Can I have a ride in your canoe, Robert?"

"If it floats. Come on Peter, let's get them into the water."

We helped launch the boats. As soon as they were afloat, Robert and Peter climbed aboard and John handed them their paddles. The canoes held their weight beautifully, so they pushed away from the bank and into the middle of the swiftly flowing river. The tide was going out, so the children ran along the bank in the seaward direction, waving and shouting as they followed the canoeists. Then Robert and Peter gave each of us a ride, and even James had a little sit in both boats.

"When are you going to start your ferry business?" said John, as he helped pull the canoes from the water.

"When the *Charley* comes in."

"How much are you going to charge for each trip?" said Elizabeth.

"Ah, that's a bit of a problem," said Robert, scratching his head. "Trouble is, everyone owes money to the Government Store and has no cash."

"We'll provide a free service until the community gets settled," said Peter. "By the time they can pay, we will have accumulated lots of goodwill."

"I'm looking forward to the *Charley* getting here," said Robert. "Peter and I will be busy all day taking the new people up the river."

But when the steamer arrived at the end of the month, most of the newcomers walked across the mudflat to their land, for their allocated blocks were on the newly surveyed north bank.

"I wish we had come later in the Michelangelo," said Anderina, at dinner that night. "Those new people have better land and they don't have to wade to the store like us. Their feet didn't even get wet."

"Only the ones with property close to the Government Reserve didn't have to wade," said Robert. "I ferried a chap called Henry Haws up Black's Creek to his land. He and a few other men went first so they could cut out spaces to pitch their tents, and then I went back for their wives and luggage. Mrs Haws was not crying like the other women, and even coped with the swamp. But when she squeezed through the trees and saw her husband pitching their tent in the tiny clearing, and realized that was her home, she sat on a stump and wept buckets of tears."

"I feel for her," said Anderina, "don't you, Robert?"

But my mind was on other things.

"Two fine animals," I said, admiring our new cows tethered at the edge of the scrub, "and by spring they'll have calves."

"Isn't it wonderful! We'll have plenty of milk for James," beamed Anderina, forgetting Suzanna Haws.

"Did you have trouble getting them off the steamer, Dad?" said Mary.

"Not too bad, having the jetty finished helped enormously."

"Did you get the turnip seeds?" said Anderina.

"Yes."

"And the potatoes?"

"Yes. Almost everything came."

"What was missing?"

"My fig tree."

"I'm sorry, Dad," said Elizabeth, putting her hand on my shoulder. "I know how much a fig tree means to you."

"I'm not. We have two beautiful cows because God knows we need them. Like Robert's surprise, he will send the fig tree at the right time, when we least expect it."

W.E. Hamilton

A Bullock, Baby, and New Tracks

In 1875, we measured life not in days or weeks, but by the arrival of the steamer. Another month had passed and the *Charley* was due any day. Since her last appearance, our cows had given two buckets of milk a day, and the house and garden were growing nicely. Robert continued surveying, while John worked with the gang cutting the bullock track to the new wharf.

"How was work today?" I asked him one evening, as the family mulched long rows of plants.

"We are getting along. Half of the track is nine-foot wide now. The worst bit is hauling the heavy timber away. I can't wait until the *Charley* arrives; a bullock will make such a difference."

"I wonder who will take charge of the animal?" said Robert, shovelling leaf mold around turnip tops.

"It belongs to the government, so probably Richard Hyland," said John.

"Hyland!" Robert spat out the name. "I hope it is fully trained."

But it wasn't.

When the steamer docked the next day, Richard went white as he watched the big beast dangling from the sling. It was bawling and pawing the air.

To Own a Fig Tree

"Steady boy, easy does it," said John, as we swung the bullock onto the jetty and his feet touched the wooden boards. John moved in front of the animal and catching hold of one horn, scratched the knobby tuft between his ears.

The bullock stopped roaring and his eyes calmed as John gentled him. Captain Leech handed Hyland a docket.

"Here you go, Overseer," he said. "One bullock."

"What am I going to do with that wild beast?" spluttered Hyland, backing away. "I'm not an animal trainer."

"No surprises there," muttered Robert.

"If I, were you, Richard," said Captain Leech, "I'd put young Johnson in charge of him. He seems to know what he is doing."

"Have you had much experience with bulls, John?" said Hyland.

"He is not a bull, and yes, I have."

"We Shetlanders were cattle folk for centuries before the lairds cleared the land for sheep," I cut in. "You won't find men better able to handle bullocks than my sons."

"Very well, John," said Hyland, "you may take charge of the bull."

"Bullock," amended John.

"Whatever, it makes no difference to me. Just get him off this wharf. You are holding up the unloading."

I unbuckled the straps of the sling, and once the bullock was free, John pulled on his horn and they ambled off the jetty. With all the commotion over the bullock, nobody noticed the two men waiting with O'Connor on the steamer. Now, as they stepped onto land, O'Connor introduced them to the gathering crowd.

W.E. Hamilton

"This is Mr Scanlan and James Simpson. Because of Mr Elliot's report, Central Government has appointed James Simpson as storekeeper, postmaster, and registrar of marriages, births, and deaths."

There was a smattering of clapping at this news.

"And," continued O'Connor, "Mr Scanlan replaces Richard Hyland, whose services are no longer required."

A storm of stomping and cheering broke out while Hyland's mouth dropped open in dismay.

"I want the twenty-two pounds-seven-shillings you owe me before I go," he said sullenly.

O'Connor brushed Hyland aside as he and his companions moved towards the store. "You'll get what you deserve," he called over his shoulder.

Unlike Hyland, Mr Simpson was decisive. By the time I had taken possession of my crate of fowls and loaded them into Robert's canoe, he had hung a blackboard outside the store itemizing the store's goods and prices.

Karamea Store Goods and Prices

Axe-handle 1/62	butter 3/6	100lb flour 18/6	1 pair of boots 27/6
sheep 26/-	60 lb sugar 30/-	2 bars soap 2/-	2 ½ lb pork 1/3
Moleskin trousers 10/6		gun 3 pounds 10/-	1 long shovel 8-
1-bushel grass seed 9/-			

I nodded towards the blackboard as I joined the queue for mail and supplies.

"Scanlan didn't waste time taking charge," I said to Thomas Lineham, who was standing next to me.

"Ah hmm, I suppose."

To Own a Fig Tree

"You seem preoccupied, Tom," said Daniel.

"Sorry," said Thomas, wiping a hand over his face. "All I can think about is the mail. I am hoping to hear Mary has had the baby safely."

He fell silent as we inched forward, so I turned to James Moffatt, Daniel, and Alfred who were standing behind me.

"My son can ferry your supplies up the river now he has a boat."

"That would be great," said Daniel. "Perhaps he could make a hot-air balloon next; getting supplies up the hill is a pig of a job. All the tracks from the sea end of the estuary link up to the terrace's 'road.' That's alright for Thomas, for he is the closest to the sea, but once the bullock road is finished, a track directly up from Johnson's Landing would be useful for you and me."

"Yes, it would," I said, stroking my beard thoughtfully. "At the moment we scramble up as best we can."

"Those of us at the other end of the terrace need a track further inland than that," said James. "My neighbours and I are going to cut a zig-zag track up from the river flats. It will make carrying the supplies up much easier."

"James has a good idea," I said to Alfred and Daniel as we shuffled into the store, "the three of us and our sons could cut a track down to Johnson's Landing. As you say, Daniel, it would be very useful, especially when O'Connor has the store built and the supplies landed there."

Daniel and Alfred nodded in agreement as Thomas (receiving his long-awaited letter) tore the envelope open.

"Yes, we could start…"

Thomas cut Daniel's words short.

"Mary's had a girl, and both are well," he said, beaming with delight.

"Congratulations," we said, slapping him on the back. "That's wonderful."

"Three girls and four boys, you'll have to have another girl to even the score, brother," said Alfred. "Fanny will be pleased to hear the news. What are you naming her?"

"Mary Anne, after her mother and aunt."

"That's nice. Fanny will be touched you've called her Anne," said Alfred.

"I am confused," said Daniel. "Is Anne, Fanny's second name?"

"No, Anne is Fanny's real name. Everybody just calls her Fanny."

"Mary and the children are coming here on the next steamer," said Thomas, scanning the rest of his letter. "That gives George and me a month to get the roof on the house."

"It is a fine house," said Alfred, "but won't it be rather a squeeze for you all?"

"Georgiana is not coming. She has found a good situation in Nelson," said Thomas, turning his letter over. "That's good, for she is fifteen and old enough to be independent."

"Caroline is thirteen, perhaps she will find something too…" said Alfred.

Scanlan called: "NEXT," and I dropped out of the conversation.

"Robert Johnson," I said.

There were no letters for me, and other than the fowls, there was nothing exciting about the supplies I had ordered, for once again there was no fig tree. Slinging the sack of potatoes on

To Own a Fig Tree

my shoulder, and gripping the top of the bag of flour, I carried them to Robert's canoe. The chooks[35] squawked as I dropped the sacks next to their crate in the middle of the boat. They squawked again as John arrived and dumped a harness on top of the sacks.

"I was afraid when I heard O'Connor dismiss Hyland, I would lose out on Bruno, but Mr Scanlan has agreed to let me take charge of him," he said, as we each took a paddle and climbed aboard.

Robert looked around.

"Where did you leave the beast?"

"I've tethered him on the other side of the river. Can I keep him on your land, Bob?"

Robert dug his paddle into the sand and pushed the canoe away from the bank.

"If you let me borrow him from time to time."

"Of course you can."

"I can help with the training," said Robert, as with smooth strokes we pulled into the centre of the river. "We could make a cart for him to pull."

"He is supposed to be a pack animal."

"Why not train him to do both?"

"That's a grand idea."

They discussed methods of training the bullock as we ferried our goods up the river. Then, leaving a pile of supplies at Johnson's Landing, Robert went back to help others while John and I toted our goods home. For the next month, my sons diligently trained the ox every evening, while I and several others cut tracks up the hillside. So, by the time the steamer

---

35   hens

arrived, we had a pack animal and two new tracks.

Laurie, who was up a tree, was the first to see the boat out at sea.

"The Charlie's coming," he shouted, scrambling down.

"Are you sure?" I said, putting down my hammer.

"Sure as sure."

And indeed, he was, for we heard her whistle blow. As soon as we heard it, everyone dropped what they were doing and the entire community rushed to the jetty. There was great rejoicing when the Lineham family reunited. Thomas, George, and all the women clucked over the baby, and none of the females cried this time, not even tiny Mary Anne. Life was looking up. Everybody had land, our houses were progressing, and the *Johnson and Coutts Ferry Service* was in great demand. Our rejoicing might have been tempered with fear, however, if we had realized it was the last day we could plot time by the steamer.

To Own a Fig Tree

The First School

Five-year-old Willie was a happy little chap. He was whistling hymns in the garden when Lawrence Lawrenson paid us a visit. After the usual greetings, Lawrence got straight to the purpose of his call.

"My wife wants our boys to begin school as soon as possible," he said, sitting on a rock within the smoking circle of our cooking fires.

"How old are they?" said Anderina, as she poured Lawrence a cup of tea.

"George is seven, James is five, and John is three."

"They are still very young," said Anderina.

"That's what I think," said Lawrence. "I told her not to fret, the boys are learning many things as they help build the house and clear the land."

"No need to rush them into letters and numbers," I agreed.

"Thank ye kindly," said Lawrence to Anderina, taking the steaming cup. He sighed. "But that's not good enough for Helen. She badgered O'Connor about it, with the result Mr Scanlon has supplied her with books and slates, and the Nelson Education Board has kindly donated a blackboard, maps, and more books."

Anderina stiffened. "Why didn't we all get books and slates for our children?"

"Oh, they are not for our personal use, my wife is merely

the custodian of the materials until the school gets built."

Anderina sniffed and relaxed.

"Oh, that's alright then, more tea, Mr Lawrenson?"

Lawrence put his hand over the mouth of his cup briefly. "I've still got plenty." He turned to me. "Helen is calling for a working bee to build the school."

"Where?" I said.

"Here on the South Terrace. John Naylor (as the future schoolmaster) has set aside a portion of his land for it."

"He won't have time to teach, he still has scrub to clear and his house to finish. This week he is helping me construct my roof, and next week I am returning the favour by helping him with his."

"True, *he* does not have time, but his wife does. Hellen will teach the young'uns in the morning until the school's built, and then Charlotte Naylor will act as schoolmistress until the community is more established."

"What happens then?" said Anderina.

"John will take over, and the school can extend lessons to the older children." Lawrence looked at me expectantly. "So, what about it, Robert? Are you willing to set aside a few days to build the school?"

I rubbed my chin and gazed into the air thoughtfully. Laurence kept quiet, waiting for me to speak. At last, I said:

"It's all very well to build a school, but how are we going to pay the Naylors for their services. I have no cash, and my account at the Government Store grows daily. I'm sorry Lawrence, I would help if I could, but my budget does not stretch to lessons. I will teach my children myself in the evening when I'm more established."

To Own a Fig Tree

"Is that all you're worried about?" said Laurence, beaming. "No money is required. Education in New Zealand is free. The Government will pay the Naylors."

"Free?" Anderina and I echoed.

 "Absolutely."

Anderina's eyes bored into him.

"For girls too?"

Lawrence nodded.

"Both boys and girls up until age twelve - provided they live within a two-mile radius of a school."

My head was reeling with this news.

"I'll ask you again, Robert," Lawrence said in a tone of triumph. "Are you available for a working bee in three weeks?"

"Yes, yes," I said, shaking his hand fervently.

"Now that is settled, I must be off for I have many others to see." He tipped his hat at Anderina. "Thank you for the tea, Mrs Johnson, send your youngsters to my wife tomorrow."

"Tell Hellen, thank you very much," said Anderina.

So, the next day Willie, Laurie, and Margret set off through the bush to the Lawrenson's place. Three weeks later, we (the fathers of the South Bank children) cleared a spot for the schoolhouse and marked the corners of the fifteen by nine-foot room, while the mothers plaited kiekie for thatch. By now we were experienced at working with local materials. We swarmed busily in and out of the bush, and the building went up quickly. The schoolhouse when it was completed looked much like our hut at home, as it was a similar size with an earthen floor, a door, and a window glazed with oiled calico. I thought we were finished when I dropped the tent flap over the doorway, but Lawrence, who was in charge of the working

W.E. Hamilton

bee, said:

"You will see by the pile of boards nearby, that James Black and David Grayney have donated lumber to the school. Come, men, let's make classroom furniture while the ladies pack the crevices of the walls with moss."

So, away we went again; this time with hammers and saws, not spades and billhooks, and soon the drafts were blocked, and we had enough tables and chairs for the school's thirty-five scholars. It was a grand moment when we set up the classroom. John Naylor fixed the blackboard on the end wall as I put the desks in rows, and Hellen pinned up a map of the world, and a poster of a fat little girl riding a square bullock under the words, 'I AM ON AN OX.'

The next day we dedicated the building with prayer, and officially opened Karamea's first school.

Inside, Charlotte Naylor had written on the blackboard:

Welcome to the Karamea South Terrace School. Est. 1875

Elizabeth, Evelyn, and John Allen.	Margret, Laurence, and William Johnson.
Beatrice and Thomas Henry.	Thomas, Walter, and Charles Lineham
Harry Delick	Samuel and Catherine Andrews
Lily and Agnes Liley	Adrian and Lillie Hill
James and Henry Castle	Maud Brown
Boy Remnant	George, Francis, and Christine Moffatt
William Scarlett	George, James, John, and Mary Lawrenson
Robert and Laurence Sinclair	James and Beatrice Pike

To Own a Fig Tree

We waited until the children filed in and sat on the split log benches before slipping away.

"It's wonderful to know our children are getting educated," said Anderina as we walked home.

The singsong sound of the two-times table floated on the breeze towards us, and I smiled with satisfaction.

"It is indeed."

That afternoon, as I nailed shingles onto the roof, it seemed very quiet without the children's chatter and William's endless whistling.

"How was it?" said Anderina, when they arrived home.

"Good," said Margret.

"Alright," said Laurence.

"What about you, Willie? Did you like school?"

William stopped whistling and folded his arms. "Mrs Naylor doesn't understand business."

"He only says that because the teacher kept telling him to pay attention," said Margret.

"You mind your manners, William," said Anderina. "It is a privilege to get an education. If you waste your time daydreaming, you will end up unable to read and write like me."

William nodded dutifully, and I thought the matter was cleared up, but a few days later Mrs Naylor accompanied the children home. "I am sorry to inform you," she said, "that I had to send William into the bush to get a supple-jack switch today. I warned him when he brought it back, that if he continued daydreaming, I would have to use it on him."

"Oh dear," said Anderina.

"What's my son been doing?" I said.

W.E. Hamilton

"While I'm writing on the blackboard and drilling the children in arithmetic and spelling, his mind is elsewhere."

"How do you know?"

"He talks to himself. We hear him muttering things like 'yes, I'll buy that fellow Cherry's section yet, and I'll raise sheep and cattle on it.'" Mrs Naylor frowned. "Unfortunately, I had to cane him, for he will not mend his ways. I would be much obliged if you would speak to him about this habit."

"Certainly," I said, "I will as soon as you've gone."

"Then I will take my leave immediately," said Mrs Naylor, looking relieved. "Good day to you."

"Good day," Anderina and I echoed.

"William," I called, when his teacher was out of sight, "come here I want to talk to you."

William skipped over, swinging a stick as he whistled.

"I understand the teacher caned you today because you were not paying attention."

William stopped whistling and hung his head.

"I told you she didn't understand business."

"If you want a business, you need to know your letters and numbers…"

Then I lectured him on the evils connected with illiteracy and a lack of education, and when I had exhausted all the troubles, I expounded on the wonderful opportunities arithmetic and science would open up for him.

"Now, son, what do you have to say for yourself?"

William drew himself up and looked me straight in the eye.

"When I grow up, Dad," he said cheerfully, "I'm going to buy that fellow Naylor's land, and turn the school into my cow shed."

To Own a Fig Tree

Truck Rears its Ugly Head

By the end of June, the walls, floor, and roof of the new house were up, but the spaces for the door and four windows gaped like large holes. The sparsely furnished room echoed and our feet made clumping noises as Anderina and I walked about, admiring it.

"We've gone as far as we can," I said, gazing up at the thin cross of light filtering through the ridges of the hipped roof. "I hope the zinc ridging comes before winter sets in."

Anderina shivered and wrapped her shawl more tightly around her body.

"That is the least of our problems. Are you sure you have written 'doors' and 'windows' on your list for Mr Scanlan?"

"Absolutely." I ran my finger over the paper I held as I read aloud:

"One house door, six feet by thirty-two inches, including hinges and lock. Two windows, twenty-eight inches high by twenty inches wide. And two windows twenty-two inches high by eighteen inches wide."

"That's good," said Anderina, sitting on the edge of a window recess. "Did you work out how many rolls of wallpaper we need?"

"Yes, I figure at three drops per roll, twenty rolls of the cheapest wallpaper will do the job.

"Quite right, there's no point paying more than a shilling per roll."

"John Naylor says you must first stretch a sort of sacking called scrim over the framework, and you paste the paper onto that, so I've ordered an equal amount of scrim."

"That man is full of useful information," Anderina nodded, her glance falling on our homemade table and benches. "What about a tablecloth?"

"Yes," my finger rubbed across the page once more, "plus twelve pairs of cups and saucers (small size) twelve pairs of knives and forks, twelve tablespoons, twelve teaspoons, twelve large side plates, and twelve small side plates." I stopped and looked up in wonder as a memory flashed through my mind. "When I was a child, my biggest goal in life was to buy twelve dinner plates and bowls." I waved my hand at the house and the view outside, "now look at us, rich beyond our imagination."

"God is good," said Anderina. "The trip was hard and it's been tough getting established, but you were right to bring us here, Robert."

I was unaccustomed to praise from my wife, so to cover my embarrassment I continued reading the list.

"Two deep plates, one large plate, two deep dishes with tops, one water jug, one milk jug, one sugar dish, and one salt dish."

"You forgot the tumblers," said Anderina.

"I'm getting to those. Twelve tumblers, (two of them small size) one twelve-cup teapot. That's the lot. Can you think of anything else we need other than our normal supplies?"

"No."

I folded the paper and put it in my pocket.

To Own a Fig Tree

"I'll be off then. I want to make sure Simpson gets my order lodged before the *Charley* comes."

Anderina hopped off the window sill, and I set off at a brisk pace to the Government Reserve.

When I arrived at the store, James Simpson took my order in the usual manner, but as I turned to go Mr Scanlan detained me.

"Your account is getting rather high, Mr Johnson," he said, flipping to the Js in the big ledger on the counter before scrutinizing the figures. "Unless I see more commitment to repaying the debt, I am afraid I will have to detain your order."

I felt my face grow warm as I took off my cap and twisted it between my hands.

"But, Sir, two of my sons are working to pay what we owe. John is on the gang cutting out the bullock track, and Robert has been away for weeks with the southward survey party.

"O'Connor says it's not enough," said the overseer, rocking on his toes and tapping the ends of his fingers together. His stern expression softened into a fatherly smile. "I have a solution to your problem, however. We are very isolated. Currently, the only way to Westport is around the gigantic obstacle of the Karamea Bluff, and sadly, the Tasman has claimed so many lives from rockfalls that freight costs are exorbitant by this route. Seeing as your son is part of the survey party, you will be doubly pleased to hear they have almost finished marking out a southern route over the hills. But before we make a start on that, I am getting a gang together to form the South Terrace Road." Scanlan's eyes bored into mine. "Are you willing to sign on or do I need to stop your order?"

I stomped home in a black mood.

"What's the matter?" said Anderina, when she saw my face.

"I start work on the road next week."

"Isn't that good? We need a proper road and the money will be useful."

"The road will be good, but I have no choice, and there will be no money," I spat out. "It's the same old *truck* system we fled from in *Zetland*. The only difference is O'Connor and Scanlan are the laird and factor. No commercial storekeeper in either Nelson or Westport will risk trading in such a remote place as Karamea, so the Government store is our only source of supplies. Scanlan was clear that those with the greatest needs have to work the most man-hours. In other words, us and the Scarletts, because we have the biggest families."

The colour drained from Anderina's cheeks.

"Oh, Robert! Clocks and sweeties again?"

"Not quite; same old slavery with a little more choice. At least we can keep cattle and own land."

My mood did not lighten as the days grew closer to the start of my new job. And I was not the only one. No difficulty we (Shetlanders) had previously encountered in our new land, soured us like the realization we were locked into *truck* once more. The only man working on the road who wasn't surly, was Thomas Lineham.

"What are you grumbling about?" he said cheerfully, as slashing and cutting we followed the straight line marked through the scrub. "Living on credit until we get established is great. Nobody in England gave me such a wonderful start in life. It will be some time before we can feed our families totally from the land, but already I have a few fowls and I eat far better here than I did in the old country."

To Own a Fig Tree

"A Sunday suit leads to three-hundred-years of bondage," I said bitterly.

"A Sunday suit? I don't follow you."

James Moffatt hacked through the base of a ponga and threw it off the track.

"He means the sheep you ate and the billhook you're using, leave you at the mercy of O'Connor and Simpson."

"You and your children, and your children's children," added Lawrence Lawrenson, digging out a flax bush.

"I think you are worrying about nothing," said Thomas, limping towards a small lancewood tree. "The Government fixed up my bad leg, and the Father-of-the-Settlement has our good at heart. If this is bush life, I don't mind it a bit."

I leaned on my billhook and raised one eyebrow.

"Does O'Connor *really* have our best interests at heart? Or is he like the lairds?"

"Perhaps he's feathering his nest at our expense," said James, grubbing out ferns. "He has land on the North Bank. If the settlement does well, his property will increase in value."

"And there is his political career," said Peter Coutts. "It won't look good for him if his pet project fails."

"Exactly," said Thomas, whacking down the lancewood. "He needs us to succeed so we have nothing to worry about. Instead of being suspicious, we should thank God there are no venomous reptiles or wild beasts for us to fear. As the Good Book says, we can 'worship God under our own vine and fig tree, none daring lawfully to make us afraid.'" He swotted a mosquito and grinned. "Only the old gnats trouble us."

As Edwin was scattering seeds a little way off, and the rest of us were unwilling to speak against the Bible, the subject was dropped (though our suspicions remained.)

For the next two-and-a-half months, we were roadmen by day, and farmers by night. While it was daylight, we laboured on the road, returning at dusk to work several more hours on our land - felling trees by the light of bonfires.

"It will be worth it when the windows and doors come," Anderina encouraged me. "Just imagine while you work that you are providing a door, windows, and zinc ridging, to make our house snug against the winter winds and rain."

"Only if the steamer comes," I said gloomily. "The order had to be sent by foot around the coast."

"How it went doesn't matter, the important thing is, it went. The *Charley* will be here soon, you'll see."

But Anderina was wrong. The steamer did not come in June, she did not come in July, and she did not come in August. All winter she bypassed us, for the seas were rough and the bar dangerous. So, there were no windows, no door, no zinc ridging, and no supplies. Only rain, hunger, and six days a week of endless work.

To Own a Fig Tree

Disaster

By August, winter had bitten into our bones and souls. Day after day of relentless rain numbed our cold hands as we miserably hacked out the road and dug drainage ditches on either side of it; and we men were not the only ones slogging in the wet. At home, within the perpetually damp bush, younger children cleared away the undergrowth, while the older ones felled small manuka trees with hatchets. One evening when I arrived home weary, Anderina met me at the door in great agitation.

"You have to do something about the house, Robert. We can't go on like this. James' cough is getting much worse." She pointed to the wet floor. "The roof is leaking and the oiled calico in the windows is not strong enough to keep the wind out."

"The windows and ridging should be here any day," I said, pulling the brim of my sou'wester forward so water stopped dripping onto my nose.

"Huh, I'm not waiting any longer for that fickle steamer."

I thought hard. "I could lie the tarpaulin over the roof and weight it down with stones."

Anderina drew herself up and put her hands on her hips. "Don't even think about taking the roof from my kitchen. Anything but that. Have you any idea how hard it is to keep a fire going in this weather?" She pulled on a woollen hat and draped a sheet of oiled calico over her shoulders before running through the rain to the camp oven.

I sploshed after her and sat on a rock by the smouldering fire.

"If only I could block the gaps on the ridges," I said, looking up at the tarpaulin as I rubbed my chin.

Anderina ladled embers onto the lid of the cast-iron vessel. "Perhaps we could thatch it with raupo," she said, wrapping a sack around the handle and jiggling the pot so its three legs were level.

I took a fistful of totara bark, and fed it into the fire absentmindedly as I pondered on the problem.

"I think water would still get in," I said at last.

Elizabeth and Laurie appeared from the bush, dragging manuka trunks which they dumped beside the nearby woodpile.

"I'll chop it into firewood tomorrow," Laurie said, sitting on a rock. "What's for dinner?"

"I've run out of oats, so I'm trying something different," said Anderina.

"What?" said Elizabeth.

"I've still got flour so I'm making bread."

"I could make ridging out of ponga trunks," I said suddenly. "Where is Mary? She can help."

"In the garden, I told her to get some turnips," said Anderina. "Here she comes now."

"There is something wrong with the turnips and potatoes," said Mary. "The tops are alright but the bottoms are rotten."

She held them out for me to inspect.

I looked at them with a sinking heart.

"What's the soil like?"

To Own a Fig Tree

"All squishy and waterlogged."

Forgetting the house, I grabbed a spade and hastening to the garden, dug out a potato plant. As I feared, the tubers dangled from the stem in slushy blobs. Feverously, I dug up another plant from a different row, and then another, and another, all with the same result. Our crops were ruined. Without saying a word, I picked up a billhook and headed into the bush. My legs moved automatically and I scarcely heard Anderina calling my name, as I mechanically hacked down pongas.

"What's wrong?" said Anderina, when I arrived home.

"Nothing," I lied, taking off my oilskin coat and shaking it out the door. "I've worked out a way to fix the roof temporarily."

"That's good."

I hung my coat and hat on a nail by a shelf of cheeses, and sat at the head of the table.

"I'm sorry, dear, my bread did not turn out well," said Anderina, handing me a plate of blackened dough.

"Oo yuck, do we have to eat this?" said Margret.

"Yes, and be grateful we have anything at all," I growled. "Bow your heads and I will give thanks."

My family, seated on benches on either side of the table, shot worried glances at me.

"Dear Lord, thank you for this food, we trust you to give us daily bread, in the name of Jesus, Amen."

"Amen," came the echo.

"What's wrong, Robert?" Anderina repeated.

I still could not bring myself to tell my wife the awful truth, so I said:

"John and I'll fix the roof tonight," I bit into the burnt mass, chewed and swallowed. "And tomorrow after work we'll board up the windows."

My heavy tone and the dismal food discouraged conversation, so we finished our meal in miserable silence. Then John and I donned our coats and once more braved the heavy downpour outside.

My idea of slicing a long segment out of each ponga trunk and jamming them over the four ridges, worked. It wasn't a perfect solution but it greatly helped.[36]

The house looked cosy in the candlelight as my son and I wearily hung up our coats and pulled off our gumboots. James was asleep in his suitcase, and the younger children dozed under sacking quilts on beds made of tea tree and flax, while Anderina, sitting on a crate, knitted. John dried his hair with a flour bag, but I dropped onto the sack on the floor and put my head into my hands.

Anderina leaned towards me.

"What's wrong? Robert," she whispered.

"Our crops are ruined, the steamer can't get here, swollen rivers block the overland route, and we are almost out of supplies."

My wife's fingers stopped moving, and we sat in silence for some time. At last, the needles started flashing again as she said:

"We have milk and eggs, fronds and grubs are in the bush, birds are in the air, and God is still in heaven. We'll get by."

I looked at her gratefully; my stoic wife was a rock in times of trouble.

---

36   Historical problem, imaginary solution

To Own a Fig Tree

Sickness and Theft

Robert was back. We clustered around him, keen to hear tales of his time away.

"How did the surveying go?" I asked, lighting the stub of a candle.

"We found a way over the Karamea bluff," he said, taking off his coat and gumboots. "What's for dinner?"

"Turnip tops, grubs, fronds, and damper," said Mary, pouring him a cup of tea.

"Sounds good to me."

Anderina eyed him with motherly concern.

"You look thin, Bob."

Robert put one foot on the bench by the table, hooked his thumbs in his belt, and puffed out his chest. We looked at him expectantly, for we recognized his story-telling stance.

"The tucker wasn't lavish on the track, especially as time went by," he said with a grin. "One chap started with a loaf of bread in the sack on his back. After it had bounced about for many days, the loaf was pulverized. 'You might as well throw it away,' we said, for by now the crumbs were so mixed with the gunny-hairs of the sack, it was impossible to separate one from the other. 'No,' he said, 'we might need them yet.' And sure enough, the day came when we were so hungry, we boiled the crumbs and sieved the liquid through our teeth!"

We laughed at Robert's look of disgust as he mimed

straining hairs from the soup.

"How is the South Terrace Road going, Dad?" he said when we settled down.

"Almost finished," I said. "And none too soon, one more miserable day in the rain and we can stop."

Robert looked troubled as he sipped his tea.

"I think Mr Scanlan has different ideas. He says now we've found a way over the bluff you can start working on the track between Little Wanganui and Seddonville."

"But it's at least seventeen miles to Little Wanganui!" exclaimed John.

"You can't walk seventeen miles there and back, plus work eight hours every day," said Anderina.

"We'd need to live in camps at the site," I said, "but in this weather, without additional tents, blankets, and food it's not practical. We'll wait until the weather improves and the steamer gets in with more supplies."

"If it takes too long, we will be busy with spring planting," said John.

"How's the garden getting on, Dad?" said Robert.

I frowned.

"Disastrous, even with all the ditches. The ground is so waterlogged our crops have rotted. If the steamer does not come soon, we will have to eat the chooks."

"Oh, Robert," exclaimed Anderina, "not our hens. They are the start of our flock."

"We may not have a choice. If they don't begin laying again, they're more useful in the pot."

A spasm of coughing shook James' frail body, and Robert's attention switched to him as Anderina wiped red flecks away from the tiny child's lips.

"Blood!"

"Only a little." Anderina slid a teaspoon of cough mixture into James' mouth.

The colour drained from Robert's face and he looked stricken.

"It's First-Elizabeth all over again." He hung his head. "If only I had run to the store quicker, she would be alive today."

"Stop blaming yourself for your sister's death, son," I said, laying my hand on his shoulder. "It was not your fault."

"Your father is right," said Anderina. "Even if you had got home with the cough medicine in time, the Lord would still have taken her."

I patted his shoulder gently. "None of us are guaranteed a long life. It was her appointed time to go."

The room was very silent, the only sound was the clattering of plates as Second-Elizabeth put them on the table. Then William also coughed, and I noticed his eyes were rather red. Anderina bustled over to him with concern on her face.

"You look flushed, Willie," she said, putting her hand on his forehead. "Do you feel well?"

William shook his head.

"I don't feel well either," grizzled Laurie.

"William Scarlett wasn't at school today because he has the measles," said Margret.

"*Measles!*" Anderina hastily unbuttoned William's shirt and pulled up his woollen singlet.

To our horror, his chest was mottled with a rash.

"It's measles alright," said Anderina, buttoning him up again. She inspected Laurance closely. "Laurie has it too. Oh dear, I wish I had thought to collect the medicine cabinet before now. Into bed with both of you."

My wife looked at me and my heart sank, for I knew what was coming.

"Robert, go to the store and get the medicine box."

"Not tonight, my love," I said apologetically.

"Why not, our children are sick and I need it?"

"It's dark, the river is running fast, and the tide is in."

"I'll go, Mum," said Robert, pulling on his oilskin, "and this time I will get back before it is too late."

"No, Bob, stop!" Mother and son locked eyes. "Your father is right; I'll not have you risk your life. One day will not make a difference, I'll get it myself at low tide tomorrow."

Anderina and Robert stared at each other and once again, the room fell silent. At last, Robert dropped his eyes and nodded slowly.

"Dinner is almost ready," said Anderina, helping him out of his coat. She replenished his cup from the teapot and pushed it towards him. "By the time you've finished your tea, I'll have dinner on the table." She pulled my oilskin on and, lifting the tent flap, disappeared out the door. As she promised, she was soon back. Once the food was on the plates, I gave thanks for the meal. Although we were used to a bush diet by now, none of the younger boys wanted to eat, and ominously, Margret picked at her food.

"How's the bullock getting on, John? said Robert, woofing down huhu grubs.

"Good, he's pulling loads and is a big help. Come and work on the track to Johnson's Landing tomorrow and see him."

Robert shook his head.

To Own a Fig Tree

"I wish I could, but Rawson wants to explore the northerly coast. Apparently, an old gold miner's trail exists over the ranges."

"A trail?"

"Yes, it's called the Heaphy Track. If we can get through to Collingwood, our way is clear to Nelson."

"That will open up our settlement to a thriving world," I said, blowing my nose.

"Only if it is feasible," said Anderina. "Hidden in those hills are sheer cliffs and raging waterways for sure."

"The only way to find out," said Robert, "is to go and see."

We continued talking as we ate. At least John and Robert did. My interest in the Heaphy Track waned as the whispers of an impending headache strengthened.

"Are you alright, Robert?" said Anderina. "You're very quiet."

"I'm fine," I said, "never felt better."

And to prove it, I went outside and slaughtered our first hen.

In the morning (despite the cold weather) I felt hot and my head thumped when I lifted it from my pillow. I pulled down the neck of my underwear and leaned close to the flickering candle, but there was no sign of a rash.

"What are you doing, Robert?" said Anderina. "Are you feeling alright?"

"I'm fine," I lied, dressing slowly.

Anderina pulled her dress over her chamise and wrapped her shawl around her body tightly. Robert was already up and preparing to leave.

"Be careful, Bob," said Anderina, giving him a small bag

of flour.

My hand wobbled and chills ran down my spine as I handed him the plucked chicken.

"Put this in your tucker bag."

Robert shook his head.

"No, Dad, I can't. You all need it more than me."

"Take it, Bob," said Anderina. "We have more if we need them." She wrapped a set of long woollen underwear in an oilcloth. "Are you wearing your woollies?"

Robert turned his head and rolled his eyes at me.

"Of course, Mum, I always wear them, summer and winter."

"Good boy, they might save your life someday." She stuffed her package into his sack. "Here's a dry set if you get wet through."

"Take care of yourself and the others, Mum," said Robert, slinging the sack onto his back and slipping his arms through its rope handles. "Are you sure you don't want me to collect the medicine box before I go?"

"No, I'll be fine," said Anderina. "Rawson won't want to wait for you."

"What about crossing the river?"

"If I make enough noise Mr Scanlan will hear, and come for me with the lighter."

"God bless and keep you, Son," I said, as he waved goodbye and disappeared through the door.

I didn't feel like breakfast that morning, and the last day of work dragged on and on. By the time I staggered home, I could barely stay upright as I unbuttoned my coat with shaking fingers.

Anderina was too agitated to notice I was sick.

To Own a Fig Tree

"Thank goodness you are home at last, Robert," she cried. "All the children are down with measles, and something *dreadful* has happened."

Her voice seemed as if it were coming and going through fog, and her face was blurry as she continued:

"I went to the store to get my medicine cabinet, but when Simpson looked for it, it was nowhere to be found. *Someone has stolen it!*"

"It must be there somewhere," I said faintly, through rapid breaths. "I saw John Naylor label it and write it in the book."

Anderina folded her arms.

"Well, I'm telling you, it's not there now. Someone is a thief! We need that medicine cabinet more than ever. What are you going to do about it?"

I did not know, but I was saved from answering by sudden shooting pains.

"Ahh," I cried, clutching my chest as I fell to the floor.

———

W.E. Hamilton

The Steamer Arrives

I had pneumonia, and I was not the only one sick. By the end of September, almost all the children of our community had measles and most of the men had pneumonia. I was still too ill to leave my bed for long, when we heard the toot of the *Charley*'s whistle one day.

"At last," said Anderina, pulling off her apron and tying on her bonnet. "I thought I'd never hear that blessed sound again."

I raised myself onto my elbow.

"Get John and the girls to help you with the supplies," I croaked. "His job and the girl's chores can wait. And if the door and windows have come, have Scanlan ferry them in the lighter for you; Robert and Peter's canoes are too tippy. Someone will drown if you use them."

Anderina nodded, and taking her flax basket from a nail beside the sou'westers, waved goodbye and went.

There was not much in her basket when she arrived back several hours later.

"Did our order arrive?" I asked, as she took off her hat.

"Yes, everything except the fig tree came. I left John and the girls packing the windows and door onto the bullock dray. They're going to bring them up the Zig-Zag."

"Good," I said, feeling relieved. "As soon as I am on my feet again, I can button up the house."

To Own a Fig Tree

Anderina's mouth was straight and her tone grim as she lifted a small bottle of vinegar and a roll of brown paper from her basket.

"Those North Bankers are sharks, the whole lot of them," she said, ripping a strip of paper from the roll. "It's first in first served; by the time I got to the store, they had made off with the fresh supplies and there was no flour, tea, coffee, cocoa, or candles."

"I suppose that means more early nights and bidi-bidi tea," I said, pulling a face.

Anderina snorted as she rubbed vinegar on the paper. "That's right. If our windows had not been in crates with 'JOHNSON' written on them, for sure they would have snatched them too." She banged the cork in the bottle. "It is hard to see folks who came months after us, get the better deal. They don't have to slog miles uphill to their farms. They don't have rotten potatoes. Instead, they have easy access to the store and harbour, their pastures are lush, and their crops are flourishing. It's so unfair."

"Did Simpson find the medicine cabinet? I said, changing the subject.

Anderina sighed.

"No, not a sign of it." Her face turned dark with suspicion. "I wouldn't be surprised if he took it himself. I smelt brandy on his breath."

"Surely not," I said disbelievingly. "It's more likely he's a sly grogger."

"Maybe, maybe not. I only have myself to blame for its loss. I knew I should have kept it with me when we first arrived." Anderina draped the damp paper across my forehead gently.

"I'm afraid without it, home remedies are the best I can do for your headache."

"It's alright," I said, "I'm getting better."

"One good thing about this sickness," said Anderina, dabbing a drop of kerosene onto a teaspoon of sugar, "is Mr Scanlan has given up insisting the men start work on the track at Little Wanganui. Walking thirty-four miles and eight hours of hard physical labour a day is ridiculous." There was a rumbling noise and the sound of voices outside. "It's John and the girls," she said, hastily giving the spoon to Margret. "Swallow this Maggie, it will help your throat. I'll be back in a minute." Then she disappeared outside.

I sat up gingerly, and taking the paper from my head, swung my feet over the side of the bed. When the room stopped spinning, I hoisted myself onto my feet, shuffled over to the door, and pushed my head around the edge of the tent flap. For the first time in months, no rain was falling from the sky. The bullock stood stock-still in the mud while my wife and children lifted the crates from the dray and leaned them against the walls of the house. I sat in the door frame and watched them peer through the slats at the goods within.

"The little panes look lovely," said Anderina, bending forward and sticking her eyeball close to a crack.

John grabbed a hammer. "Shall I open the crate so you can see them better, Mum?"

"No, John," I intervened, "keep the windows boxed up until we are ready to install them."

"Your father is right," said Anderina, with a sigh. "Glass is fragile and if we break a pane, it could be months before we can get it repaired." A light entered her eyes. "But we could

To Own a Fig Tree

take the door out."

There was a flurry of activity, and soon a handsome door appeared. When I saw it, I felt frustrated at my weakened condition.

"If I had my usual strength, I'd put that door in right now."

"Never mind, Rob, the weather is improving every day, another week won't make much difference. Put it inside, John, so the littlies can see it."

I stood up stiffly and hobbled out of John's way as he carried the door in and set it against a wall.

"Don't forget this," said Mary, pointing to a large wooden box.

"The dinner set," cried Anderina, "quick, girls, bring it in. Don't forget the hammer, Elizabeth."

I sat on a bench as Mary and Elizabeth (staggering under the weight of the box) stumped inside and slid it onto the table. Then Elizabeth stood on the bench and slickly whisked the nails out of the top boards with the claw of the hammer. The dinner set was nestled in straw.

"Such a pretty blue," said Mary, as her mother lifted a stack of small side plates.

"I always loved willow pattern," said Anderina, touching them reverently. Elizabeth sat on the table and picked up a cup and saucer while Mary dug out a pile of large plates.

"Count them; make sure we have got what we are charged for, John," I said. "There should be twelve of everything."

"Where are the teapot and deep dishes?" said Anderina, suddenly.

"There are still two boxes on the dray," said John. "I'll get them."

"Did you see Peter Coutts, Mary?" giggled Elizabeth as John disappeared?

"Yes, he looked very spiffed up in his Sunday suit."

"His cousin, Barbara, told me he's going back to Nelson on the *Charley* to ask Jemima Jamieson to marry him."

Mary's face lit up.

"Really?"

Elizabeth beamed and nodded violently.

"She might already be married," croaked Margret from her bed. "Single women are snaffled up quickly."

"Nah, not her," said Elizabeth, putting tumblers on the table. "She and Peter have been sweethearts for years. They were only waiting for Peter to build a house."

"Thomas and Margret will be relieved," said Anderina, admiring the cup she held. "That's one old maid off their hands."

"Perhaps even their older girls, Agnes and Janet, will be married by the time he gets there," said Mary.

"Here we are," said John, cutting the conversation short as he dumped the crate on the table.

"Careful," Anderina admonished, as Elizabeth levered off the lid.

"Where do you want the zinc ridging stored, Dad?" said John.

"By the windows."

"Nice wallpaper," said Mary, ignoring her brother's interruption.

"The deep dishes and jugs must be in the other box," said Anderina, taking the roll Mary handed her.

Mary grabbed another roll, and pulling a length of paper

To Own a Fig Tree

out, inspected the pattern. "Very pretty. We've never had flowers all over the wall before."

"Frippery and fuddling nonsense," said Anderina, trying in vain to suppress a smile of delight. "The paper is only to stop the drafts."

"Is the lock for the door in there?" I said.

"Yes, Dad." Mary handed me a handsome lock and three door-hinges. "And the scrim."

Anderina's smile disappeared and her face turned grim again. "I hope we have enough flour left to make wallpaper paste. Those North Bankers got it all."

"Never mind, there will be more flour soon, for now the weather has turned, the steamer will call once a month again."

"You are quite right, Robert. I am silly to worry," said Anderina, abandoning herself to the pleasure of unpacking the rest of our goods. "The steamer will be back before we are ready to wallpaper."

But I was wrong. The windows and doors were in, the zinc ridging was on the roof, and our spring crops were planted before we heard the shrill blast of the *Charley*'s whistle once more.

W.E. Hamilton

Lost, Saved, and Found

Our cows had calved and Karamea now boasted four cows, two calves, one bull, twelve goats, two sows, one bore pig, sixty-one pair of fowls, four ducks, and the bullock; at least it did until a day ago. We had lost a cow and her calf, and the King brothers were hunting for two missing pigs.

"Bessy, Bessy," called Anderina.

"Come on, come on," I shouted.

"They can't be on the terrace," said Anderina at last. "If they were, Bessy would have called out by now."

I nodded.

"That's true, she always moos when we call her name. We'll have to try further inland."

"But, Rob, the bush is thick, and the light is fading, we might get lost."

"Nonsense. I've been up and down the rivers and over these hills many times. We have to keep looking for if she has time to get further away, we will have lost her and the calf for good."

Anderina sighed. "Alright, we'll keep going. We can't afford to lose them. Do you think they will have headed into the hills or down to the river?"

"Uphill, they'll feel safer higher up," I said, turning inland.

We saved our breath until we started climbing, then the hills and valleys rang with shouts of: "Bessy."

To Own a Fig Tree

At first, it was not too dim in the bush, but as we pushed our way deeper and deeper into the tangled jungle of supplejack and mighty trees, it got darker and darker, until finally, we could see nothing. At last, Anderina had had enough.

"We should go home, if we continue much further there will be two cows, two pigs, and two Johnsons missing."

"Alright." I turned to make my way home and suddenly realized I was lost. I did not want to admit my mistake but there was no way around it. "Anderina, I don't know the way home."

"Oh, *Robert!* I told you this might happen. What are we going to do?"

"The only thing we can." Then I prayed: "Dear Lord Jesus, we are lost, please keep us safe and help us find our way home."

"Amen," said Anderina.

We stood still for a few moments.

"I think we should go this way," said Anderina, turning around and moving to the left.

The way seemed as good as any other, so together we tunnelled our way like earthworms through the dense undergrowth. After some time, I suddenly had the strongest impression we were in danger.

"STOP!" I shouted, throwing my arms in front of my wife, "lie down, something doesn't feel right."

Anderina, without questioning, dropped with me to the ground. Then I groped among the dirt and leaf mold. There was earth to the right and left of us, but when I pushed my hand forward, it shot into nothingness. I broke into a cold sweat and my voice shook as I said:

"One more step and we would have fallen over a cliff."

"Thank you, Lord, for saving us," said Anderina, looking upwards.

We lay there without speaking for a few minutes to let the shakes pass. Around us were the usual night sounds of the bush. Crickets sang, *moreporks*[37] hooted, and kiwis whistled their long repetitive call over and over. But as my heart stopped thudding, I noticed another noise. It was the soft roar of falling water. Hmm, a cliff in front and a waterfall to my right. I mulled over the reference points and then I knew where we were.

"Anderina, I know the way home," I shouted, pulling her to her feet. "This way." And turning, I led her home.

We met Robert and John on the way back. They were holding lanterns high and calling for us.

"I'm glad to see you," said Robert, with relief in his voice.

"We thought you had fallen over a cliff," said John.

"We almost did."

"But the grace of God and your father's quick thinking saved us."

"Has Bessy come home?"

"No sign of her or the calf," said John.

I shrugged.

"Oh well, we'll try again tomorrow."

My wife's face was grim in the lantern light.

"Not in the hills, Robert, and not in the dark!"

I nodded.

"We'll try along the river if she is not back by morning."

I half expected to see Bessy when I went out to milk Daisy, but there was no sign of her, so after breakfast, I wrapped a rope around my waist, and Anderina and I set off in search of

---

37   owls

To Own a Fig Tree

her once more. This time we went along the Karamea river flats below the high perch of the South Terrace.

"Bessy, Bessy," we shouted as we tramped in and out of the bush along the riverbank.

Suddenly I heard something. "Listen, is that a moo?"

We stood stock-still, straining our ears in the sound's direction.

"Flossie… Arabella," the call floated on the breeze towards us.

"That's not Bessy, it's Edwin shouting for his pigs," said Anderina, her face falling. "He must be looking for them down here too." "Perhaps we will find his pigs, and he will find our cows," I said with a grin.

But instead, three miles up the river we all stumbled upon our lost animals at the same time, in the same place. The cow and her calf were grazing, and the pigs were grubbing about on the edge of a lovely clearing filled with gigantic flowers. It was so unexpected both my wife and I, and the King brothers, momentarily forgot our livestock. Anderina sucked in her breath sharply and her hand flew to her mouth in wonder.

"Oh, my goodness, who would have thought such a little patch of heaven would exist in this wilderness?"

Edwin knelt and examined them carefully.

"These are seeds I planted a couple of months ago when I went for a ramble along the river," he said.

His brother picked a vigorous bloom and poked it through his buttonhole.

"Are they the same type as the little ones you planted at home, Eddy?"

"Yes, though you would hardly know, mine are so small

and frail. I can't believe the difference. I planted both crops in August but you would not guess it." He dug his fingers in the ground and scooping up some earth, crumbled it between his fingers speculatively. "This soil must be extremely fertile."

I whacked the back of my heel into the ground, and it made a thumping not squishing sound.

"The drainage is good too."

"This is marvellous," said Edwin, his eyes shining. "I was beginning to think all the land on the south side was no good. I must tell O'Connor of my find when he next comes."

I unwrapped the rope from around my waist and tied it around Bessy's horns with conflicting emotions.

"Are you saying our land has more problems than just drainage, Edwin, that it is infertile as well?"

Edwin snapped a thick stalk and held it up.

"More is happening here than just good drainage. Look at the health of this plant. These flowers are three times the size I'd expect. I wish I'd planted potatoes instead. If we swapped our properties for blocks down here, we could equal or better the conditions of the North Bankers."

I thought of my rotted crop, my spring planting and my finished house, and felt hope seesaw with despair.

"If Edwin is right, and O'Connor gives us new land," said Anderina, picking a bunch of flowers, "we may never suffer last year's troubles again."

'And all my labour is in vain,' I thought, but did not say. Instead, I smiled and pulling on the rope, said:

"That which was lost is found. Come Bessy, time for you and your calf to come home."

To Own a Fig Tree

A Miserable Anniversary

James was steadily getting worse. He survived the measles, but instead of red flecks, he now coughed up pools of blood, and all the handkerchiefs in the house were stained with reminders of what we would rather forget. We were within days of our anniversary of landing in Karamea, but it was obvious our youngest was unlikely to make the full year.

"He is fading fast," whispered Anderina, as she cradled James in her lap.

We gathered around in a tight knot, listening to his irregular gurgling breaths.

"I can hear the death rattle," said Anderina. "Pray Robert."

I nodded and laid my hand gently on James' head, and shut my eyes

"Dear Heavenly Father, thank you for this little life you loaned to us for a short while. We thank you that there is a better life for James beyond this one. You have promised him a room in your mansion, land and fig trees. We release James into your care, and ask you will be with us through our sorrow and loss. Amen.

"Amen," echoed my family.

Then we fell silent, listening to the laboured breathing that grew fainter and fainter until it stopped altogether.

"He's gone," said Anderina. She laid him gently in his suitcase, put a penny on each closed eye, and crossed his arms over his chest. "Do you need his measurements, Robert?"

W.E. Hamilton

"No, I've already got them."

My heart was heavy as I went to our old ponga hut and pulled a bundle of pre-cut boards out from behind the cow's manger. Although I had known for a long time this day would come, it did not make it any easier. I wiped tears from my eyes as I hammered the small coffin together, and lined it with wallpaper offcuts. We mourned in private for a day, and then the whole community (all two-hundred-and-twenty-seven of us) came to the funeral on the South Terrace, where we buried him near the Zig-Zag track on the plot Rawson had set aside as a cemetery. Mr Scanlan, who had been away for two weeks, was back in time to take the service.

"And a very nice job he did of it," neighbours comforted us, as clods of dirt fell with hollow thumps on the lid of the homemade box.

But public approval for Scanlan evaporated, when the next day he rebuked us for not returning to work.

"O'Connor will be here any day and you have not even started on the track between Little Wanganui and Seddonville."

We crossed our arms, stood our ground and glowered at him.

"The track is thirteen miles away, and the weather is still volatile," I said. "It is impractical to walk there and back every day, and we don't have adequate clothing or equipment to camp there in the rain. When summer comes, we will work on the track."

"I shall have to report you to O'Connor when he comes on the twenty-sixth, and I'm warning you, he won't be happy."

It was not the right answer.

"Let him say what he will," someone shouted, "it's our

To Own a Fig Tree

right to down tools and strike."

"We will see about that," said Scanlan, red spots of anger appearing on his cheeks.

"Yes, we will," we jeered.

But his threat was more than just words, for when the *Charley* arrived, even the first man to the store got nothing.

"No work, no supplies, and no further credit," said O'Connor to the milling crowd, as he stood before the locked door. "And men with the biggest debt must work the most hours."

"You're just trying to feather your own nest," someone shouted angrily.

"My sole anxiety (apart from establishing a direct link to the Seddonville railway line,)" O'Connor shouted back, "is to keep suspicious men from getting deeply into debt."

"It's too late for that!"

"For suspicion maybe," said O'Connor, "but not too late for you to work off your debt." He put his hand on the shoulder of the man standing next to him.

"This is Mr Jennings, the surveyor in charge of roadworks. He waits here ready to sign up all who want work and supplies. Who will be the first to join the roading gang?"

The animosity in the silence that fell, was almost tangible.

"What about you, Johnson?" shouted O'Connor, singling me out.

"You have the biggest debt."

I hung my head.

"One-hundred-and-fifteen pounds. Just how do you propose to repay that huge amount without signing up for work immediately? Have you, endless flour and potatoes, or does your family need more supplies today?"

W.E. Hamilton

I said nothing, so his gimlet eye searched through the crowd for another victim. "And Scarlett," he said, picking on Daniel, "your debt is the second biggest; one-hundred pounds. Do you have a rich uncle in your back pocket or will you be signing up?"

Daniel also hung his head and shuffled his feet.

"Come on Johnson," said O'Connor, holding out a pencil. "Act the man, be the first to sign on."

I had no choice; he knew it and I knew it. I stepped forward, took the pencil from him and signed my name in Jennings' book, then Daniel signed, and after him, Frederick Liley, for we had the biggest families. After that, a queue rapidly formed as men waited to sign on, each one looking like a condemned criminal awaiting the gallows. When the last man placed his signature in the book, O'Connor said in a genial tone:

"Now the serious business is over, onto happier things. Congratulations Peter Coutts on your recent marriage." He waved him forward. "Come up here Peter and bring your lovely bride with you."

It was a smart political move. Our attention shifted from the track to blushing Jemima.

"Three cheers for Mr and Mrs Coutts," called O'Connor.

The first hip-hip-hooray was subdued, for we were still smarting over our defeat, but as Peter was one of us and deserved our support, the second cheer was louder, and the last 'HOORAY' sounded almost cheerful.

"And there is more good news," said O'Connor, as Peter and Jemima slid back into the crowd, "Edwin King informs me he has found extremely fertile ground on the river flats of the South Bank. Later this afternoon I will investigate this find. I

To Own a Fig Tree

have hopes it will be very beneficial for those struggling on the South Terrace."

There was a smattering of clapping from the women among us.

"One more thing before I open the store," said O'Connor, hooking his thumbs in the pockets of his waistcoat, and leaning back like an all-providing-patriarch. "Election time is coming up. For most of you, this is the first time you have been eligible to vote. It is a great privilege. You will receive voting papers next month. Fill them out and send them back by the middle of January."

"What happens if the steamer can't get the papers here in time?" came a shout.

"I will personally see they are sent overland from Collingwood," said O'Connor.

"Of course, he will," muttered Liley, "he wants our vote."

"Well, he's not getting mine," growled Daniel.

O'Connor, sensing our darkening mood, motioned Fanny Lineham forward and plucking little Mary Anne from her arms, kissed the baby on her cheek before giving her back to her mother.

"We may have our differences," he said smoothly, "but just remember when you make your choice, that I am your neighbour, and I will fight for this district for I am the Father-of-Karamea."

Then before anyone could jeer, he quickly added:

"Unlock the store, Simpson. As a celebration of our first anniversary, free sweeties for all the children."

Because of the lollypops, Margret, Laurance, and William, remember our first anniversary as a great time. But I shall

W.E. Hamilton

always remember the twenty-sixth of November 1875, as a miserable day; the fitting marker of a year pocked with small oases of joy, in a big desert of trouble and heartache.

―――――――――

To Own a Fig Tree

Camp Life

The sun had not yet peeped over the horizon when Robert, John, and I prepared to leave for our first week of working on the track.

"Take all the cheeses," said Anderina, pushing a circular cheese into each of our sacks.

"But what about you?"

"The girls and I can make more; the cows are giving plenty of milk. Have you all got a spare set of woollies?"

"Yes, Mum, don't baby us," said John.

Anderina bit her lip and looked troubled.

"Three loaves of bread, cheese, and oats does not seem much to keep you going for a week of hard labour."

"There's bush food and O'Connor's providing a whole bullock for the gang," said Robert.

"Thirteen miles is a long way to carry heavy meat," said Anderina.

"The bullock will carry himself there, we will butcher him on Tuesday."

The worry lines on Anderina's face smoothed away and she smiled.

"Red meat is just the thing for physical toil."

"Get everyone to mound the soil around the potatoes," I said, giving my wife last minute instructions. "And start planting the crops. Thomas Lineham has already got half an acre in barley, oats and a variety of other vegetables." I looked at my wife and children doubtfully; they were sturdy, but the full burden of breaking in the land and farming, was heavy for such small shoulders. "I wish I didn't have to leave you and the kids with all this work, Drena."

"Don't worry, Rob, it's no different to *Zetland*, we always bore the brunt of the work when the men were out at sea. At least we don't have to worry about you drowning."

"You're right, it's no different to Shetland," I said, as I pulled on my sou'wester. "We've come all this way and we are still in bondage."

"Ah, but it is different," said Anderina, helping me on with my backpack. "Here you can own land and vote. Now pray for us and go, or you'll be late."

I did as she said, and then my boys and I picked up our swags and an implement each, and strode along our driveway and onto the road.

Although building the road had been a hassle, now it was done, it was lovely to have a wide clear path through the scrub. In bush country, visibility was limited to a few feet, so to see men many yards in front and behind was novel.

"It feels like the whole world is on the move," said John, as more and more men, all with a long stick in one hand, a tool in the other and a sack and swag on their back, stepped out of the scrub and marched seaward. At the end of the road, we filed down several tracks to the estuary and headed south along the coast. It was thirteen miles to Little Wanganui. Mr Jennings strode in front, and we straggled behind him in groups, with James Moffatt at the end of the line, leading the bullock.

"Where have you been, Robert?" said Charles Scarlett, as

we plodded along the shore. "I haven't seen you lately."

Robert hitched his swag higher.

"I went north along the coast with Rawson, towards the Heaphy Valley. We were looking for a way to Nelson that avoids the snowline."

"Did you have success?" said Charles, dodging the long fingers of a wave.

"Yes and no, we surveyed a connecting track to the Salisbury Open, and the Aorere Valley that leads to Collingwood and on to Nelson, but Rawson estimates it would cost five thousand pounds at least to get a road through, and the government are unlikely to loosen their purse strings to that extent."

Charles whistled and his eyebrows shot up.

"Why so much?"

"Sheer cliffs and raging waterways are expensive to get around. A man on foot can find his way over them, but you'd never get a carriage through without bridges and extensive road work. I'm afraid the only feasible route is over the Karamea Bluff."

At the mention of the Karamea Bluff, our mood darkened and we stabbed our sticks into the wet sand with unnecessary force.

"If O'Connor had waited one more month, I could have got all my crops in," Daniel scowled. "It's a lot to expect Harriet and the children to plant and clear the land by themselves."

I opened my mouth to agree, but John, looking up at the gathering clouds with an experienced eye, cut in sourly:

"Rain! Great, just what we need!"

"And that is another thing," I said, my train of thought shifting, "O'Connor should have waited until summer, we are ill-equipped for lousy weather."

Daniel nodded. "Not enough tents or waterproof clothing. I don't want to get pneumonia again."

"How did you camp on the Heaphy Track, Robert?" said Charles.

"We came across a few huts left by old gold miners, but mostly we made *bivouacs*[38] because we were travelling light."

A few fat raindrops fell.

"I think we will have to do the same," I said, buttoning the front of my oilskin.

As we knew they would, the raindrops quickly deteriorated into a deluge. Water poured from the hem of my raincoat, and my feet squelched as my gumboots rhythmically passed under the waterfall. After four hours, we reached the lower Taffytown Hill where Jennings stopped. I stood on one leg and emptied the water from my boots as we waited for the stragglers to catch up. When at last James and the bullock arrived, Jennings gathered us around and said:

"Men, there is no point taking a break; the ground is sodden so there is nowhere to sit. As we have a full eight hours of work ahead of us, we might as well get started. Best to get your quoter done before dark."

We huddled in grim misery and said nothing, so he continued:

"If you look hard, you will see crosses painted on some of the tree trunks. This is the trail. Follow the white marks, and cut out a path wide and smooth enough for a horse to pass through easily. Find a dry place for your gear and then get to work."

---

38   rough shelters made from ferns and scrub

To Own a Fig Tree

Grumbling and muttering, we did as he said. It was difficult finding somewhere dry, but John found a large overhanging rock on the lea side of the hill, big enough to shelter our and the Scarlett's sacks and swags. Then, picking up our tools some of us began slashing and cutting out trees, while those behind dug the forest floor into a pathway.

"It's not very level or smooth," said Jennings critically, when he inspected our work. "It's so rough, men and horses will trip and tumble over it in the dark."

"A rough and tumble track is the best we can do under these beastly circumstances," growled Fredrick Liley.

Alfred Lineham gave a shout of laughter. "The Rough and Tumble Track, what an apt name, I like it."

The name passed with sniggers from man to man as we toiled in the hosing rain, and by knock-off time the trail was dubbed the Rough and Tumble Track. That night, after a meagre meal of cheese sandwiches, and tea made from manuka shoots, we scouted about for somewhere to sleep.

"Of all the miserable nights I've endured in my life, this must be the worst," I said, looking around at the dismal scene. "I think under the rock is the best we can do."

"Unfortunately, you are right," said Daniel. He took his spade and smoothed the ground, while the rest of our group piled branches and ponga fronds against the rock until we had something resembling a ferny beaver's dam. We left an opening just large enough for a man to crawl through. It was a tight squeeze to get the five of us in, but the increase in body heat made up for the discomfort.

"What a rotten way to live," said John, settling down on his bed of sacks and pig fern.

W.E. Hamilton

"Focus on tomorrow's grand meal," I said, wrapping my oilskin around my body tightly.

"Mm yum, I'd like a T bone steak," said John, licking his lips.

"I'd like a rib-eye steak," said Daniel.

"I don't care what part I get so long as its meat," said Charles, swapping his wet gumboots for a dry pair of socks and hobnail boots.

With this glorious promise before us, we eventually dropped into the deep sleep of exhaustion. It was still raining in the morning when we awoke, stiff and cold.

"Not much hope of getting something hot," said Daniel, crawling out of our hollow.

"You'll get used to it," said Robert unruffled. "I've cooked in worse weather than this."

He broke dead twigs off a silver birch, and (coaxing a little heat from a smouldering fire) made the tea.

I took my Bible from my sack and read a portion of the scripture aloud. Then I thanked God for our meal, and we ate thick doorsteps of bread with slabs of cheese sandwiched between them. All day, as we slaved like a chain gang, we thought about the wonderful meal we were going to have that evening. But when the blessed moment to stop work finally arrived, a dreadful thing had happened; our dinner had wandered off.

"Why didn't you tie the bullock up, Moffatt?" said Jennings.

"I did," said James, his chin sticking out aggressively.

"Well, you didn't tie the rope tight enough for he's gone."

Hunger and disappointment made us angry.

"You should have kept a better eye on him," shouted

To Own a Fig Tree

Fredrick Liley.

"How could I? I had to work like the rest of you."

"Let's hunt around, perhaps he has not gone far," said Alfred Lineham.

Our spirits rose at this thought, but after an hour of fruitless searching, we concluded the wily beast had escaped the butcher's knife and fled home. That night, instead of beef we ate young ponga fronds and grubs.

"I wish the bullock had never come," said Charles, as we made a bivouac beneath the trunk and enormous roots of an upended tree. "Eating pongas when you expected meat makes bush food taste worse than usual."

"It certainly does," said John, biting the head off a huhu grub savagely. "Camp life stinks."

We all heartily agreed with him. Life on the track was hard, even when the rains stopped and summer kicked in. Often, as we slogged upwards, higher and higher, our souls were embittered by treacherous slips and unexpected washouts. Moreover, debt robbed any sense of reward from our labour. The West Coast Times (who kept an interested eye on our efforts) succinctly summed up our position when a wit reported:

'The Karamea settlers are still plodding on, and have the satisfaction of knowing that they are all in debt to the Provincial Treasury. Working off dead horses is found to be as slow a process at Karamea as elsewhere.'

W.E. Hamilton

Political Sabotage

The Rough and Tumble Track went inland from Little Wanganui, and followed the Rough and Tumble creek to the Mokihinui River at the top end of Seddonville. Like the year before, Christmas came and went with little more to mark it than an extra sabbath of rest. On the day after Christmas, as we painstakingly chipped our way up the Karamea Bluff, we talked politics between the blows of axes and picks.

"The voting papers were supposed to be here on the twentieth of December, and they are still not here," said Daniel anxiously. "This is the first time in my life I have been eligible to vote, and I don't want to miss out because the papers came too late to get them back in time.

"Relax," said James Moffatt, swinging his axe at an enormous tree trunk. "There are plenty of days between now and the twenty-ninth of January."

I grubbed out a big flax bush and wished I could feel as easy in my mind as James did.

"But the seas have been too rough for the steamer to get in this month," I said.

"O'Connor promised to send a man overland if the steamer couldn't make it," said James, wriggling his axe out of the trunk, "and it's in his interest to make sure we get the papers, for he knows we will vote for him."

Daniel prised a rock out from under his feet with his pick.

To Own a Fig Tree

"Will we? Are you sure about that? After the way he treated us last visit, I think I will vote for his opposition."

I agreed with Daniel, but I kept quiet.

"As the old saying goes," said James, swinging his axe again. "Better the devil you know than the devil you don't. O'Connor has a stake in Karamea, whereas the other chap does not. Even if O'Connor's only motivation is to feather his own nest and save face politically, he'll fight for the settlement."

"Hmm, you have a point," I said. "Perhaps I will vote for him after all."

"Maybe you will, maybe you won't; you might not get the choice," said Frederick Liley darkly. "If the mail courier favours the opposition, he might decide to 'lose' his way."

"You are a suspicious fellow," said Samuel Friend, slapping his buddy on the shoulder in a chummy way. "The courier will come, you'll see."

I agreed with Samuel, but when the courier arrived a few days later, I changed my mind and thought Liley was a prophet, for all our voting papers were mysteriously lost in the bush.

"Did you come from Westport or over the Heaphy from Collingwood?" said Jennings, as we downed tools and gathered around the mailman.

"Over the Heaphy. I don't know what happened," he said, opening his eyes extra wide to ape innocence. "They were in my mailbag when I started, but they must have fallen out somewhere along the way, for they are not there now."

There was a pregnant silence of suppressed rage as we glared at the little weasel.

"*You devious rat,*" Edwin burst out, "by the time you go back and return, it will be too late for our vote to be counted."

Robert turned to Mr Jennings.

"I know where they are," he blurted out. "I know the Heaphy track, and if you let me go now, I can get them in time, for I can guess where he has hidden them."

A shadow of concern flitted across the mailman's face, but recovering quickly, he said:

"I hope you find them, young man, for I feel bad about losing them."

"Yeah, right," said Liley disbelievingly, "pull the other leg it has bells on it."

"Go, Robert," said Jennings, "I hope your guess is right."

Then Robert, taking a billy and swinging his swag onto his back, strode quickly away. The mailman, eyeing our glowering faces and clenched fists, was eager to go. He left as soon as Robert was out of sight.

"And I dare say the cowardly weasel will keep a distance between himself and Johnson," said Samuel.

"It would serve him right if Robert spotted him and gave him a thrashing," said Edwin, smiling at the thought.

"He won't do that," I said. "Vengeance is the Lord's. God Almighty will repay the wrongdoer, not us."

"That will take too long. I should have gone with him," said Edwin, his mouth drooping. "I'd be happy to give him what he deserves."

"Then it is just as well you didn't go," said Jennings. "Everyone back to work, for until Johnson returns there is nothing more we can do."

John tugged my sleeve as I picked up my spade.

"I don't like to tell you this, Dad, but Robert's like Edwin; he likes to take things into his own hands."

To Own a Fig Tree

I stared at him.

"Are you saying he might punch the mailman if there was nobody around?"

"No, he wouldn't do that. I'm just saying Robert doesn't hold to the faith as much as the rest of us."

My heart plummeted.

"An infidel like the King brothers?"

"I wouldn't go that far, but definitely leaning in that direction."

My shoulders sagged and I felt energy drain from my body.

"He keeps the trappings of religion, but only for your sake. He doesn't have the real thing. I'm sorry, Dad," said John patting my shoulder, "I've held off telling you the truth about Robert, but I think you need to know."

I wiped my hand over my face and nodded.

"It is a terrible blow, but you did right to tell me. God gives everyone freedom to choose or reject him. We must pray fervently that Robert will encounter God and wake up."

Robert was away for two days. When he arrived back, he carried a thick wad of voting papers. As soon as we saw him, we downed tools and clustered around.

"Where did you find them?" said Jennings, as Robert handed us each a paper.

"There is a rough hut with a bunk in it on the track. I went there and searched under the bed, and sure enough, I found the papers hidden in the back corner."

"So, the lousy weasel was lying," said Edwin King. "*I knew it!*"

I took a pencil from my pocket and hovered it between the two names.

W.E. Hamilton

"Are you having trouble deciding," said James, noticing my hesitation.

"Yes."

"As I said before," said James, circling O'Connor's name, "better the devil you know than the devil you don't."

"The devil we know is still a devil."

"Aye, but the other devil tried to take away our right to vote."

As soon as he said that, I knew what to do. Carefully, I drew a circle around 'O'CONNOR'. An arrogant devil was better than a devil who stomped on the freedom of choice.

To Own a Fig Tree

An Unsettling Letter for Samuel Friend

In our isolated community, news from the outside world seldom filtered in, and visitors were even rarer. So, when the school inspector, Mr W.C. Hodgson, arrived in March, 1876, it was a big occasion. He examined everything and we awaited his verdict with trepidation, for we felt the honour of the community was at stake. Nobody was more concerned about the school's reputation than Charlotte Naylor.

"I shan't sleep a wink until I know what Mr Hodgson says about us," she confided to Anderina.

But she had no need to worry, for when the inspector's report came out, he wrote:

Mrs Naylor, the teacher of this remote and indeed almost inaccessible school, has contrived in a short space of time and under unusual difficulties to produce excellent results. When I examined the school at the end of March 1876, it had been open for only nine months. The thirty-five children present were huddled together in a room measuring only fifteen-foot by nine-foot. Yet the older scholars read and wrote tolerably well from dictation, and worked money questions in arithmetic very correctly, not one in the first-class failing to pass the school standard. The other class was equally well taught, and all the scholars were remarkably well drilled and orderly. Despite the hardships, there is a keen desire of the settlers to give their children the benefit of an organized system of education[39].

And that was not the end of our fleeting limelight, for shortly after, a newspaper headline informed us that the *Ocean Mail* had sunk. The shipwreck was the talk of the week.

"Didn't you come out on the *Ocean Mail*?" said Fredrick Liley, as we picked at the limestone at the top of the Karamea Bluff.

"Yes," said Robert, "and she was a fine ship. Such a pity to hear she was wrecked off the Chatham Islands."

"Ruin of some sort is the natural outcome of racing and betting," I said piously. "It's a wonder the *Avalanche* and the *Crusader* didn't also come to a wretched end."

"What rot, Dad," said Robert. "It was just one of those things. The wind hauled suddenly to the south-west and blew her hard onto the reefs."

"There must have been more to it than that," said Samuel Friend, "for Captain Watson's certificate is suspended for nine months, and they suspended the first and second mate for six months."

"The Court found the mishap was due mainly to negligence by the captain and officers in not keeping dead-reckoning by the log," said Liley, picking up a long and heavy iron bar.

"Such a pity," said Robert. "Captain Watson is a good man."

"She had a full cargo of wool, tallow, and other colonial produce," said Samuel.

"I know," Liley puffed as he hit the hard ground repetitively. "The cargo was worth seventy-eight thousand pounds."

"Was anyone drowned?" I said, levering out a rock.

"No," said Robert. The passengers and crew got ashore,

---

[39]   W.C. Hodgson's report to the Central Board of Education

and went to the house of a Maori who lived a couple of miles from the wreck. Stores were also taken ashore and carried up into the bush where tents were pitched for the crew."

"Nobody died, that is the main thing," I said, throwing the rock to the side of the path.

"The article said the master made a survey of the wreck, and she was sold to one of the Chatham Island run holders for nine-hundred-and-forty-five pounds," said Samuel. "The owners of the goods have protested to their insurance companies, for there were nearly five-thousand bales of wool aboard, and four-hundred tons of this was saved in a very short while, not to mention many casks of tallow."

Frederick straightened up and leaned on his bar.

"What a bargain, I wish I had the luck of that run holder. If I had heaps of money, I would leave this miserable place in a heartbeat."

"Do you mean that?" said Samuel, with quickening interest in his tone.

"Yes, I do."

"Well, you could. I got a letter from my brother the other day," said Samuel, "and he told me something very interesting."

"Smoko time," shouted Jennings, as he walked down the line of toiling men.

We threw down our tools with relief.

"Hold that thought until the tea's made, Sam," said Frederick.

He searched in the bushes for the billy of water and our tucker sack, while Robert and I hunted for dry sticks. Meanwhile, Samuel cleared a bald spot on the ground and made a ring of stones. Before long, the fire was burning merrily, and the billy made little fizzing sounds as drops of water rolled down its side. I found a nice big stone with a flat top, dragged it over to the fire, and sat down. At an altitude of one-thousand-four-hundred-and-twenty feet, the thick bush had given way to more sparse vegetation. From my perch on the crest of the Karamea Bluff, I had a panoramic view of the sea and surrounding hills and mountains.

"Now, Sam, what's this business about leaving Karamea?" said Frederick, opening a twist of paper and shaking tea into the boiling water.

"As I said, I got a letter from my brother."

"Which one?"

"Thomas the gas worker. Tom and his wife and four children came out to Nelson recently on the *Fern Glen*. He had difficulty finding gas work, but now he has a nice position as the manager of a small farm at Richmond."

"Good for him," said Frederick, squatting and stirring the tea with a stick. "I always liked him. Tom was one of the better blokes of Westerham."

"He's provided with a large house and garden, and ground to keep a milch goat, pigs and fowls. He even has a horse to ride and thirty-shillings a week in wages. Things are going so well for him he says he is twenty-one pounds heavier since leaving London."

"That is all very nice, Sam, but how does that help me?"

"I'm coming to that. I told him of the rotten time you and I were having, and said I regretted coming here. He says he's sure he could get us work."

"Even me?" said Frederick.

"Yes, listen said Samuel, pulling a letter from his pocket.

To Own a Fig Tree

His eyes scanned the page until he found the portion he was looking for.

"I'm sure I could get you a job, brother," Samuel read aloud, *"this farm could do with another worker. If you are interested, I could put in a good word to the boss for you. Also, tell Fred, pit sawyers are in great demand here and command big money, and if that doesn't work out, there are plenty of houses in need of painting. Us Kent men should stick together, so throw off the shackles of Karamea and come as soon as you can."*

A faraway look came into Frederick's eyes as I pulled cups from the tucker sack. It was obvious he had forgotten the tea, so I slipped a stout stick under the billy's wire handle and lifted it off the fire.

"Have a cuppa while you are thinking about it, Fred," I said, dipping a tin cup into the brew before handing it to him.

He took it without comment, and stared down the track absentmindedly at the groups of men clustered around small fires. After a long silence, he spoke.

"I'd have to ask my wife first."

"Of course, you must discuss it with Caroline," said Samuel. "I would not go if Harriet was against it."

Frederick stroked his chin and gazed into the air. "Caroline won't mind leaving the house, it's not much of a house, but my son and I have put I lot of work into clearing the land. I'd have to ask him too." He shielded his eyes with his hand and squinted down the track. "I wonder which group he is working with today?"

"I think he's with the advance team chopping out the bigger trees," said Robert, taking a sip of tea.

Frederick stood up, swivelled around and peered down the

track over the Bluff.

"I can't see him," he said, sitting on a fallen log. "I'll have to wait until we finish work tonight to ask him."

I could see Samuel had decided to leave, but Liley was wavering.

"Are you thinking of packing it in, Fred?"

"Maybe. Let's face it, Robert, the land on the South Terrace is rubbish, I fear nothing of value is going to grow there."

"The summer harvest failed because we planted our crops too late," I said, leaping to defend the land.

"The North Bankers planted at the same time but they had a bumper harvest," said Fredrick.

"That's true," said Samuel, "some of them were even later than us."

"Our new crops are doing alright," I said.

"At the moment they are, for it's only April. What happens when the heavy winter rains set in? Will our drains work better than last year, or will everything rot in the ground once more?"

"Our crops will be alright this time," I said with more conviction than I felt.

"Even if they are, I'm not a farmer," said Liley. "I was hoping to get work at the new timber mill, but Mr Baigent has decided not to go ahead with it."

"Why?" I said, "this is the first I've heard of it."

"Because the price of timber is falling, and the bar is fickle."

Jennings came up the track shouting:

"Smoko's over, back to work."

Frederick threw the dregs of his tea on the ground.

"The more I think about it, the more I like the idea of cutting my losses and moving on."

To Own a Fig Tree

Samuel banged his friend on the back.

"Good for you, Fred, we can have a better life in Nelson."

I scoured my cup with a handful of dirt and wiped it out with the corner of the tucker sack.

"What about your debt? You can't just walk out if you owe money."

Now that Liley could see a door out of his predicament, desire to leave was growing at a rapid rate.

"Hmm, that is a problem." He put his cup in the tucker bag. "I know," he said, his face lighting up. "We won't do a lick more work on our houses or land, Sam. Then you and I can work longer on the track, and as soon as we have paid off our debt, we'll leave."

"Longer hours on the track!" Samuel's face was full of dismay.

"It means we can get out of here quicker."

"What about Caroline and William?" I said.

Liley waved his hand dismissively.

"Oh, they'll agree." He turned back to Samuel. "You and I will work together from now on, Sam. That way we can encourage each other."

"Alright, Fred."

"I think you are mad to throw away the opportunity of owning land!" I said, kicking dirt over the fire.

"And I think you are mad to stay with a sinking ship!" said Frederick. "The Colonist reported that abandonment of this settlement is imminent."

"It's a pack of lies," I said indignantly. "You know you can't believe half of what you read in the paper, they are just looking for a sensational story."

W.E. Hamilton

"We are all entitled to our own opinion, Robert. I hope you are right about the land, for your sake. As for me, I'm going to get out while I can."

I put my cup in the tucker bag and went back to work with a sinking heart. If Frederick was right about the land being infertile, I was in deep trouble.

To Own a Fig Tree

The South Terrace is Abandoned

The District Surveyor, Mr Jennings, was a good sort once we got to know him. He worked with us on the track and took our grievances seriously.

"Twelve to sixteen pounds for a cow is far too high a price," said Daniel, shovelling dirt into a hollow. "They're going for half that in Westport and Nelson."

Jennings wiped the sweat off his brow.

"I suppose the cost of shipping pushes them up, Dan."

"A pound or two, maybe but not six or eight pounds."

"It's the Government Store," I said, flattening a hump. "It was the same way in *Zetland*, the merchants set the price for both our labour and their goods. Labour was always cheap, and goods were always limited and expensive. The outcome was the same there as here, no man ever had a credit balance under the evil *truck* system."

"Don't you think 'evil' might be laying it on a bit thick?" said Jennings mildly.

"No, I don't. Every day we get deeper in debt despite the long hours we work."

"Sixteen hours a day, six days a week is long, I'll not dispute that," said Jennings, pushing a rock off the track. "But I swear before God, I faithfully record every hour every man works."

"The fault does not lie with you," I hastened to assure him.

"No, indeed," said Daniel, "we trust you. The discrepancy lies elsewhere."

"You don't set the prices in the store," I said, "have you seen how much they charge for tea and flour?"

"You got me there. That is a definite drawback to the place," said Jennings. "Although the track is almost finished and I should be moving onto the next job, I like this area and I'm thinking of settling here permanently…"

"Staying permanently! Good one." Daniel banged him on the back in a friendly way.

"That's wonderful," I smiled.

Jennings held up a hand.

"Whoa, slow down. I've not decided yet, for I said to the Missis only the other day, 'Karamea is lovely but the cost of living is very high.'"

Robert, who was listening to our conversation as he worked, suddenly spoke up.

"What we need is our own steamer."

"That is a good idea, Robert," said Jennings, "but it is beyond our means to get one."

"Maybe one day," I said, with doubt in my tone.

Robert was not daunted by our disbelief.

"There are ninety cows and one-hundred pigs in the settlement already. If we had a steamer, we could sell butter, cheese, and pork to Westport and Nelson. Plus, we could bring in our own stores and set up a shop in opposition to the Government Store."

"You forget most of the cows belong to Hubert Dolphin," said Daniel. "That Irishman will not need an independent steamer to make money because he's related to Eugene

To Own a Fig Tree

O'Connor."

"I know people think Dolphin and O'Connor are kinsfolk," said Jennings, "but it's not true."

There was an awkward silence.

"How far are we off finishing the track?" I said, changing the subject.

"A few more weeks and we should be done, end of June beginning of July at the latest I'm guessing."

Spits fell from the dark clouds hovering overhead.

"I wish it was sooner," I said, as the spits rapidly turned into a heavy downpour.

Jennings was right. June had just ticked into July when we reached our goal of the Seddonville railway line. But there were no celebrations when we chopped down the final tree, and dug out the last spadeful of dirt, our minds were on more serious matters, for the South Terrace crops had rotted once more. Frederick Liley, Samuel Friend, and their families were the only smiling faces in a sea of gloominess, when the *Charley*'s whistle blew and she slipped over the bar. They had moved all their luggage to the store several days ago to be ready to leave as soon as possible. Now they stood near the dock, surrounded by bags and trunks.

"Our time in Karamea has not been a complete disaster," said Samuel, pocketing a wad of notes. "Scanlan paid me thirty-six pounds; eighteen pounds for my house and eighteen pounds for land improvements. What did you get, Fred?"

"Forty pounds; five pounds for the house and thirty-five pounds for improvements," said Frederick, handing the money to his wife.

"Five pounds for the house is fair," said Caroline Liley. Her beaded purse made a loud click as she snapped it shut. "Our house was only grass and thatch, while yours was slab and thatch."

"But I had five acres felled and three-quarters of an acre planted out," said Frederick, "that's why I got more. How much did you clear, Sam?"

"Just over an acre with a quarter of an acre in garden. I didn't follow the overseer's advice to concentrate on the land, not the house."

"And Samuel Junior is much younger than William," cut in Harriet, laying a hand on her son's shoulder. "He did very well for his age, but there is a world of difference in the labour of an eleven-year-old boy and an eighteen-year-old man."

By now, the steamer was at the jetty. Robert caught the rope a sailor threw him, and tied it to a heavy post as Caroline and Harriet fluttered around their carpet bags and trunks. O'Connor, leaping lightly off the boat, strode down the wharf.

"All the best in your new venture," I said, stepping forward and shaking Fredrick's hand. "I hope you do well."

He nodded.

"Thanks, Robert, I hope everything works out for you too."

"If you decide you want to work in Nelson, let me know," said Samuel, as we shook hands. "My brother might find something for you."

"Thanks, I'll keep it in mind," I said evasively. I picked up a trunk and slung it onto my shoulder. "I'll help you with your luggage."

"That would be good," said Frederick, "I know we have plenty of time before the tide rises again, but the ladies are eager to be aboard."

To Own a Fig Tree

While I carried trunks to the steamer and supplies to the land, O'Connor roamed the beach calling:

"GATHER ROUND, GATHER ROUND, I HAVE AN ANNOUNCEMENT TO MAKE."

By the time I had finished, a large crowd had collected around him. I walked over and stood at the edge of the group, curious to hear what he had to say.

"First of all, congratulations men, on completing the track. You have made history by ending Karamea's total isolation. For those of you still heavily in debt…"

I strained my ears, for he meant me.

"There is ongoing work in the form of road maintenance."

My heart sank.

"Now concerning the problems on the South Terrace."

The mood electrified as half the settlers gave him their undivided attention.

"It's confirmed, the ground of the south plateau is infertile pakihi."

There was a collective groan and someone shouted:

"I wish you had discovered this a bit earlier; I've wasted eighteen months on useless land."

O'Connor held up his hand to quieten us.

"Don't despair. Last November, Edwin King found fertile ground three miles inland on the river flats of the South Bank. Since then, I have had Rawson survey it into five-acre blocks. As laid out in the first prospectus, you are entitled to an extra five-acres. Instead of choosing a town allotment, I suggest you take your five acres from the land Edwin found."

"But we have fifty acres?" came another shout.

"You may swap it for another fifty acres when we find

better land," said O'Connor smoothly. "In the meantime, I strongly suggest you take advantage of this offer, for the land is superior." He held up a wooden box. "I am ready to draw the ballots. If you are interested, put up your hand."

We, the folk of the South Terrace, were suddenly engulphed in seesawing emotions. We milled about uncertainly. I was not sure whether to rejoice or grieve, when Anderina materialized from the crowd. Sidling up to me, she plucked at my sleeve.

"Oh, Rob, what shall we do?"

"We don't have a choice, Drena," I said, sadly. "Our land is worthless."

"But all your hard work."

"We can start again. Five acres of fertile soil is better than fifty acres of rubbish."

A look of horror crossed her face. "But our home! It is the most substantial house in the whole district. We can't leave that."

"It certainly is a problem," I agreed, "for we have had double our allotted amount of free lumber and there will be no more. If we want extra timber, we shall have to cut it ourselves or move the house."

"Move the house! "How will we do that?"

I patted my wife's hand reassuringly.

"There will be a solution, I just don't know what it is yet."

"I dare say God will show us the way," Anderina nodded slowly.

"Come now, don't be shy," called O'Connor. "Who will be the first man to take advantage of this generous offer?"

"I WILL," I shouted, raising my hand high.

To Own a Fig Tree

House Moving

The answer from heaven concerning our house came in the very earthly forms of John Naylor and the Scarlett family. They stood in the centre of our one-room cottage, staring up at the framework under the roofing-shingles. John tapped his tooth with a pencil as he thought, and at last, he said:

"If we number and label the purlins and rafters, we could pull the roof apart and reassemble it without too much trouble, I think."

I nodded.

"What about the walls, Naylor?" said Daniel. We walked outside and Daniel, Naylor, and I examined the four corners while our families milled about talking.

"The timber is new so the corner boards should come off without splitting," said Naylor, wriggling a board. "Then it's just a matter of pulling out the nails that hold the walls together. Once we have it in pieces, we should be able to shift it."

"How?" I said

"Roll it on posts one section at a time, starting with the floor."

"Oh, my poor wallpaper and windowpanes," groaned Anderina.

"We could remove the windows and move them separately," said Naylor. "But you are right, the wallpaper will take a beating. It's a good thing your new land is near the bottom of the Zig-Zag."

"How long will it take to clear a spot big enough for the house, Mr Johnson?" said Harriet.

"The boys and I are getting on pretty well, Mrs Scarlett. We will have an acre cleared within a few weeks."

"When you are ready, call me," said Daniel. "I and the family will come and give you and Naylor a hand if you like."

"The more the better," said Naylor," he rubbed William on the head, "even this budding businessman (the bane of his teacher) can carry roofing shingles."

William ducked and dodging around Elizabeth Scarlett, whistled his way over to a mud puddle. Elizabeth looked at Robert from under her eyelashes.

"How is your land getting on, Bob?"

Robert flushed under her gaze and loosened the neck of his collar with his finger.

"Quite well," he stuttered. "I've got some of it cleared."

"When are you going to build your house?"

Robert swallowed before answering. "As soon as I've finished helping Dad with his place."

"Robert likes Elizabeth," chanted Margret in a sing-song tone.

Robert's face flamed into redness and Elizabeth (pretending she had not heard) put her hands behind her back and looked the other way.

"Stop that silliness, Margret!" Anderina said sharply. "Have more respect for your older brother."

Margret was unabashed. "Mary likes John McHarrie."

Now it was Mary's turn to blush.

"Little girls who can't control their tongues can talk to

cattle," said Anderina, handing Margret a bucket. "Milk the cows."

Laurie sniggered with delight for it was his turn to milk.

"Who's this John McHarrie, Mary?" said Harriet. "I've not heard of him."

"He's new to the area," said Mary.

"A good catch," said Anderina, raising her eyebrows at Harriet. "A gold miner from Stranrauer in Scotland, and he has his eye on Mary."

"Oh, Mum, stop it!"

"He's looking to settle in the Land of Promise," said Anderina, ignoring Mary.

"Is that our side or the North Bankers' side of the river?" said Harriet.

"The north side, we're the Promised Land."

"Land of Promise, the Promised Land, I can never remember which is which, the names are too similar."

"It is confusing, Karamea Jack suggested we use the Maori translation to make more of a distinction between the names."

"That's a good idea. What are they in Maori?"

"I can't remember."

"Our teacher says we're Arapito," said William, puddling his feet in the mud. "The others are Umere."

"Trust the youngsters to remember," said Anderina proudly, "they soak up knowledge like a sponge."

The women stopped talking and stepped to the side as Daniel, Naylor and I passed them and peered under the house.

"It shouldn't be too hard to get the floor detached from the piles," said Naylor, "provided you haven't done too good a job, Robert."

"If I'd known we were going to pull it apart, I would have been a lot shoddier."

While we prodded the rimu stumps the floor sat on, the women returned to their fascinating subject.

"Has John McHarrie said anything to you, Mary?" said Harriet.

"No."

"Ah, but his eyes say a lot," said Anderina. "Mark my words, the Johnsons will see their first wedding before the end of August."

"Oh, Mum, you don't know that. I wish you would stop saying such things. I don't even know if he is interested."

"There is no need to be bashful; at twenty-two, it is alright for you to look around."

I cut through the chatter.

"How long do you think it will take to move the house, Naylor?"

"If we start early, I think we could move it and reassemble it in a day."

"That's not too bad."

"The trick is to get a full day without rain," said Anderina grimly.

My wife was right, in July every day was patchy with rain. After cancelling the house-moving several times, I made a firm decision.

"It says in the Good Book, *'whoever watches the wind will not plant, he who looks at the clouds will not reap.'* We will take the Lord's advice and shift the house tomorrow regardless of the weather."

We were up long before dawn. The rafters and beams were

To Own a Fig Tree

numbered and a plan for their reconstruction was tucked away in my pocket. Anderina took care of breakfast and household matters while Robert, John, and I made preparations to dismantle the house.

"Oh, my poor wallpaper," groaned Anderina, as I ran a sharp knife down the corners. "It will never look the same again."

"If I don't do this it is ruined for certain," I said, hacking through the scrim backing. "But if I slit it, we might salvage most of it."

"Are we going to take the windows out?" said Robert, fingering around the edge of the sill for nails.

"I think we will get away with leaving them in if we strengthen them with a couple of boards. So long as they don't twist or move, the glass won't break."

"You forgot dropping the wall down the Zig-Zag as a hazard," said John.

I frowned at him and glanced at Anderina; she was still getting over James' death and, therefore, easily rattled. Right on cue, she burst out:

"Drop it down the Zig-Zag! We shall be homeless before the day is out, I just know it."

I in turn, was more impatient than usual.

"We won't drop it, woman!"

I turned to Robert, who was fixing a board horizontally across the window frame. "Diagonal, boy, diagonal!" I barked, "fix them like an X."

"I'm not a boy!" said Robert, throwing the hammer down. "If you speak to me like that, you can move the house by yourself! I've got my own house to build."

Margret started crying and John said:

"Shut up, Willie, can't you tell this is not the time for whistling?"

There was a knock on the door and Daniel called:

"Hello, folks, is anybody home?"

We fell silent.

"Come in Scarletts," I said, opening the door wide.

"Are you all ready for the big move today?" said Daniel.

"Oh, Harriet," said Anderina, "I am so embarrassed. I don't know what has got into us all? Lately, we seem to fight and get upset at the least little thing."

Harriet put a big basket of food on the table and hugged Anderina.

"It's this," she said, smoothing the black band around Anderina's sleeve. "You don't get over losing a little one in five minutes."

Anderina nodded sadly. "What about you, how are you getting on Harriet?"

"Much better, it gets easier after two years."

"I bought a hammer and a ladder, Robert," said Daniel, "and as soon as the sun rises, I'll remove the ridging and strip the shingles off the roof."

"Do you want a hand, Bob?" said Charles.

"Yeah, that would be good. I'll do the front windows while you do the two on the back wall."

"While you're waiting for some light, Daniel, perhaps you and John could move the furniture outside," I said.

"Sure thing," said Daniel, lifting his wife's basket off the table.

At that, everyone exploded into action. Men marched

To Own a Fig Tree

methodically in and out of the door carrying household goods, while the women, with swirling skirts, rolled up the bedding and packed the trunks, until at last, the house was empty and the sun was up. Then the mountains echoed with the sound of screeching nails and groaning timber as we carefully pulled the house to bits.

"Looking good," said Naylor, turning up as we lifted the last wall from the floor. He dropped a bundle of short posts on the ground. "I've brought your wheels."

"They are not wheels, Mr Naylor," said Margret.

Naylor grinned "Quite right, Missy, they are more like rollers, and once we get them under these walls, we can roll them wherever we want to go."

He turned to me.

"I went down to your place this morning, and I've positioned the piles where you have marked out the house site, so we can just drop the floor on top of them."

"Thank you, John," I said, shaking his hand, "I appreciate your help." I pointed at the men busy at work around the perimeter of the floor. "We've almost got it loose."

"Good. If you've got a spade handy, I'll get our rollers ready."

"Over there," I said, pointing to a spade in the ruined garden. "William, run over and get it for Mr Naylor."

A shout of triumph came from the demolition team as the last nail linking the floor to the foundation posts came out.

"Looks like we are ready to go," said Naylor, taking the spade from William and swiftly skimming a flat line in the ground. "Once I've got the rollers in place, I want everyone to help lift the floor onto them."

W.E. Hamilton

"It won't fit on those skinny little things," said Anderina, watching Naylor drop posts at intervals along the smoothed earth.

"The floor stands on its edge, Mrs Johnson," said Naylor. "Now everyone, bring it over here."

So, we gathered around the floor and lifting it, carried it over to Naylor, where we tilted it upright and dropped it onto the rollers.

"We need an equal number of people on both sides," said Naylor, directing us into place. "Strongest men at the back to push, Charles and Daniel Scarlett at the front to pull, boys over nine and girls in short skirts in the middle to keep everything upright. Mrs Johnson, I'll leave you and the women in charge of the younger children and the roof shingles. I will go ahead of the rollers to smooth the way."

Then we took our positions, and I and Daniel, Robert, Charles, my John, Dan junior, Jimmy, William S, Laurie, Margret, and Sarah pushed and heaved the floor, while Anderina, Harriet, Rose, both Elizabeths, and Willie, wandered behind us carrying baskets loaded with shingles. Along the flat terrace everything was straightforward, but when we got to the Zig-Zag, things became trickier.

"Roll it past the track so the men at the back automatically become the men at the front," instructed Naylor.

We groaned and grunted, and when we had done it, stopped and stood puffing.

"Now, Robert and Daniel, I want you to lift when I say to, and I'll pull the rollers across a bit so they are on the same angle as the track. When I've got them lined up, swivel your end onto them. Got it?"

To Own a Fig Tree

We nodded.

"LIFT," shouted Naylor, adroitly whisking rollers out and repositioning them at an angle. "AND SWIVEL."

We staggered with our burden over to the new line while Charles and Bob held the other end steady.

"NOW DROP IT INTO PLACE."

Once that was done, Naylor said:

"Robert and Daniel, you won't need to pull downhill as gravity will do most of the work. Your main job will be to slow it down if the momentum gets too strong. I've hacked out the trees at the end of each bend, so you should be able to get it far enough off the track to swivel it past the corner."

"I don't understand," I said.

"He means we will become the tail again, and Dan and Charles will be the front until the next sharp bend," said Daniel.

"That's right," Naylor nodded. "Is everyone ready?"

There was a collective shout of, "YES," so away we went.

I won't say getting down the Zig-Zag was trouble-free, but it was not as bad as Anderina feared, and moving along the river flats was easy by comparison. We were in high spirits and the feeling of accomplishment was great, when we dropped the floor onto its new foundation, and nailed it firmly in place.

"You only have to do that four more times," said Naylor, smiling.

We groaned and a round of good-natured-bantering broke out.

"We will shift the side walls before attempting the window-walls," said Naylor, ignoring accusations of slave-driving, "by then we'll know what we are doing."

The idea was sound, for after three successful moves our

confidence was up, and the last two walls went down the Zig-Zag without mishap.

"What next?" said Harriet, sitting on the floor and opening up her basket.

"After lunch, the men and I will assemble the walls," said Naylor, taking the bread and cheese Harriet handed him, "while you and the others bring down the rest of the roof. Leave any long rafters that are too heavy and one of us will collect them."

"The weather is holding up alright," said Daniel, "looking up at the grey clouds hovering overhead as he added sticks to a nearby fire.

"I hope it stays that way until we get the roof back on," said Anderina. "If water gets on my wallpaper, it's done for."

"So far it isn't too badly damaged," said Harriet.

Anderina put her hands on her hips and inspected the walls lying inside-up on the ground.

"Better than I expected, once we tape the corners and put a few pictures over the rips it should be alright. Fortunately, the windows are fine and the door is only a bit scratched."

Harriet took a tin from her basket and handed it to Daniel, who opened it and sprinkled tea into the bubbling billy.

"Cover what you can with your kitchen tarpaulin," she said, passing Anderina a sandwich. "And I'll bring mine next time we come down, just in case it rains."

"Good idea," said Anderina.

Lunch was a pleasant meal. The project added zest to our conversation and warmed the community spirit. Once everyone was fed and watered, we divided and went about our business once more. The walls came together rapidly, but the roof was another matter.

To Own a Fig Tree

"Lie it out like a giant jigsaw puzzle," said Naylor, "where is the diagram, Robert?"

I took the plan from my pocket and handed it to him. He spread it out and nailed it to a tree so we could all see it.

"Bob, you and Daniel get the ladders and help me with the roof. Robert, find the central rafters and hand them up to us," said Naylor. "Ladies, find the purlins and lie them on the ground according to their numbers.

So, away we went again. The women solved the giant puzzle, then some of the men passed the beams onto the roof while others fastened them in place. When the frame was up, half of us shingled the roof while the rest carried household goods down from the terrace. The shadows were lengthening by the time we fixed the final strip of ridging onto the roof.

"We have done it," said Anderina, as they carried the last trunk inside. "Thanks be to God, we've had not a drop of rain!"

"Yoo-hoo," called a woman's voice, and from between the trees stepped Charlotte Naylor. Beside her walked John McHarrie, carrying a large cauldron and a sack of tin plates and cutlery. "I thought all the hard workers would be hungry," she said, "so I made you a stew for dinner. Where do you want it?"

"That is very kind," said Anderina, slapping at a mosquito as she moved to meet them. "Put the pot next to the fire John."

"Perhaps I should make a ring of smoke," said John, also slapping at the pests. "It's that time of the day."

"Yes please, we don't want to be eaten alive."

John made a ring of little fires and pulled logs into the centre of the circle. I pondered on the man's chivalry concerning the heavy pot as I built up the cooking fire and hung a billy of water over it. Then my family and our 'angels' sat on the logs and ate stew. And everybody noticed Robert sat next to Elizabeth Scarlett, and John McHarrie sat next to Mary, but not even Margret ruined the moment by commenting on it.

———————————

To Own a Fig Tree

A Wedding

Mary married John McHarrie on August the seventh, 1876. The day was a milestone because it was the first wedding for both the Johnsons and Karamea.[40]

On the morning of the event, Anderina was fluffing about the house.

"Roll up the bedding and stow it in the corner, John," she said, "and, Robert, make some sort of lectern for the preacher."

Mary glanced out the window at the dirty weather as she packed her clothes into a suitcase.

"Do you think the Reverend will get here?" she said anxiously.

"We must allow for the possibility of disappointment," I said, stacking two trunks on top of each other. "It is unlikely Captain Leech will risk crossing the bar."

Mary groaned and threw her apron over her head.

"Stop that silly behaviour, Mary, you'll muss your hair and get your Sunday dress dirty," said Anderina sharply. "We must hope for the best. There is much to do, and I shall not rest until I know for sure the Reverend is not coming, for I do not wish to be caught unprepared." She handed Mary a stack of paper and added in a softer tone, "Pin these pictures over the worst rips in the wallpaper."

Mary took them and stuck one of Elizabeth's drawings

---

40   The wedding is historical, the ceremony is imaginary

over a long rent, while I dragged the trunks to the centre of the back wall.

"Where do you want the table, Mum?" said Robert.

Anderina opened the lid of the almost-pirate chest. "Push it against the wall, Bob, and set the benches facing the lectern. Beth, lay the tea set and small plates on the table." She swivelled her head and swept Margret, Laurence, and William a 'look.' "Tin cups for the young'uns and one piece of cake, but only after the adults have been served."

William stopped whistling momentarily.

"What if they eat it all?"

"Then you will politely pretend you never wanted any," said Anderina.

William's mouth drooped.

"Cut thin slices when you carve up the cake, Elizabeth," he said solemnly.

"And that's another thing, William," said Anderina, lifting the clock from the chest and setting it in pride of place on the table. "No whistling during the ceremony." She put the key next to the clock and the Family Bible next to the key.

"Do we sign the marriage certificate before or after starting the clock?" said Mary, pinning up the last picture.

"Before, of course," said Anderina, "then your father will write your names in the Bible, and after that, you wind the clock."

"Why are they winding the clock?" said William.

"It symbolizes the beginning of Mary and John's life together," said Anderina.

"And Mum wants to get some use out of her clock," giggled Margret.

To Own a Fig Tree

"Well, we need *something* to mark the occasion," said Anderina.

"I've got something," I said. "Today I'm starting a new tradition. I was going to keep it secret until the end of the ceremony, but as the weather might interfere with the surprise, I'll tell you now."

The eyes of my family were on me as I took from the corner where I had hidden it, a small seedling in a pot. "As soon as you got engaged, Mary, I ordered a tree which we will plant in the orchard as a living monument to this significant day."

"Is it a fig tree, Dad?" said Mary, her eyes growing wide.

I put the plant next to the clock.

"No, unfortunately. I wanted a fig but the best I could get is this apple."

"An apple is an excellent choice for the first tree of our orchard," said Anderina, "and a fitting tribute to Mary and John.

"Yes, Dad," said Mary, kissing me on the cheek. "For if John and my marriage is as sweet and sustaining as an apple, we will do well indeed."

"What's the time, Robert?" said Anderina looking flustered.

"I'll go and look."

I pulled on my oilskin and wandered the short distance down to the river and back.

"Almost full tide, so I'm guessing it's half-past-nine," I said, taking off my coat and hanging it on the nail by the door.

"Hurry," said Anderina, handing Elizabeth the broom. "As soon as the *Charley* blows her whistle John and our guests will arrive."

I shook my head slowly.

"The river is so turbulent I doubt the steamer will come. It will be a miracle if the preacher gets here."

"Does that mean we can eat the cake by ourselves?" said William, his face brightening.

"No," said Anderina. "Our guests will still come, and if the preacher can't get to us, your father will go over the track with Mary and John so they can marry in Westport. We will eat the cake as a farewell blessing."

Margret pressed her nose against the window and her breath misted the glass.

"Come away from there, Maggie," said Anderina, "you'll leave a mark."

"Oh, Mum, nobody will notice." Her bored tone quickened into sudden interest. "Here comes John running up the driveway."

Mary's face lit up, then she rushed to the door and flung it open. "Oh, John!" she lamented, as he strode in. "It looks like the preacher won't get here today."

"Hello, Mr and Mrs Johnson," said John, removing his hat respectfully. "Hello, Mary."

Mary pulled the door shut. "I just know we shall have to go over the track," she said mournfully.

"Don't fret, love, he might still come," said John, taking off his coat and brushing drips off his Sunday suit. "Although looking at the river, I admit the chances are slim."

The Scarletts were the next to turn up, and after them our old friends from Shetland arrived in dribs and drabs. Although our house was the most substantial one in Karamea, within a few hours it was so crowded there was standing room only. By midday, we had given up hope. The prayers of blessing had begun, and Elizabeth had the knife at hand for the cake, when (with a thundering of hooves) the preacher arrived.

"Praise be," said Anderina, ushering him in while Bob slipped out to take care of the horse.

"How did you get here?" I asked, as the blessings changed to shouts of thanksgiving.

"When Captain Leech said we would not land in Karamea," said the Reverend, "I persuaded him to set me ashore at Old Man Rock.[41]"

"But that's halfway between Little Wanganui and Mokihinui," gasped Mary.

"You didn't walk around the coast to Wanganui in this weather? said Harriet, her hand flying to her mouth in horror.

"I certainly did, Mam," said the Reverend chuckling. "I leapt from rock to rock dodging the waves, repeating the words of an old hymn; 'I do not wish to see the distant scene, one step enough for me.'"

We laughed as Elizabeth took his oilskin coat and Mary handed him a towel.

"Once I got back to Little Wanganui I caught the ferry over the river, where I borrowed a horse and galloped all the way here."

"You have had an ordeal," said Jemima Coutts.

"All in the line of duty," he said, rubbing his hair dry, "although I'm afraid it has rather spoiled that hymn, for I shall never again sing, 'I do not wish to see the distant scene,' without thinking of wet feet."

We laughed once more. And even though it was not usual to

---

41   Inspired by an event that happened to Reverend Dart in 1912

eat and drink before the wedding ceremony, we all had a cup of tea and ate the cake because the Reverend was shivering. After cake and several cups of tea, he was warm and rested enough to marry John and Mary. Then everyone sang hymns as the happy couple signed the marriage certificate, and I recorded their union in the front of the Family Bible.

"The winding of the clock was a nice touch," said Harriet, once the ceremony was over. "I've never seen that done before, is it a Shetland custom, Anderina?"

"No, I just thought the idea up."

"I think it was lovely," said Jemima. She smiled at her husband. "I wish we had thought of doing that, Peter."

"Robert also wanted to plant our first tree as a memorial," said Anderina, "but I think it will be too wet."

As if God had heard her and turned off a heavenly hose, the rain stopped and the sun peeped through the clouds.

"Come, John and Mary," I shouted, picking up the seedling. "We have one more thing to do."

They followed me, and the guests followed them, and we wandered over to the area I had set aside for my orchard. I handed the little tree to Mary and the spade to John, and they planted it together. Then I laid my hands on them both and prayed:

"John and Mary, may the Lord bless your marriage, may you be like a well-watered tree beside a river that produces beautiful fruit. Amen."

"Amen," said the people.

Then John collected his new wife's suitcase from the house, and with Mary leaning on his arm, we escorted the newlyweds to the river, for it was low tide by now.

To Own a Fig Tree

"Hubert Dolphin, Hubert Dolphin," we shouted across the water.

James Simpson came out of the Post Office.

"He's busy sorting goods," he shouted, pretending he had no idea what was happening. "What do you want?"

"He's the ferryman and we want to get across," we shouted.

"Alright, I'll send him out," said Simpson, trying (but failing) to suppress a wide smile.

He disappeared into the store and shortly after, Hubert came out and rowed the lighter over to us.

"Then John and Mary climbed in the boat, and we cheered and whistled as Hubert rowed them to the Government Reserve, and Simpson entered their marriage into the town register.

By now, the winter daylight was drawing to a close and we were in high spirits.

"Wait until they've had time to get home and then we will creep over and tin-can them," said Robert gleefully. "Everyone, get anything that will make a loud noise and meet back here."

The idea seemed good to us, so we scurried off and returned with cans and cowbells. It took Hubert several trips to get us all over the river, but once we were on the North Bank, we snuck down the river flats until we came to John's ponga hut.

"Keep quiet," hissed Robert, as we stifled laughs. "Don't make a noise until I wave my hand."

We gathered around the hut and Laurie scrambled on the roof. Robert, standing by the closed door, held his hand in the air. He waited a few moments before dropping his hand. Instantly a huge cacophony broke out as with shouts and yahoos, we banged tins and bells. Peter Coutts, who had a ram's horn, was blowing a loud blast when John came out, and

W.E. Hamilton

entering into the fun, pretended to drive us away. When at last we tired of the game, we shouted goodnight and went home.

Of course, it was too late for the Reverend to leave; the way back was long and the night was dark. He was unperturbed by having to stay overnight, however, for as he said:

"The first requirement of any preacher who performs weddings at Karamea is bravery, and the second is flexibility, for you never know what will happen on the perilous trip there or back."

To Own a Fig Tree

The Second Anniversary

Unlike the first anniversary that passed uneventfully, we celebrated Karamea's second year with a sports day at the Government reserve. The weather kindly cooperated with our plans. The sun shone, the water was still, and the illusive *Charley* sat by the jetty. In every house on the morning of the twenty-sixth of November, 1876, Karameans were getting ready for a day out. In our home, Anderina was inspecting produce on the table, while Laurie was making a hoop from supplejack, and Elizabeth and Margret were clapping and singing:

"*A sailor went to sea, sea, sea,*" the girls chanted, as they smacked their hands together rhythmically.

"*To see what he could see, see, see,*"

"*But all that he could see, see, see,*"

"*Was the bottom of the deep blue, sea, sea, sea.*"

"Girls, girls, stop it!" cried Anderina, throwing up her hands! "I can't concentrate on what I am doing with that din going on. You are too old for such childish games, especially you Elizabeth. Can't you find something more constructive to do?"

Elizabeth looked crestfallen at the rebuke, but Margret merely plucked up a large handkerchief and twirled around the room waving it.

I rolled the cricket ball in my hands.

"Don't take it to heart, Lizzy," I said, "Mum is just busy."
Elizabeth's pride was still smarting.
"She said I was childish!"
"Not you, only the game, and today is the perfect day for playing games. What do you think of this?" I said, holding the cricket ball aloft.
"It's fine, Dad. You must have saved every hair Bessy and Daisy shed to make that."
William stopped whistling long enough to say:
"I helped groom the cows so it's half mine."
"It is indeed, Son," I said, handing the ball to him.
"You could have the whole thing and it won't do you much good," said Laurie, checking the join in his hoop was secure. "Johnsons are no good at games and sports."
"I know." William was unperturbed. "I'm not going to *throw or catch* it! I only want it as a sample."
"A sample of what?"
"A sample of the cricket balls I make. If I find there is a big enough demand for them, I shall offer to groom all the cows of the neighbourhood, and sell sports equipment."
"Puh, a sport's business!" snorted Laurence distainfully.
"The King brothers say I can have the bladders of the pigs they slaughter," said William, putting his hands in his pockets and whistling a few notes.
Laurence looked more respectful.
"Pig's bladders make good footballs."
William nodded.
"If you want to sell your hoops, Laurie, I'll give you a penny each for them."
"I suppose you will sell them for two pennies?"

To Own a Fig Tree

"Of course, I need money to turn the school into a cowshed."

"I might as well sell them myself then," said Laurie. "I don't know why you think you can make cricket balls? Dad made that one."

"He could do it, it's easy enough," I said. "It's only soapy water rubbed into the hairs until they matt into a hard ball. The hardest part is persistence," I pulled a face. "And enough hot weather to dry them out."

"Willie's persistent enough," said Laurie, ruffling his little brother's blond hair.

"Would you buy this for a penny?" said Margret, holding her handkerchief in front of William. "They are perfect for 'Drop the Handkerchief.'"

William tilted his head and eyed the cloth speculatively.

"I might. Let me have it today and I'll see if I can get orders for some."

"Alright," said Margret, "But only until they start the games, for I shall need it once they start playing 'Drop the Handkerchief.'"

Anderina's voice cut across the conversation:

"I need help. I can't decide which vegetables to enter in the competition." She pointed to two cabbages. "Which do you think is the best, this one or that one?"

We gathered around the table and considered them thoughtfully. I felt their weight, Elizabeth checked their density, and William hunted for caterpillars (for in the world of small boys, insects were marketable.) Then, because the outcome was divided, we drew straws and Anderina popped the winner into her basket. Now the cabbages were sorted, we voted on the potatoes, turnips and carrots. The bread and cake were easy for there was only one of each, but the butter was trickier as there were several pats to choose from. Anderina scraped a slither off each of the three yellow bricks and we tasted the tiny lumps of butter thoughtfully. One sample was under-salted, one over-salted, and one just right, so Anderina wrapped the last pat in waxed paper and laid it in her basket.

"We can go now," she said, putting on her bonnet and tying the strings under her chin.

I lifted the heavy basket off the table as Anderina picked up the picnic hamper, and we walked towards the door.

"Where is Bob?" said Anderina, looking around as she stepped outside.

"He left after he milked the cows," said Elizabeth, following everyone out and shutting the door behind her. "He wants to register his canoe for the race."

"I'm glad we don't have to climb up and down that steep bank anymore," said Anderina, as our three youngest sped down the narrow track along the river's edge. "We may have a little further to walk to get to the store now, but at least it's all on one level."

I nodded. "Shifting was a hassle but now we are getting re-established it has been a good move. The corn is already sprouting."

Anderina stopped walking. "Thursday, Friday, Saturday, Sunday…" she counted, ticking the days off with her fingers. "…Friday, Saturday. But you only planted the seeds ten days ago," she said, her eyes growing wide. "That is incredibly quick. I expected to see nothing for three weeks."

"It's the wonderful soil," I said, as we resumed walking. "By the end of next summer, I hope to harvest enough wheat

To Own a Fig Tree

to mill our own flour."

"Oh, Robert, do you think that is possible?" said Anderina, her eyes shining.

"Absolutely," I pulled a funny face. "Even if our entire crop can be ground by a peppermill!"

Anderina laughed.

"I hope we'll need more than a peppermill."

"As do I. My goal is self-sufficiency. The key to getting a good crop of wheat is clearing enough ground by fall, for we have to get the winter wheat in before it gets cold."

"Self-sufficiency, free from debt and truck," said Anderina, with a sigh of pleasure. "If we accomplish that, we have done a great thing for our children."

"And their children and all future generations," I added.

"Indeed," said Anderina.

The track widened significantly as we reached Johnson's Landing.

"Bob's idea of shifting the store here was good," I said, looking at the small shed on the end of the new wharf.

"It certainly was, wading the river to get our supplies was not practical. I only wish the store was properly stocked, tea and flour are a shocking price."

I was silent, for we had thrashed the subject of tea and flour so many times there was nothing left to say about it. Anderina twisted her head and considered the clearing at the end of the wharf.

"Bob's land is coming on well."

I nodded and pointed to a neatly stacked pile of lumber under the trees. "Our son is not lazy, split-slabbing with a mall and wedges is hard work."

"Our children are industrious like their father," Anderina smiled. "I suppose Bob will start building a house for his bride soon."

"No," I shook my head. "There is no girl in his sights, so he will concentrate on clearing the land."

"Robert Johnson, are you blind? 'No girl in his sights' you say! Haven't you seen the way his eyes follow Elizabeth Scarlett? Even you noticed they sat together on the night we shifted our house."

"Well, yes," I admitted. "But she is rather young for him. Wouldn't her sister, Rose, be closer to his age?"

"There is not much difference between nineteen and seventeen," said Anderina, skirting around bullock-dung. "And Bob is only twenty-three."

"It seems rather odd," I said. "If we were still in Shetland, he would choose a woman in her thirties."

"He can have a younger wife here," said Anderina, as the crowd queuing for the lighter came into view, "for he can feed a bigger brood."

I shifted the basket into my other hand.

"True, but a healthy girl like Elizabeth could produce up to fourteen children if she gets started early enough, and even in New Zealand, that is a big family to provide for. Lilias Coutts is a nice girl, and thirty-two is a much better age. I'll speak to him about her."

"You can try, dear, but intuition tells me you won't have any success."

"Hello Johnsons," said Daniel, making room for us in the queue as we arrived. "I saw young William has a nice cricket ball, how's your batting arm feeling, Robert?"

To Own a Fig Tree

"You won't want me on your team, Daniel," I said, "I'm better at swinging a hammer than a cricket bat."

"What about rounders then?"

"Same problem, I'm afraid. I can't catch or throw."

"Pity," said Daniel, helping his wife into the lighter. "What about racing?"

"Too short and slow for running, but I might have a shot at the sack race."

"What about you Anderina?" said Harriet, taking the picnic hamper from her. "Are you entering anything?"

Anderina scooped up her skirts and climbed into the boat.

"Produce, baking, and dairy products."

"Me too."

Daniel and I took off our boots, rolled up the bottoms of our trousers and waded into the shallow water. Hubert Dolphin took the oars of the lighter, and together we crossed the river. When we got to the shore, I helped Anderina out of the boat, and we made our way over to the Exhibition Marquee (ingeniously cobbled together from tarpaulins.) Anderina handed her exhibits to Mrs Scanlan, and then we wandered up the beach to look at the canoes. As we got close, I noticed James Simpson and Edwin King, lifting a barrel off the *Charley*.

"I don't like the look of this," I said stiffening. "That looks like a hogshead of beer to me."

Anderina sucked in her breath sharply.

"I told you I smelt brandy on James Simpson's breath the day the medicine cabinet went missing."

"Sly grogging is one thing," I said, frowning, "but fifty-four gallons of the devil's brew is quite another."

"O'Connor has seen it," said Anderina, as he followed them

off the steamer. "Perhaps he will stop them bringing it ashore."

"He's an Irishman, he'll not have a problem with it. And if something's not done swiftly, it will be too late to do anything about it. For once the Irish get a whiff of liquor, the day will deteriorate into a drunken brawl."

Anderina's mouth straightened into a grim line and her lips went thin. "Go over there and stop them bringing it down the jetty, Robert, while I inform the Leading Brothers of this sin."

We parted company, and I hurried up the beach and onto the wharf, where I met "O'Connor.

"I object to the alcohol," I said, pointing to the barrel sitting on the jetty.

"It's Simpson's business, nothing to do with me," said O'Connor, preparing to walk on.

A crowd of militant elders was marching towards us as I stepped in front of him. "That much alcohol will ruin the day."

"You're being melodramatic, Johnson," said O'Connor, as the sailor handed James a five-gallon cask of brandy.

"Another cask! How much more has he got?"

"Not enough to cause trouble."

"It's causing trouble already and the lid is not even open," said Daniel, coming up.

"That's right," said Alfred Lineham, standing astride and crossing his arms.

"This is a family day," said James Moffatt, wagging his finger. "This is not the place for liquor."

But old Benjamin Coutts was the most persuasive. He shook his walking stick at O'Connor and thundered:

"That demon-drink oils the pathway to hell for sinners, and is an offence to God Almighty. You call yourself the Father-of

Karamea, be a man and do something about it!"

O'Connor held up his hands and took a step backwards.

"Alright, alright, I'll speak to Simpson."

We followed him down the jetty and stood glowering at Simpson and Edwin.

"James, I'm sorry, but the alcohol is causing trouble with the steadier settlers," said O'Connor, "I have to ask you to return the cask and barrel to Nelson."

"But I wanted it for the opening of my new hotel and boarding house," said Simpson, sticking out his chin aggressively. "How I spend my money is my business."

"Yes, yes," said O'Connor, "I don't have a problem with it, but for the sake of peace, you must return the brandy. You may keep the barrel of beer provided you take it home and do not open it today."

"Alright," said James, sighing as he gave the cask back to the sailor. "I knew it was a risk." He glared at us. "Karamea is full of religious do-gooders."

"Good man," said O'Connor. "I know this is irritating for you, but the religious unity here is one of the things holding this community together. The Special Settlement of Jackson is falling apart without it."

"No hard feelings, James," I said, sticking out my hand.

"No hard feelings," he echoed, shaking it.

"The canoe race will start in five minutes," shouted Mr Scanlan through a homemade speaking trumpet. "All boats out of the water."

Robert and Peter, and a few other canoeists pulled their boats onto the sand and lined them up in a row as a crowd of spectators gathered.

"At the count of three," shouted Scanlan, "drag your boats into the water. The first canoe to reach Johnson's Landing is the winner."

We cheered and clapped.

"ON YOUR MARKS, GET SET, ONE, TWO, THREE, GO!"

There was a flurry of activity as canoes whooshed into the river, and paddles seesawed in and out of the water at a furious rate. Everyone (unencumbered with a long skirt) ran along the bank cheering the racers onward. Peter and Robert soon outstripped the other boats by a good distance, for they were the most experienced canoeists.

"GO BOB, GO BOB," we shouted as he and Peter slashed through the water neck and neck.

We thought for sure one of them would win, but close to the finish line Peter's canoe suddenly wobbled and rolled over.

Jemimah screamed.

The crowd gasped.

But Robert, leaping from his boat, dived and pulled Peter to the surface.

Some of us waded in and helped them onto the bank, while others corralled the drifting boats and paddles. A canoe slid past us to the finishing post, but nobody took any notice of the winner.

"What happened, Pete?" Robert panted, as they sat on the bank recovering from their fright.

Peter frowned and wiped the water off his face.

"I don't know. Suddenly the canoe twisted and I found myself upside-down in the water. Thanks for rescuing me, Bob, I was having trouble getting out from under the canoe."

To Own a Fig Tree

"Oh, Peter, you were almost drowned!" cried Jemimah, running up and throwing her arms around her husband. "Are you alright?"

"I'm fine, only a little wet."

"Come home and get dry," she said, hustling him off.

After such a tumultuous beginning, the day settled down. Friendly rivalry sprang up between the North and South Bankers as they formed teams for cricket and rounders. The North Bankers won the cricket match before the picnic, but The South Bankers won the rounders in the afternoon. Then Margret retrieved her hanky from William and the kids played, Drop the Handkerchief, Twos and Threes, Prisoners Base, Tip the Finger, Nuts and May, Fall Over, and Hot Rice.

"Little Mary Anne Lineham won the baby contest," said Anderina, as we wandered among the trestle tables laden with baking and vegetables. "But The North Bankers won all the produce prizes."

"That is hardly surprising, their gardens are more established for they have not had the same setbacks as us."

Anderina sighed and nodded.

"We did better in the livestock. Thomas Lineham took first place with his cow, and Edwin got Prize Pig. Henry Haws won first place with one of his goats, but The North Bankers can't count that as a win, for he owns both Karamea's goats."

"Who won best butter?" I said.

"Mr O'Connor and Mr Scanlan are judging it now," said Anderina, leading me over to the table of yellow bricks.

"It was very hard to choose a winner in this section," said O'Connor, "for all the butter we have tasted today is far better quality than we normally see on the Westcoast. After much deliberation, however, we have picked a winner."

And he pinned a blue rosette on my wife's butter.

It was a glorious finish to our second year. We helped clear up and started for home. Anderina, in a bubble of happiness, talked about her prize-winning butter and blue ribbon as we walked. I was glad for her, but I did not share her joy, for I was uneasy; earlier in the day, I'd seen O'Connor nail a for-sale sign on the Government store.

To Own a Fig Tree

God's Provision in a Tight Spot

Christmas was coming, and I could tell by the wrinkles on her brow, Anderina was worried about finance. She was not troubled by lack of money for presents and fancy food, for we never had gifts or turkey; payment of our lease was due.

"How was your visit with Mary?" I asked, taking off my dirty boots before I came inside.

"Nice," said Anderina, in a preoccupied tone. She handed me a newspaper with a circle drawn around an article. "What is this? It looks important."

I sat on a bench by the table, and glancing at the heading, said:

"The Government is withdrawing Karamea's financial support, because they fear Julius Vogel has overspent."

Anderina's hand flew to her mouth and the worry lines deepened.

"And you didn't tell me about it!"

"I didn't want to distress you."

"Read the article to me, Robert."

I cleared my throat and read aloud:

"*After the lavish and explosive development by the Vogel Government, a more prudent leadership chooses to consolidate rather than expand. Subsequently, the general assembly in Wellington has decided to suspend financial support to its*

W.E. Hamilton

Special Settlement at Karamea. Instead, it has proclaimed the area as a road district under the Nelson highway Act of 1871. The services of Mr Scanlan and J Simpson, the overseer and storekeeper respectively, will shortly be dispensed with as the store is to be sold. Eugene O'Connor, the acknowledged 'Father of Karamea,' will continue to keep a kindly eye on the settlement. Mr Oswald Curtis (Executive Officer of the Nelson Provincial Council) is instructed to pay him fifteen pounds for each monthly visit. In anticipation of the untimely winding up of state sponsorship, O'Connor will distribute three months of rations to impoverished families. Job opportunities resulting from future public works in Karamea are restricted to those in debt to the Government."

Anderina was silent for a few minutes.

"Mary says there's talk of closing down the settlement and moving us to a more accessible location," she said in a small voice.

"Well yes, there was, but this paper is old, and when O'Connor announced he would live permanently at Westport, parliament backed down."

"Does that mean we can stay?"

"Yes."

Anderina blew out a long stream of air and the crinkles in her forehead smoothed out.

"That's a relief." Her eyes bored into me. "How long have you known about this?"

"Since Anniversary Day. There are rumours of an impending depression, and when I saw O'Connor nail a for-sale sign on the shed at Johnson's Landing, I guessed the Government was pulling out."

To Own a Fig Tree

"Three weeks! You could have told me sooner."

"The corn is growing at an enormous speed," I said, changing the subject. "At the rate it's going it will grow twelve feet high."

"Don't be silly, Robert," said Anderina, laying a plate of oatcakes on the table. "Corn does not grow that tall."

"This corn might."

My wife was not so easily distracted.

"How are we going to pay the lease?" she said, the worry lines returning. "We have no money and we owe more than anyone else to the store."

"That makes me eligible for Government work. I'm not keen on road maintenance but it is better than nothing. And if we are still short, God will provide somehow."

Anderina took the kettle off the fire and nodded as she poured boiling water into the teapot.

"We have had some close shaves, but he has never failed us. Nevertheless, I wish now we had not gone to the expense of building a brick chimney," she said, hanging the kettle back on the crane in the fireplace.

"You had to have a way to cook indoors," I said, "it's not practical cooking outside in the rain."

"I suppose so. Call everyone in for morning tea, Robert."

I picked up a pot and spoon, but as I opened the door, the wind caught it and blew it hard against the wall with a bang.

"I don't like the look of the weather," I said over my shoulder, as I belted the bottom of the pot with the spoon. "I think we are in for a storm."

"Oh dear, I hope it doesn't flatten the corn."

"It should be alright, it's in a sheltered spot. I just hope there are no vessels out at sea."

But there was.

We had barely finished our tea when James Simpson came sprinting down the driveway.

"A ship is stranded on the bar and the captain is offering a shilling and sixpence an hour to dig her out," he shouted, before running off to tell others.

"A shilling and sixpence!" Robert cried, snatching his sou'wester off the peg by the door and pulling on his boots. "That's good wages!"

"And all in cash," said John, dragging on his coat.

Anderina looked at the ceiling. "Thank you, God, for your provision."

"I don't think the captain of the ship will think much of God's answer," said Robert, grabbing a shovel. "This will cost him a pretty penny."

"God's ways are wondrous his mercies to perform, Bob," said Anderina tartly, as she put on her hat.

"What does that mean?"

"It means we will pay our lease with money from heaven," I said, lacing up my boots before reaching for a spade.

We hurried down to the mouth of the river. When we got there, a crowd of sightseers were watching the crew of the ship digging around her stern. John, Robert and I took off our boots and left them on the bank with Anderina and the children.

"It's the *S.S. Kennedy*," said Margret, her voice was shrill with excitement.

"Stuck in the sand," said William.

"She must weigh at least a-hundred-and-forty tons," said Robert, putting his sou'wester on his head as spits of rain

To Own a Fig Tree

turned into a downpour. "She'll take some digging out."

"If we dig behind and around her, we might float her off the bar at full tide," said Daniel, as we waded over to the stricken vessel.

"That's the plan," said the captain overhearing us. "One shilling and sixpence an hour to dig her out. Are you men signing up?"

"Aye, aye, captain," said Robert.

"Give your names to the first mate then," said the captain, "and a bonus of a tot of rum each if you get her free by high tide."

"We'll have her floating by then," said old Benjamin Coutts, as we signed on. "But you can keep your rum, we're a Godfearing community."

"Speak for yourself, Granddad," said Edwin, "I'll take my tot and be glad of it."

"Granddad!" said Benjamin offended. "I can dig as well as you can, you cheeky whippersnapper!"

And just to show him, Benjamin dug his spade deep into the bar, and threw a huge spadeful of sand towards the beach.

"You may be able to dig, Granddad," said the irrepressible Edwin, "but you can't go as long as me."

And he was right. For the gallant old man was quickly tuckered out, and after a while, Peter escorted him back to the shore. The rest of us, however, kept digging without a break.

"I felt her lift a little," shouted the captain after six hours slog. "A little more and I think she will be free."

We dug and dug and an hour later she was afloat.

The captain paid us, and we tucked our money into our shirt pockets before pushing the *S.S. Kennedy* into deeper water. Then the sailors built up a head of steam, and slowly, taking frequent soundings, she sailed out of the river and into the ocean.

Anderina was full of smiles when I handed her the money I had made.

"We may be too poor to give gifts at Christmas time," she said, putting it in her purse. "But thankfully God still gives Christmas presents."

To Own a Fig Tree

Big Trouble

In our isolated community, many days passed between significant events. But today there were two things to gossip about. The *Charley* had arrived, and (after months of no interest) the store was sold to Hubert Dolphin.

"Fifty pounds for the store, and a hundred-and-fifty for the goods, is a pittance!" said James Simpson, as we waited at Johnson's Landing for Hubert to bring the fresh supplies down the river. "He got a bargain because he and Eugene are related. If I'd tendered that little, O'Connor would have turned me down flat."

"Did you make an offer?"

"Well, no, after building my hotel and accommodation house, I don't have any money," Simpson admitted. He looked sheepish, but only for a moment. Recovering, he straightened and stabbed his finger in the air. "But if I did, he would have turned me down flat. I can't compete with kin."

"Eugene and Hubert swear they are not related," said Daniel. "You can't assume all Irishmen are cousins."

"They may deny the relationship," said Simpson, rubbing his nose and shooting us a glance full of suspicion. "But is it the truth! Why would Hubert suddenly employ Eugene's brother, A.C. O'Connor, as the storeman if they are not related?"

"Perhaps it was part of the deal," said Thomas Lineham.

"That does not make it any better," said Simpson, "it's still nepotism. I am going to check my account, and I suggest you blokes do the same. I don't trust that Dolphin fellow. I bet nobody has a credit balance."

"You are being overly suspicious," said Thomas Lineham cheerfully. "I'm sure I have cleared my debt, for in August I only owed twenty-two pounds, and George and I earned sixteen pounds the following month. So, with that, and what we earnt digging out the *S.S. Kennedy,* I'm confident I'm in the black at last."

But when Hubert Dolphin arrived at the store and the books were opened, nobody had a credit balance, not even Thomas.

"I can't understand it," Thomas said, bewildered. "I felt certain I was squared up."

"It's quite simple, Lineham," said Hubert smoothly, "your wife bought tea and flour."

"Why you weaselly little Irish hound," snarled Simpson, "no Scotsman would stoop to price gouging on necessities."

"No Scotsman parts with his money without squealing," said Hubert, "so I hardly think that furthers your argument. And while we are discussing tight Scotsmen, don't think you can continue keeping your fowls and pigs on crown land for free, James Simpson."

"I'm still the postmaster, I have rights, Dolphin."

"I have leased all the crown land and have control of it, Simpson."

James thrust his chin forward and the veins on his neck stuck out.

"I shall continue keeping fowls and pigs, and you'll not get one penny out of me, you Irish *Jackeen*."

Hubert thrust his face close to James.

To Own a Fig Tree

"Take that back, Simpson!"

"*Jackeen, Jackeen, Jackeen.*"

"You'll be sorry, *Bampot*."

"*Bampot!* You're the idiot, Dolphin!"

"If you don't have your pigs and hens off crown land by the end of the week, Simpson, I shall set my cattle dog on them!"

"If you set your dog on my livestock, I'll shoot him."

"I thought it was going to come to cuffs," I said to Anderina, as we unpacked our supplies later in the day.

"Oh dear," she said, opening a packet of tea leaves before pouring them into the tea caddy.

I put a bag of flour in a dark corner next to a mound of potatoes and covered everything with sacks.

"As it is, the dispute is threatening to split the Scots and the Irish," I said. "We can only hope everything calms down and nothing comes of it."

But when the shots rang out at the end of the week, my hope of peace was ruined. I, along with the rest of the community, hot-footed it to the Government Reserve. We found Simpson by his henhouse in the yard of his new hotel.

"I warned him," said James, unrepentantly, as he dabbed his black eye with a hanky. "I told him I'd shoot his dog if it worried my pigs and poultry."

"Did you ask Hubert to call it off?"

"I didn't have time, his cur was about to rip the heads off my chooks," said James shutting his hens in the chicken coop. "You heard the man threaten to set his dog on my livestock."

"Where is Hubert?" said Benjamin Coutts suddenly.

"He took his dead dog, and has gone to round up the Irishmen," said Simpson. "I told him I'll shoot him or any of his cronies if they try to throw me or my animals off my land."

My heart started racing.

"Put the gun down, James," I said, holding out my hand and taking a step forward.

James swivelled and pointed the nozzle at me.

"Get back, Johnson, if you take another step, I'll fill you with lead."

His gaze swept over the crowd as I retreated,

"Who thinks the store is ripping us off?" he shouted."

"Aye."

"Who thinks they have not paid us fairly?"

"Aye."

"Who thinks they have rigged the accounts?"

"Yes!"

The agreements were growing louder and heartier.

"Who hates the evil *truck* system?

"MEEE!"

By now I was shouting along with the loudest of them.

"Dolphin and the O'Connors are related. The Irish will oppress the Scotch and we will miss out on the supplies, especially now *N. Edwards and Co* have discontinued shipping to Karamea."

There was a shocked silence.

"How do you know?" said Daniel at last.

"I'm the postmaster, I'm the first to know everything."

"Why would they do that?"

"Mishaps like the *SS Kennedy*, weigh too heavily against its continuation."

"But the Government subsidizes it fifty pounds a trip."

"It's not enough. The *Charley* is not coming again."

To Own a Fig Tree

This news was like lighting a keg of dynamite.

"DOWN WITH DOLPHIN, O'CONNOR, AND ALL IRISHMEN," shouted someone.

We took up the chant and the mountains echoed with ugly shouts.

Only Jennings kept his head. He whipped a pencil and pad from his pocket and scribbled two notes. Turning to Charles and Robert, he said urgently:

"Run over the track to Westport, boys, go as fast as you can and don't stop. He gave a note to Charles. "Take this letter to a man called Mr Ings, and, Robert," he gave him the second note, "find Eugene O'Connor and tell him to come at once. Karamea is on the brink of war."

W.E. Hamilton

Worse Trouble

James reloaded his shotgun.

"It's a good thing the hotel is finished," he said, "we can shelter in it if it comes down to a shootout."

The door of the hotel flew open and Mrs Simpson appeared, her face looking like a thundercloud. The crowd parted before her as, with lowered head and stomping strides, she marched over to her husband.

"I heard that, James Simpson!" she said, putting her hands on her hips. "Any shooting is to be done well away from here. I'm not having the glass blown out of my new windows or bullets shot through the curtains!"

"But, sweetheart, the swine, Dolphin, is swindling us."

At this, we cheered and shouted:

"SWINDLING SWINE."

Ignoring the commotion, Mrs Simpson zoned in on her husband.

"Don't you, *sweetheart,* me!" she hissed, wagging her finger at him, "I'll not have our new hotel turned into a wild west saloon with bullets embedded in its fresh paint."

"Your wife is right," said Mr Jennings, pushing his way forward. He pointed at the front wall of the hotel. "Three windows and two fine doors; it would be a pity to mar the best building of Karamea with bullets."

Mrs Simpson simpered. "The roof was my idea," she said.

To Own a Fig Tree

"Very nice," said Jennings, admiring the central gable flattening into a lean-to on either side. "I am sure this establishment is fine enough to house Julius Vogel, should he visit Karamea."

"Julius Vogel!" Mrs Simpson fluttered her hands. "He wouldn't come here! Would he?"

Jennings turned to the crowd.

"The best way to resolve our current trouble is not through guns, but a petition to parliament."

"*Parliament,*" Mrs Simpson exclaimed, "oh, my!"

"So," Jennings continued, "I've sent Robert and Charles to get O'Connor."

"O'Connor! What use is he to us?" Simpson snarled. "He's on the side of the Irish Oppressor."

"IRISH OPPRESSOR, IRISH OPPRESSOR," we chanted.

"Be quiet, James," said Mrs Simpson. "Mr Jennings is quite right." She turned to Jennings. "Simpson's Karamea Hotel and Accommodation House, has a very nice parlour where the petition could be signed. We imported the wallpaper from England."

"Thank you, Mrs Simpson."

Jennings turned to us and lifted his voice.

"My friends, I am well aware of your complaints and suspicions…"

With these words, he caught our interest. We quietened and gave him our full attention.

"As we worked on the track, I listened to your grievances and know the dissatisfaction you feel over the imbalance between your hard labour and the existing state of affairs. I also know you no longer trust O'Connor. Therefore, I recommend you go over his head and send a list of complaints directly to the house of representatives."

The idea that agricultural workers had the right to complain to Parliament was novel. We nodded and murmured agreement.

"With this in mind," continued Jennings, "I have sent word to Mr Ings, a Westport lawyer. He will work with you to draw up a petition outlining all your concerns."

"Tell him to inform Mr Vogel," cut in Mrs Simpson, "that Karamea has a five-star Accommodation House with English wallpaper, clean sheets, and no bedbugs."

Jennings smiled and patted the little lady on the arm.

"Madam, I'm sure he will inform Parliament of everything it needs to know."

Mrs Simpson beamed, while Mr Simpson bent his shotgun and took the cartridges from the double-barrel.

"I like the idea of making O'Connor squirm before parliament," he said. "That has got to hurt a politician."

We were about to disperse peacefully when a large crowd came towards us. We tensed, ready for a fight, but when they got close, we realized something much worse had happened.

"It's Peter!" Old Benjamin cried out, running to meet the group carrying the body. "What has happened to my son?"

"We found him floating in the river, his canoe overturned," said Hubert.

"Drowned! My only son drowned!"

Old Benjamin's vitality popped like a balloon pricked by a pin.

"Bring Peter inside and lay him out on the table," said Mrs Simpson, ushering them into the parlour. "James, bring a drop of brandy for Benjamin."

To Own a Fig Tree

"Does Jemima know?" groaned Old Benjamin, stroking the wet hair off his son's face. "Not yet."

"Leave me to tell the news of Peter's death to my daughter," said Thomas Jamieson, wiping tears from his eyes. "It is not a job any father wishes to do, but I would not have her hear of the death of her husband from anyone else."

"I'll run and tell auntie and the girls about Peter, Uncle Ben," said James Coutts.

"No, James," said Old Benjamin, rallying. "Like Thomas, I will have no one other than myself impart the dreadful tidings. Send for the Reverend and make arrangements for a casket." He groaned again. "My poor girls, I am eighty-one and not long for this world, who will look after them once I'm gone?"

"John and I will, Uncle," said James, "we will care for them along with our sisters."

"Two widows and seven unmarried women, is a heavy load for two lads of thirteen and twenty to support," said Benjamin laying his hand on his nephew's shoulder.

"I'll help," said Harry Lineham, stepping forward. "I'll chop firewood for Jemima and plant her crops."

"And the rest of us will chip in and care for your girls," I said. "Between us, we will not see them hungry or without a roof over their heads."

"You are good men," said Old Benjamin.

James Simpson offered him a small glass of brandy.

"Drink this as a restorative."

"Thank you, James, but no," said Old Benjamin, holding up the palm of his hand. "My heart is sick, not my body."

And yet, his upright frame was suddenly stooped, and he looked twenty years older as he crept out of the room.

W.E. Hamilton

A Petition is Sent to Parliament

Word spread like wildfire that O'Connor had arrived. He looked hot and dishevelled as we gathered around. Already troubled by Jennings' note, meeting the Reverend on the way to perform a burial service increased his alarm.

"Who was killed and who killed him?" he asked.

"Nobody was killed," said Mr Jennings. "Peter Coutts was drowned."

"I am relieved to hear it," said O'Connor, drawing a deep breath. "I thought as the Father of Karamea, you called me here to stop my children fighting."

"*Father of Karamea, puh!*" James Simpson snorted and spat on the ground disdainfully.

"You mean, Karamea's oppressive laird!"

"And Dolphin's your crooked merchant!"

There was derisive laughter and the mood of the crowd was on the brink of growing ugly.

"Come now," said the Reverend, stepping forward and holding up his hands. "This is not the time for recriminations. Have respect for the dead and grieving by not adding to their sorrows with more trouble. Let us go quietly to the cemetery and lay Peter to rest."

"The Reverend is right," said Jennings. "This is a day for paying our respects. Mr Ings will come in a few days and then

To Own a Fig Tree

we will draft up a formal complaint."

The reasonableness of this suggestion was apparent to all, so six men collected the coffin, and we quietly followed them to the cemetery at the top of the Zig-Zag track. Benjamin and Barbara, both looking ancient and frail, stood with their arms around Jemima as the Reverend said:

"Life is fleeting and full of trouble."

Then, as our entire community watched, he sprinkled soil onto the lid of the coffin.

"Ashes to ashes, dust to dust," he said, motioning the pallbearers to lower the coffin into the grave. "We commit Peter Coutts to the ground, trusting in the resurrection of the dead at God's appointed time."

The sadness was almost tangible as the elderly couple and the tragic young widow, dropped cowslips into the grave.

As soon as the funeral was over, O'Connor slunk away. Nobody bid him farewell, and I did not press him to attend the memorial tree planting at my place. I wanted to plant a fig, of course, but there was no hope of acquiring one without the steamer. Instead, Edwin kindly gave me a pear seedling, which we planted in a spot overlooking the river. The tree had not been in the ground many days when Mr Ings arrived. Then, for the good of the community, we pushed the dark shadow of Peter's death aside as best we could, and concentrated on the petition. Mr Ings listened to our grievances carefully and took copious notes.

"In a nutshell," he said, "you think there has been mismanagement of this settlement by O'Connor, inflated prices in the Dolphin owned and operated store, and inequity in the *truck* system."

W.E. Hamilton

"That's right."

"And you want an investigation into matters, O'Connor removed as the director of Karamea, and the steamer service reinstated."

"That's right."

He put his notebook back in his leather case and slid the catch shut.

"I shall go back to Westport, where I will draft up a list of grievances to send to the House of Representatives. As soon as I get that done, I will bring it back here for you to look over and sign."

He left, and it was some months before we saw him again. When he came back, he had the petition which read:

Petition of Karamea Special Settlers

(Petition of the Karamea Special Settlers AJHR, 1877, D7 pg. 17-18) To the Honourable, the Speaker and the members of the House of Representatives of New Zealand, in Parliament assembled.
The petition of the undersigned special settlers, resident at the Karamea, Buller County, in the Colony of New Zealand showeth

That as special settlers, we have been permitted to take up land at the Karamea on deferred payments.

That in occupying land in such a remote locality, we were assured by the Nelson provincial authorities,

- That we should be supplied with stores at moderate prices.
- That work would be given us whereby we might earn money sufficient to pay for such stores, and also to pay the instalments of money falling due on our land.
- That a subsidized steamer would call at the port.

To Own a Fig Tree

For some time, provisions were supplied at moderate prices in return for labour done on roads, but that we received little or no cash.

But without notice to your petitioners, the Government store and its contents has been sold to the director of the settlement, or his trading partners, and that the price of the provisions has been raised to an exorbitant degree.

Moreover, the distribution of labour has been made in a most capricious manner, many of your petitioners getting little or no work while others have been fully employed.

Furthermore, no steamer has called at the port for many months past, and that therefore your petitioners have been debarred from obtaining stores from a cheaper market, and also from getting rid of any produce they have for sale.

Your petitioners have grave reasons for supposing and verily believe that large profits have been made by the present director of the settlement in trading transactions with your petitioners, in excess of any profits contemplated in the original scheme of the settlement. They believe it would conduce to the progress of the settlement if the present director was relieved of his charge thereof, and that any further expenditure of public money on the Karamea Special Settlement should be under the control of the Buller County Council.

In addition, the subsidizing of a steamer to call periodically at the port, and the outlay of a moderate amount of money on public works within the Karamea District, will make the settlers a success.

Your petitioners, therefore, pray that your honourable House will investigate the matters complained of, and that such relief be granted as may seem just.

And your petitioners, as in duty bound, will ever pray.

W.E. Hamilton

"Look this over," said Mr Ings, writing seventeenth of August, 1877 on the bottom of the paper. "And if you agree, sign your name to it."

The paper passed from hand to hand. I was last in line. When it came around to me, I scrutinized it and added my signature to the list of thirty-eight other names.

"What happens now, Ings?" said Jennings.

"The under-secretary for immigration will appoint a man to hear the submission, and arrange a time for the hearing," said Ings, slipping the document into his briefcase. Then bidding us goodbye, he left. And it was some time before we saw him again.

To Own a Fig Tree

The Hearing

In spite of Mrs Simpson's hopes, Julius Vogel did not come to Karamea. Instead, Magistrate Alexandra MacKay, was appointed to hear our petition. He, his secretary, O'Connor, and Mr Ings came by foot over the track.

"Such an arduous journey," said MacKay, as we (the thirty-nine petitioners) escorted him and his party to the Simpson's hotel. "Surely there is an easier way to get here?"

"Not since the steamer service stopped," O'Connor said, pulling a face.

"Come in and restore yourself with a beer," said Simpson, rushing forward and opening one of the two front doors.

"And after that, I will show you to your rooms," said Mrs Simpson, pointing to the other door. "The sheets are clean, there are no bedbugs, and the wallpaper is English."

"Madam, your hotel is an unexpected oasis in a briar patch," said McKay, limping across the threshold and dropping thankfully into a chair.

"I have a handsome parlour, Sir, where you can hold your hearing tomorrow," Mrs Simpson simpered. "The curtains are real lace made by Mary Lineham, a local woman."

McKay took the glass Simpson handed him.

"That sounds very good," he said, taking a long pull on his beer. He turned to Mr Ings. "My dear wife's father, William Gibbs, was a magistrate and a goldfield's warden at one time.

He had some rough journeys out to remote goldfields in the back of beyond, but I doubt even he had a worse trip than the one we have just had."

"Indeed," Ings agreed. "I wish this case had come to our attention before the steamer stopped running."

We could see they were eager to rest, so we arranged a time for the meeting, and bid them farewell.

Robert and I were two of the forty-six people notified to attend the inquiry; accordingly, we presented ourselves at Simpson's Hotel early the next morning. The parlour, though spacious by Karamea's standards, was hard-pressed to accommodate such a crowd.

"All rise, the Court is in session," shouted the secretary, as MacKay entered the room.

The command was unnecessary, for sitting was not an option.

"Welcome to this hearing," said MacKay, taking a seat at the table. "The Government has no wish to appoint a full commission of inquiry into your case, as it believes the charges laid do not warrant the time or expense. That being said, Parliament desires that justice is accessible to all. I propose, gentlemen, we dispense with formality." He put on his reading glasses and his secretary handed him a copy of our petition. "I have before me a list of your grievances…"

"Excuse me, Your Honour," cut in O'Connor, "I request the evidence be taken on oath."

"Denied," said MacKay, "as I am not a Judge I am not empowered to do as you request."

"But the inquiry might treat me unfavourably without sworn oaths!"

To Own a Fig Tree

MacKay lowered his glasses slowly, and gave O'Connor an icy stare before saying in measured tones:

"In my hearings, Sir, justice is not compromised through lack of sworn oaths."

"Your Honour, I did not mean to imply disrespect," said O'Connor.

MacKay held O'Connor in his gaze until O'Connor dropped his eyes. Then he leisurely perused the document before him.

"I will start with hearing the Special Settler's evidence."

Several of the settlers got up and gave (in my opinion) lucid and factual accounts of O'Connor's deficiencies of management and payment of labour. O'Connor stood glowering but silent, until Robert got up to speak.

"Your Honour," cut in O'Connor, "I object to this man's evidence on the grounds he is not a Special Settler."

"Mr Johnson," said MacKay, "are you one of the thirty heads of families that arrived in Karamea on the *Charles Edward* on Thursday the twenty-sixth of November, 1874?"

"Yes, Sir, I was one of the men who came to Karamea on that day."

"You are very young. Are you sure you are the head of the Johnson family?"

"Well, not exactly. The actual head of our family is my father, Robert Johnson Senior."

"Then your evidence is not relevant."

"Not relevant," Robert spluttered! "I have worked as hard as any of the men. I have felled trees, pit-sawn lumber, surveyed the land, and toiled on the track, all without bullock or horse! How can you say my evidence is not relevant?"

"While your contribution to this community is indeed

significant, Mr Johnson, the law is confined to hearing the evidence of the original party of thirty men who hold Crown Leases in this Special Settlement of Karamea."

At this, a buzz of consternation broke out in the room. Robert's shoulders slumped as MacKay's words sank in, and as he shrank, O'Connor expanded.

"Your Honour," O'Connor shouted over the noise, "fourteen more men who are not Special Settlers signed the petition and expect to give irrelevant evidence. Some of them, like Robert Johnson, are not the head of their family, others are Old Colonists, miners, and others have forfeited their rights as Special Settlers through not fulfilling the legal regulations."

The buzz escalated into shouts of anger, and MacKay banged his hammer on Mrs Simpson's best table in a manner guaranteed to distress the good woman. When we had settled down, he said:

"This hearing is adjourned until I have determined who may give evidence."

"O'Connor won that round," said James Moffatt, as we milled about waiting. "But he won't get away as easily once he is on the stand."

To our delight James was right. We may have lost fifteen witnesses, but Mr MacKay had some hard questions for our opponent.

"Eugene O'Connor, the settlers complain about your method of payment for labour. Please explain why they were paid only in goods, never in cash?"

"Your Honour, it is better to say that payment for goods was, for the most part made in labour. The debt came first, usually incurred for clothes, tools, and other items incidental

To Own a Fig Tree

to settlement before work started."

"You objected to us earning cash any other way," we shouted.

MacKay held up his hand, and when we had quietened, his secretary handed him a newspaper cutting.

"I have in my hand, Mr O'Connor, a report in the West Coast Times, describing how several settlers had been working for *N. Edwards and Company*. It claims you wanted their wages handed over to the Provincial Government, and even visited the settlement to obtain this object."

"I was working in the interests of the settlers for their good," said O'Connor.

"But the paper says (and I quote) *'O'Connor abused the settlers in unmeasured terms in language more forcible than polite, until a threat of corporal castigation put a stop to the struggle.'*"

"Your Honour, the settlers are no good with money, and I was determined they repay their debts before they got out of control."

"Such a highhanded manner could scarcely convince the settlers of your good intentions," said MacKay. "Moving on, however, the settlers claim the visits of the steamer were not regular enough, and thus, denied the chance to obtain cheaper supplies and export their produce."

There was a pause in which we nodded and murmured agreement.

"The settlers have no produce to market," O'Connor sneered.

"Yet you informed Curtis (and I quote) *'Karamea should this year be producing field and dairy produce for the Westcoast markets.*'"

For once smooth-talking O'Connor had nothing to say, so MacKay called James Simpson to give evidence.

"Mr Simpson, as storekeeper, in your own words describe O'Connor's management of the store."

"Your Honour, while working as the storekeeper, O'Connor repeatedly told me the store was to be sold, and I was to stock only enough goods to grant bare rations."

"And did you do this?"

"Yes, Sir."

"What was the result?"

"Well Sir, as the steamer called erratically, we often ran out of supplies."

"Mr Jennings," MacKay called.

"Yes, your Honour."

"How do you think the erratic steamer service impacted the community?"

"It inconvenienced the settlers and denied them the opportunity of disposing their produce."

"O'Connor asserts," said MacKay, "the settlers had nothing to sell because of setbacks."

"That is true of the settlers on the South Bank, but not of those on the North Bank, who have not been thus hindered."

"Hubert Dolphin," said MacKay, "you and O'Connor both deny the prices at the store are excessive, and have provided a list comparing the prices of similar goods in Nelson, Mokihinui, and Karamea."

"That's right."

"The settlers claim the prices in Karamea are much higher."

"Any price difference is the cost of transportation to such a

To Own a Fig Tree

remote location," said Hubert.

"What do you have to say about this, O'Connor?" said MacKay.

"There are 'persons' in this community (who I will not name)," hissed O'Connor, "who have duped these inexperienced and ignorant settlers into believing false rumours about me."

We glowered at the word ignorant.

"These 'persons' are currying favour with the Buller County Council, to take over control of the settlement. This settlement cannot succeed while the settler's minds are disturbed by persons seeking only selfish objectives, regardless of the interests of the community as a whole. Moreover, it is often hard to explain matters concerning the accounts at the store, for many of these men can neither read nor write. They are wary of each other and don't trust me, yet I have gone out of my way to see that the settlement is a success; even to the point of giving some men work at my own expense. I have personally expended (most unprofitably) about two-hundred-and-fifty pounds of my own money."

After O'Connor's burst of self-justification, other settlers complained that O'Connor favoured certain settlers above others in the distribution of work.

"I don't get enough work," said one.

"He is capricious," said another.

"Regarding survey work," said J Blackburn, "I fear I will be penalized for not voting for O'Connor in the election."

There were many more witnesses who said similar things. After a time, my legs ached, and it was hard to keep track of everything said, as the accusations flew back and forth for three days. On the fourth day, Mr MacKay summed up with these words:

"I find the charges against Eugene O'Connor have been created by a feeling of distrust by the memorialists against him, combined with a feeling of jealousy and suspicion against each other, and that this combination of causes has led them to magnify suspicion into certainties, and to form conclusions in many instances altogether unwarrantable.[42]"

There was a stunned and unhappy silence, as we were not satisfied with the findings of the enquiry. Not even O'Connor (who was exonerated) gloated, because his pride was wounded.

"What does he mean by 'memorialists?'" said Daniel, as MacKay slipped the documents and papers into his case. Everyone looked blank.

"Gossips perhaps?" said Henry Haws.

As nobody had a better idea, we agreed it was so.

"No account books were produced," I grumbled, as we shuffled one by one out the door. "He should have delved into the thousands of pounds that have mysteriously vanished."

Daniel picked up a stick and slashed the air with it.

"Not only that, a great deal of relevant evidence for our side was struck out and omitted."

"It's not all bad," said Thomas Lineham, "the steamer is to call again."

Alfred smiled and clapped Thomas on his back. "My ever-cheerful brother. Trust you to find something good, Tom."

"Well, it is good."

"Alright, I don't deny the steamer coming again, and more often than every six weeks, is great."

"I think the Official Party's journey over the Rough and

42   Taken from the report by Mr A MacKay concerning the petition of the Karamea Special Settlement

To Own a Fig Tree

Tumble Track might have played a big part in that decision," Jennings chuckled. "If they could have reinstated the steamer service in time for the *Charley* to take them home, they would have!"

When we stopped laughing, I said:

"We must also thank God the evil system of *Truck* has ended, and O'Connor is kicked out."

Unfortunately, O'Connor overheard my comment as he came out the door. He strode a short distance past us before turning and yelling:

"You can crow now, Robert Johnson, but Karamea will not benefit from being under the Buller County Council, if the Council does not make better use of expenditure at Karamea than they are doing with the county funds! You wait, in a few years, you will wish you had stayed with me, but it will be too late."

Then the deposed Father-of-Karamea, turned on his heel and stalked off.

"That was awkward," said Daniel. "It is a pity he has cattle and land in Karamea."

"He's a busy politician who lives in Westport," said Jennings, "he won't be here much."

There was a small commotion behind us and turning we saw the Simpsons bidding the Official Party goodbye.

We stepped to either side of the doorway and lifted our hats as MacKay, his secretary, and Ings hobbled out. They nodded to us before limping away slowly.

"Poor things," said Mrs Simpson, waving. "They have more blisters than skin on their feet. It's good I had plenty of sticking plasters in my medicine box."

W.E. Hamilton

I remembered Andrena's accusations. Narrowing my eyes, I said sharply:

"When did you get a medicine box?"

Mrs Simpson stamped her foot. "Long before we came here, Robert Johnson. The Magistrate was right when he called you all a suspicious and jealous lot!" She sniffed, and put her nose in the air. "And he should know, for he is a Parliament-Gentleman, and what's more, he appreciates lace curtains and English wallpaper."

To Own a Fig Tree

The Great Flood

It was spring at last, and life was good. Yellow flowers dripped from the bare branches of the kowhai tree, and glorious white swathes of clematis flowers dotted the bush. On the Johnson farm, winter corn towered twelve feet into the air, and Bessy had calved again. There was a pleasant breeze as we stood around her, admiring the new calf.

"Little Dewdrop makes five cows! We are going up in the world," said Andrena, stroking the calf as she suckled. "And when Daisy calves, we will have six."

William stopped whistling. "Not if he is a bobby-calf."

"We will still have six even if he is a boy," said Margret, scratching the root of Dewdrop's tail.

"No," William put his hands in his pockets and rocked back and forth on his toes. "We will have five cows and a good dinner."

"Willie!" squealed Margret, "don't be so awful!" She turned puppy eyes on me. "We won't really eat Daisy's calf if it is a boy, will we, Dad?"

"Not until he is as big as Clarabelle and Buttercup," I said, looking at the sleek yearlings munching ferns at the edge of our clearing.

Robert turned a sailor's eye on the gathering clouds. "A storm is coming. You should shut Bessy and Dewdrop in the shed."

"And Daisy too," said Anderina, "she is due to calf."

I looked at the ponga hut behind the house and stroked my chin thoughtfully. "It will be a bit of a squeeze."

"There will be enough room," said Anderina, "we don't want Daisy running off in a storm and having her calf somewhere in the bush."

The little breeze suddenly quickened into blustery wind, and the cornstalks shook.

"Tether Bessy and Daisy up the hill, Margret," I said, my mind on the corn, "so we can get them into the shed quickly if we need to."

"Do you think we should harvest some of the corn, Dad?" said John, noticing my preoccupation.

"I don't know," I said slowly. "It could do with a bit longer."

"It wouldn't be a bad idea to bring in the corn closest to the river," said Robert, "with thawing snow from the mountains, the river could rise quickly."

I hesitated, but spits of rain and a rumble of thunder wiped indecision away.

"Everyone put on coats and grab a basket."

We ran to the house and were back within minutes. I pulled a stalk down, and grasping an ear, twisted it off and prised the leaves apart. The kernels were small and hard.

"I'd rather wait a week, but I think it is wiser to get it in now," I said, putting my hat on as the spits turned into rain, and the rain became a deluge.

We picked furiously, but we had hardly finished harvesting the first row when we heard a loud rumbling.

"I can hear the Westport train," said Anderina, pausing in surprise.

To Own a Fig Tree

"It can't be the train, we're too far away!"

Robert went white and let go of the stalk he was holding.

"IT'S A FLASH FLOOD," he yelled, "RUN TO HIGHER GROUND!"

Margret and Elizabeth screamed, threw down their baskets, and along with their brothers ran towards the Zig-Zag track. I also started running, but Anderina bent to pick up fallen ears.

"FORGET THE CORN, ANDERINA," I shouted, grabbing her hand and pulling her. "WE ARE TOO CLOSE TO THE RIVER!"

Then we both ran swifter than we thought possible, past the house and up the hill. And not a moment too soon, for mounting headwaters sent a mighty flow of water rampaging from the mountains. Gaining momentum and debris as it rushed in its headlong flight, the river disgorged tons of silt and boulders over the farms it passed. It missed the cows, but swamped the house, and swept the entire corn crop away. When the storm was over and the water had receded, we surveyed the damage.

"Once again the North Bankers got off easier than we did," I said jealously.

"I hope Mary and John are alright," said Anderina.

"They're fine," said Laurie, "I climbed a tree and saw them putting more thatch on the roof of their hut."

"Thank God for that," said Anderina, sighing in relief. "I couldn't bear it if anything happened to Mary."

"We didn't get to eat our corn," said Margret, her mouth drooping. "All that work and nothing to show for it."

"Our baskets and even Peter's little pear tree are gone," said Elizabeth, as she hung wet bedding over a line stretched between two trees.

Anderina wrung water from a blanket.

"We can plant more corn and another pear. The main thing is none of us were killed. I hope Robert's house is alright."

William stopped whistling long enough to say cheerfully:

"I saw someone's roof floating down the river."

"It won't be Robert's roof, you awful child," said Margret, "Robert's house is downstream."

"Hello, Johnsons," called a voice, and out of the bush came Daniel and Harriet.

"Hello, Scarletts."

"I see like us you lost your corn," said Daniel. "Is the house very damaged?"

"Only the bottom of my wallpaper," said Anderina with a sigh. "And that's not much of a loss for it was already banged up."

"What about you?"

"A couple of gaps in the walls but nothing a few ponga trunks won't fix," said Harriet. "Not like our poor brethren up Paradise Road."

"What of them?"

"Have you not heard?"

"No."

"Their farms are ruined by silt and boulders."

"If they can't get more land, they will have to leave Karamea," said Robert, overhearing us as he came up the driveway. "So much for this being God's Land of Promise! We have had one trouble after another."

"Don't speak like that, Son," I said, "before you take the land, there are always giants to fight. Faith WILL prevail, and we WILL become established."

To Own a Fig Tree

Robert rolled his eyes.

"Yeah right! Like your fig tree that never comes."

"It's all about timing, Bob; God will send the fig tree when we most need it."

Fear suddenly flooded Anderina's face.

"Does this cynicism mean you've lost your house, Bob?"

"No, no, it's fine. It's far enough up the hill that the river never got to it."

Anderina relaxed.

"That's a relief. You have put so much work into it I'd hate to think it had been destroyed."

"The floor is soaked, of course," said Robert, "because the rain came in through the gaps for the door and windows, but it will soon dry out."

"Are you going to ask Elizabeth Scarlett to marry you once the windows and doors are in?" said Margret, winking cheekily at her brother.

Robert's face flamed as he hissed under his breath:

"*Shut up! I haven't asked her father yet.*"

Daniel looked the other way and pretended he was deaf, but Harriet squeezed Robert's hand and whispered:

"Don't worry, Bob, we heard nothing."

Daisy saved the awkward moment. She had separated herself from the other cows, and was sitting down and standing up repeatedly; all the while making little grunting sounds.

"I think your cow is about to give birth, Robert," said Daniel, observing the cow's unusual behaviour.

"Your right," I said, "I can see the water-bag protruding."

"Harriet and I will go," said Daniel, "the less disturbance around her the better."

Daniel and I shook hands, and they left.

We went about our business while quietly keeping an eye on Daisy, and within two hours, a spotty little calf staggered to her feet.

"Six cows, how wonderful," said Anderina, watching Daisy lick the calf as it suckled.

"The black circles around her eyes are so pretty," said Margret. "We should call her Spotty."

Only William was disappointed. He stopped whistling a hymn and surveyed Spotty glumly.

"What a pity. I was looking forward to a good dinner."

To Own a Fig Tree

Be Fruitful and Increase

In hindsight, Karamea's third anniversary was a turning point. It marked the end of our turbulent beginning, and the start of the settled years. The garden was growing enormous vegetables and the memorial trees in the orchard were flourishing. As well as Mary and John's apple, there was a replacement pear for Peter Coutts, and James' death tree was a peach. Then it was time for Anderina to blow the dust off her midwifery bag, starting with John and Mary's first daughter, Jemima Anne McHarrie.

"A nice touch calling her after that poor young widow," said Anderina, rocking the baby as John and Mary planted a second pear tree.

"I think she will not be a widow for much longer," said Robert. "Harry is very faithful in keeping his pledge to look after her." He took Elizabeth's hand. "If I'm not mistaken, they'll marry shortly after Elizabeth and me."

He was right. Robert married Elizabeth Scarlett on Christmas Eve, 1877, and Harry Lineham married Jemima Coutts less than two months later.

"If you don't mind, Dad, I'd like my marriage tree on my own land," said Robert, when he saw me perusing a farming catalogue. "And I'd rather have something bigger and showier than a fruit tree."

So, I sent for a jacaranda and he planted it by himself.

W.E. Hamilton

While it delighted us that Robert and Elizabeth's marriage joined the Johnson and Scarletts together, the union brought a novel problem in its wake. Until July, 1878, we had two Elizabeth Johnsons in the family.

"Which was jolly confusing," said Mary, patting baby Jemima Anne on the back. "Thank you, Charles, for marrying Our-Liz and solving the problem."

"It is me you should thank for the Elizabeths swapping names," said Margret with a cheeky grin, as Charles and Elizabeth planted an apricot seedling, "I suggested it."

"You think too much of yourself, sister-in-law," Charles laughed, as he tamped the soil around the tree. "It was my own idea."

Like our grandchildren's names, the trees at first were common varieties. We planted another apple for Harriet Anne Johnson, and plums for Mary Jane McHarrie, Mary Anne Scarlett, Andrena Alice Johnson, and Jan Margret McHarry.

Technically, Dobbin should not have got a tree, but we planted a crab apple in his honour because, besides being my first horse, he was the first horse of Karamea.

After the first horse came the first grandson.

"His name is Robert," said Elizabeth, as we clustered around the new arrival.

Laurence sighed.

"Three Robert Johnsons is worse than two Elizabeths, with no hope of marriage changing their names."

"We can't break the family tradition, Laurie," said Robert-the-second.

"We will call him Bobby," said Elizabeth.

Little Bobby's tree was a chestnut.

To Own a Fig Tree

"I plant this as a symbol of Robert-the-thirds life," I said, as I watered it. "May he grow into a strong man of God, a sheltering tree to those who depend on him, a man mighty in faith, full of kindness and wisdom. Amen."

"Amen," said everyone but his father.

Instead of amen, Robert said:

"Are you still waiting in vain for your fig tree, Dad?"

I nodded.

"God's timing is perfect; he will send the tree when we need it most."

"Yeah, right," said Robert, rolling his eyes.

Although I believed my words, I did not enjoy my son taunting me. When John Scarlett was born, I tried extra hard to get a fig tree, and for a brief time I thought I had tracked one down, but it was a false hope for when the steamer came, I found they had sent me a bay tree.

"It's a good thing I kept the fig tree a surprise," I said to Anderina, "for if Robert knew I'd been expecting a fig, he would never let me live it down."

After the fig fiasco, there was a grapefruit for little William Scarlett, and a lemon for Margret Elizabeth Johnson.

The school we built at Arapito had to be honoured.

"Not a tree," said William, rubbing the seat of his trousers, "a cane is more appropriate."

We laughed and planted a raspberry in, 1880. The blackberry came four years later when the school burnt down, and the boysenberry was to thank the Education Board for replacing it.

Then we were back to babies, and a dispute blew up between Laurie and Anderina over the tree for John and Mary's third daughter.

"We need another lemon," said Anderina, "they are so useful one is not enough."

"*A sour lemon,*" said Laurie, his face a mask of horror. "The poor kid needs some sort of compensation for the name Euphemia."

He had a valid point. So, Jessie Euphemia McHarrie got a pawpaw tree, and her sister Isabell Catherine got the lemon.

"Such a little pet," said Anderina, when Rose Ellen Scarlett arrived. "And perfect timing, for I saw in the catalogue there is a special on orange trees."

After so many girls, it was nice when Robert and Elizabeth's next four children were boys.

I cleared a wide strip of land and planted a macadamia, pecan, and walnut tree, for Daniel, John-the-Second, Laurence William, and George Cooper Johnson.

In 1888, we became the proud owners of twenty-five acres.

"Only half of what we were promised, but better than nothing," I said.

"The horse and school have monuments," said Anderina, "the farm must also be honoured."

So, I planted two grapevines; one on each block of land.

"Thank you, Lord, for delivering us from three-hundred-years of bondage," I prayed, planting a black grape near the house.

"Thank you God for giving us the Promised Land," Anderina prayed, digging a green grape into the new land.

The herb garden went in when William Morris-Jenkins settled in Little Wanganui.

"Our very own doctor," said Andrena, planting lavender and rosemary.

To Own a Fig Tree

"Not quite," said Our-Elizabeth, digging in camomile and feverfew. "Fourteen miles is a long way away, and he isn't fully qualified."

"Doctor Jenkins finished his medical course before leaving England," said Anderina defensively, "and he would have passed his final examinations if he hadn't sailed here instead. We can rely on him to attend to accidents and render first aid."

"If he waited a little longer," said Our-Elizabeth, reaching for the parsley, "he would have been able to perform surgical operations as well."

"Give it up, Sis," said Willie, "Mum is his biggest fan since he praised her for her midwifery skills."

"Ninety babies and I've not lost one," said Anderina, with justifiable pride.

After Doctor Jenkins and the herbs, we were back to girls and apple trees with Martha Mary Scarlett, and Emily Alice McHarrie, before swapping to nut trees with David Scarlett and William McHarrie. Twins, Laura Ida, and Wilimiena Martha McHarrie, broke the pattern with a tamarillo plant and kiwi fruit vine.

The flour mill was a grand enterprise.

"Not a tree for my husband's new business," said Our-Elizabeth, "plant grain, for Charles and his partner, George Allen, need something to grind."

So, I cleared a field and planted it in wheat.

By 1892, an extensive orchard surrounded our house, and we were running out of recycled names; Sarah Emma Case Johnson enjoyed three brand-new names and a banana palm.

"We have so many grandchildren I can't keep track of them all," I said to Anderina, as we watched them running around under the shady trees. "And now Margret has married Norman Winstanley, and John is married to Martha Crabb, there will be a lot more on the way. I keep muddling Arthur Thomas up with Robert William, and I have no idea which twin is which."

Andrena eyed me thoughtfully.

"What you need is a pipe."

"A pipe?"

"Yes, a pipe. Now that you are a sixty-seven-year-old grandfather, a pipe would be just the thing. It would make you look distinguished and sophisticated."

"How does that help me with the grandchildren?"

"On Sunday, when the whole family comes to dinner, you can sit under the trees in summer, or beside the fire in winter, contentedly smoking, and when Arthur Thomas or Robert William come past, you can take a nice little suck on your pipe before saying, 'hello boys.'"

"Couldn't I do that without smoking?"

"No, no." Anderina shook her head emphatically. "It wouldn't be the same. When you get around to ordering the pigs, let me know and I will pick out a handsome pipe for you."

When our order came on the *Charley*, I was satisfied with my choice, but not Anderina's.

"Those pigs are good eaters, they'll eat anything," I said to her, as I settled into my rocking chair by the fire. "I tipped corncobs, potato and onion skins into their troughs and they woofed them down. At this rate, they will fatten up fast."

"Here is your pipe and baccy, Robert," said Anderina, as I pulled off my boots and put on my slippers.

"Do I have to smoke?"

"Yes."

To Own a Fig Tree

"But I don't like it."

"You will grow to like it."

"If God wanted us to smoke, he would have given us chimneys on our heads."

My wife put her hands on her hips. "Fiddle-dee-dee. That's like saying if God wanted you to wear clothes you would have been born in trousers."

To please my wife, I filled the bowl of the beastly thing and lit it.

"Ah," said Anderina, inhaling deeply. "Such a nice smell."

"Here," I stretched out my hand with the pipe. "You smoke it."

My wife, looking scandalized, pushed my hand away. "Don't be silly, Robert, only vulgar rough women smoke pipes."

I sucked tentatively on the pipe's stem, and was rewarded with a bout of coughing.

"That is not the way to do it, Robert, you are supposed to look contented - like a cat lying by the fire."

"I'd like to see you do better," I spluttered between coughs.

"Keep at it," said my wife hardheartedly as she picked up her knitting. "Other men manage to be ornamental."

Then she sat in the rocking chair on the other side of the fire, and the clock on the mantlepiece ticked loudly in the companionable silence.

"The house is empty without all the children," said Anderina, casting on stitches.

"We still have Laurie and Willie at home."

"I know, but it is not the same. They are either working, or Willie is visiting young Jane Ogg, while Laurie is wooing

Augusta Fullen."

"Perhaps I'll find fig trees for their weddings," I said, considering Anderina's fingers.

"You never know," said Anderina, knitting purl and plain stitches alternatively. "With, God, anything is possible."

"What's happened to your hands, Rina? They used to be slim and smooth."

Anderina stopped knitting and flexed them stiffly. Her once nimble fingers were thick and knobby. "Arthritis, the occupational hazard of growing old."

"Are they painful?"

"Terribly, when the weather gets cold or a storm is brewing." She took up her needles and wool and started knitting again. "But they are alright tonight."

I watched the old fingers moving methodically and slowly, as I took the occasional puff.

"Where has the time gone?"

"Where indeed?"

The smoke from the pipe was dwindling and with further neglect, quietly went out. The evening suddenly took a turn for the better as Anderina was preoccupied and I did not draw attention to the pipe's demise. Instead, I rocked back and forth sucking the cold stem in a relaxed manner.

"Now you are getting the hang of it. That's the look I wanted," said Andrena. "Take your pipe around the farm with you tomorrow, and practice throughout the day."

I was not keen, nevertheless, to please my wife I put it in my pocket before I went to feed the pigs the next morning. I had mixed feelings that evening when I found it gone, for I did not want to face my wife's wrath. I hunted about for it, but as

To Own a Fig Tree

I had not bothered to smoke that day, I had no idea where or when I'd lost it.

"You've hidden it," said Andrena, glaring at me.

"No," I said, laying my hand on the Bible. "I declare before, God, I have not hidden or destroyed it."

"Well, I'll have to believe you because you are a truthful man," said Anderina, sulkily, "but it seems rather convenient."

It was Willie who found it, because it was his turn to slop the pigs.

"Look what I found in the pig's trough," he said, holding my pipe aloft? "It was sitting on top of a corncob. The pigs had eaten everything except it and the cob. They must hate the smell of tobacco if they refuse to eat the cob under it."

I got out of my chair and taking my pipe from Willie, threw it into the fire.

"What did you do that for, Robert?" said Anderina, looking cross. "We could have washed it."

"The pipe is where it should be," I said, unmoved by her annoyance. "There must be something very wrong with smoking if the pigs won't touch it."

W.E. Hamilton

Two Sorts of Blindness

Robert's house stood in a clearing amid tall trees. Anderina and I admired it as we walked up the hill towards the open door.

"Our son's house is superior to most of the settler's houses," said Anderina, her breath hanging like mist in the early morning air. "It would not look out of place in Nelson."

I picked up a long tea-tree stick with my gloved hand.

"Much better than a raupo hut or a cabin covered with a tarpaulin," I agreed.

"If I were twenty years younger, I'd like a two-storied place, myself," said Anderina. "The way the attic room peeps out from under the gable is charming."

I nodded, and dug my stick into the ground as the path steepened.

"I hope Bob passes his captain's certificate," I said, switching to the purpose of our visit. "He will be gutted if he misses it."

"Don't fret, Robert, I'm sure he will. The time you have spent drilling him on his questions will give him confidence."

Two small heads popped up at the attic window, waved and disappeared abruptly. Shortly after, seven-year-old Daniel and six-year-old John, burst out the door and flung themselves at us.

"Hello, Granny and Granddad."

To Own a Fig Tree

"Hello boys," I said, ruffling their hair as Anderina stooped to kiss them. "How is the cow-riding going?"

"Pretty good," said Dan. "Come and watch Bobby and us ride the bull."

"Bull riding!" Anderina exclaimed. "I don't like the sound of that!"

"Oh Granny, he's blind and very tame."

"You can't trust a bull," said Anderina, unconvinced, "not even a blind one."

"You can trust this one," said John. "Come and see him, Granddad."

"After I have helped your father."

By now Robert-the-third and Margret Elizabeth were running down the path.

"Hello, Bobby and Margret."

"I caught an eel yesterday," shouted Bobby.

"And I finished knitting my first shawl," said Margret, bouncing up and down as they all ushered us onto the veranda and into the house.

"Where is your father, dear?" said Anderina, as we removed our hats and gloves.

Margret took our things and put them on the hall table beside the sloping wall of the staircase. "He's in the parlour."

"Hello, Mum and Dad," said Robert, coming out of a front room. "I thought I heard voices."

"We're in the kitchen," Elizabeth called from the end of the hallway. "Come and have tea before you start."

"That's a good idea," I said, stepping into the large kitchen that ran the full width of the house. "Perhaps I will."

"It's nice and warm in here," said Anderina, kissing Harriet,

Anderina Alice, and baby Sarah.

"Partitioning the house into spaces makes it much easier to heat small pockets," Robert said. "You should think about dividing your house into rooms, Dad."

"We don't need five rooms, a hall, and an attic, like this one," said Anderina, "the rooms would be tiny, for our house is smaller." She looked around the timber-lined room with the big fireplace. "I wouldn't mind a kitchen like this though. It's warm and cosy but there is plenty of space for the table and sofa."

"Not five rooms, Mum," said Robert, "three. A short hallway with a room off each side and the kitchen at the back like this."

"Hmm," I said, "I like that idea."

The baby grizzled and Anderina forgot everything else.

"Come to Granny, Poppet," she cooed, taking Sarah from Harriet before easing into a rocking chair by the hearth.

The fourteen-year-old relinquished her charge with relief.

"Put the kettle on, Reena," said Elizabeth, wiping a strand of hair off her face with a flour-covered hand. "I'll make the tea as soon as I finish kneading this dough."

Anderina Alice spun around and her skirts flared out as she twirled towards the open fire.

"Careful, watch your skirt, Reena!" Anderina cried out in alarm.

"I've told you not to dance in the kitchen," Elizabeth scolded her second daughter. "Thirteen is too old for that sort of silliness."

"Far too dangerous," I said.

Anderina nodded.

To Own a Fig Tree

"In *Zetland*, we used to say the men die in the sea and the women die over their fire."

"Oh, Granny," said Anderina Alice, pulling the iron crane over the flames. "That was in the olden days. Things like that don't happen now."

"Granny Johnson is right, young lady," said her mother. "Where there is water and fire there is always danger." She scooped up the smooth dough and dumped it into a camp oven.

"Speaking of dangerous," said Anderina, "the boys say they are riding your bull, Bob."

"He's not dangerous," said Robert. "I got him dirt cheap, and I'm training him to pull a cart and plough."

"I still don't like it."

"Oh, Mum! The worst he's done is sit on the road. Henry Wood came careening down the hill on his bike on a dark night, and rode into him."

"Serves Henry right," said Elizabeth, rolling her eyes. "I told him he needed a light on his bike, but he wouldn't listen."

Anderina Alice giggled and took up the story.

"We heard someone pounding on the door, and when Dad opened it, there was Mr Wood looking as white as a sheet, shouting that the bull had attacked him."

"Actually, he attacked the poor old bull," said Dan.

While we were talking, Harriet was laying cups and saucers on the large wooden table surrounded by spindle-back chairs.

"Dad, pass me the sugar, please,"

Robert twisted around and gazed at the preserves and bottles on the shelves of the hutch dresser.

"Which is which?" he said, looking at two identical jars.

"The one with the red lid is the sugar."

W.E. Hamilton

Robert hesitated before handing Harriet the jar with the green lid.

"Not the salt, Dad. I said the sugar is in the red jar."

"Hold on a minute, son," I said, taking both jars in my hands and putting them behind my back.

I shuffled them around and held them out. "Point to the red one, Bob."

Robert started to point at one jar, then looking confused pointed at the other.

"That one, ah no, that one."

"What colour is the tea caddy?" I asked as Elizabeth (with little George clinging to her skirts) opened a green canister and spooned leaves into the teapot.

"I dunno, red?"

Anderina gasped and opened her mouth, but I held up my hand to silence her.

"And what colour is that?" I said, pointing to the scarlet tea cosy lying beside the teapot.

"Green?"

"Oh, Bob," said Anderina, "you're colour blind! How did I not realize?"

"Dad's blind like the bull," said Daniel in dismay.

"Don't be silly, Dan," said his mother, "of course your father can see."

"Colour blind, fancy that!" said Robert, a light dawning in his eyes. "That explains why red and green look the same to me." He picked up a thick maritime manual lying on the hutch dresser. "There is another fire in the parlour, Dad. You can test me in there where it is quieter."

I took the two cups Elizabeth handed me, and followed him

To Own a Fig Tree

out of the kitchen, past the staircase in the hallway and into the front room. Robert dropped the manual onto an easy chair and threw another couple of logs in the grate.

"Just let me get this going better," he said, taking down a pair of bellows and pumping air until the embers leapt into flames.

I put our tea on a low table, pulled a chair closer to the fire, and taking up the manual sat down. The square room with its single window overlooking the river, was pleasant. Signs of Elizabeth's excellent housekeeping skills abounded; from the tidy curtains to the braided rag-rug on the floor, and the flowers in the jampot on the mantelpiece. When the fire was crackling merrily, Robert took his cup and after several sips, said:

"Pick a question at random and read it out, Dad."

I put my cup down and leafed through the pages.

"Alright. What is the rule of good seamanship?"

"Nothing excuses a mariner who doesn't take prudent steps for special circumstances requiring extra precautions."

I scanned the document.

"Yarda yarda yar, yes, that's roughly it."

"Ask me another one."

"What is dead reckoning?"

"Calculating the current position by applying the course and speed to a previously calculated position."

"Correct."

I flipped through more pages and my heart suddenly sank.

"Identify a red and green signal."

"Let me see that," said Robert, snatching the manual from me. His eyes roamed over the page and when he saw the sentence, his shoulders sagged and he ran his hand over his face in a despairing gesture. "That's it, I can't pass this."

"It's not completely over."

"Yes, it is. I can't tell the difference."

"Well, how do you manage when you are out at sea?"

"The red buoys are on the starboard side of the channel, and the green buoys are on the port side. Besides, there is always someone on the boat who can see colours."

"My advice to you, son, is don't give up. Take your exam and just guess. Who knows? you might get them right!"

Robert sighed and picked up his hat and coat.

"I wish there was a more certain way. It is a long trek to Westport if it is for nothing."

"Like they say, 'nothing ventured, nothing gained,'" I said, following him out of the room. "I'll keep you company for the first few miles."

Robert was away for several days. When we next saw him, he was driving a cart made of logs.

"Don't call me Robert Junior anymore," he shouted, drawing the bull to a halt before jumping down. "I am Captain Johnson of Johnson's Landing."

"Congratulations, Bob," I said, shaking his hand. "Did they ask about red and green signals?"

"Yes. The fellow taking me through the questions flashed two cards in front of me and said 'which is red and which is green.' Of course, I had no idea, but I took a wild guess and got it right. So now," he pulled his new captain's cap onto a jaunty angle, "I have a Certificate of Competence with a provisional Captain's ticket." He leaned against the placid bull and scratched behind his horns. "This old fellow and I might be blind, but it does not stop us from doing our jobs well."

To Own a Fig Tree

The Dairy Cooperative

Buttercup stood in the ponga cowshed munching hay from the manger. The gentle hissing sound stopped, and Anderina got off the low milking stool slowly.

"I can't keep this up much longer," she said, pulling the pail out from under Buttercup. "A dozen cows are a lot for an old couple to milk."

"Are your hands hurting, Dreena?"

"Something fierce. And not just my hands these days. Arthritis has moved into my knees and feet."

"Oh dear," I said, feeling very sorry for my wife. "Don't worry about milking anymore, I can manage by myself."

"Twelve cows are too much for you, love. Perhaps Willie could help?"

"I can't ask him now that he has his own farm to break in. He is too busy bush felling and milking his own cows."

"You are right. He has enough to do without us adding to his burden." Anderina bent to pick up her pail, but I stopped her.

"Leave that. I'll carry the milk," I said, lifting two buckets.

Anderina smiled at me gratefully as she untied Buttercup and led her out of the cowshed.

"Harriet is a big girl," she said, letting the cow go.

"How old is she now?" I said, as we plodded towards the house.

"Fifteen. Perhaps Elizabeth could spare her a few mornings a week."

"That's a good idea," I said, clomping onto our new veranda and down the hallway to the kitchen.

"Not in there, put it in the front room, Robert. You'll find the bowls in there because the room is cooler."

"It was a good idea to divide the house," I said, backtracking and turning into the room on the left.

"It certainly was."

I poured the milk into the bowls on the table, while Anderina pulled the roller blind down.

"Leave that up until I get the milk poured; it's hard to see what I'm doing."

Anderina yanked the blind's string and the brown canvass shot up the window with a rattle.

"It does a good job of keeping the room dark and cool," said Anderina, covering the bowls of milk with clean cheesecloths. She bustled out to the kitchen and returned with a flat wide spoon and the butter churn.

"Does churning hurt too, love?"

"Yes," she admitted, scooping cream off the top of yesterday's milk. "But I try not to think about it."

"Dan and John would turn the handle for a piece of toffee each," I expect.

Anderina smiled as she filled the wooden barrel with cream.

"You're right. Those two scallywags would walk to Westport for toffee. I will make some this afternoon."

I chuckled before returning to the cowshed for the rest of the milk. When I got back to the house Anderina had skimmed all the cream, so after tipping the fresh milk into pans, I collected

To Own a Fig Tree

the skim milk and fed it to the pigs. That afternoon, as soon as I heard the rumble of wooden wheels, I went to the end of our driveway, and looking to the right, saw my son coming towards me in his homemade cart. I could see by the tilt of his cap he was not plain old Robert Junior driving a cattle cart, but Captain Johnson sailing his steamer through the sea.

"Ahoy Captain Johnson," I called, waving.

"HEAVE TO," the captain shouted, and the bull and cow stopped.

"I see you've made modifications to your ship," I said, looking at the contraption made from two logs sawn from the trunk of a large tree.

Dan and John laughed while Margret pouted.

"We had a little accident earlier today," said Captain Johnson, touching his captain's cap, "so the boys built the bow higher."

"Was anyone hurt?" I said alarmed.

"Only Maggie's pride."

"And my white pinafore," said Margret, "all the bluing in the world won't take the stains out of it."

"The bull pooped over her," chuckled Robert, momentarily forgetting he was a captain. "Too much lush grass."

"It shot out like brown liquid from a hose," said Dan. "Serve you right Margret for hogging the front seat. You should have sat in the stern."

"Now, now, enough of that," said his father. "I want to talk to you about something, Dad. But first, what did you want to see me about?"

"Milk and butter."

Robert slapped his knee in delight.

"That is exactly what I wanted to talk about. No settlers are happy with the way the store pays us for our butter. *Truck* is degrading. Moreover, cash has bargaining power when buying equipment and stock. We are independent farmers and we want cash, not truck."

"Woah! You're thinking so much bigger than I am. I was only going to ask if the children could help with milking and churning."

"Of course," said Robert with a dismissive wave of his hand. "I'll send Harriet and John tomorrow." His gaze intensified as he returned to his former subject. "I am calling a community meeting at Johnson's Landing tomorrow, will you come?

"Certainly."

"Good, I'll see you there then." He twitched his hat and reverting to Captain Johnson, called:

"ALL ABOARD."

At this, John and Dan, who were scratching sticks in the dust, leapt onto the cart.

"WEIGH THE ANCHOR," shouted Captain Johnson.

Then, flicking the rope running through the sacking yokes on the beasts, they trundled off.

Accordingly, on April the twenty-sixth, 1893, I made my way along the bullock track to Johnson's Landing. When I got there, many rafts and dugouts were tied to the piles of the wharf. It was a pleasant day, so we gathered outside in the clearing at the end of the wharf. Then Captain Johnson, looking splendid in his cap and full beard, addressed the owner of the store.

"Hubert Dolphin, we request you pay us in cash for our butter. What do you say to that?"

"I say, no," said Hubert. "Some of you still owe me money

To Own a Fig Tree

and I can't afford to pay in cash."

The crowd rumbled and shuffled their feet in a dissatisfied manner.

"Is that your last word on the matter, Hubert Dolphin?"

"It is, *Robert Johnson Junior.*"

"It's *Captain Johnson,* Dolphin, and don't you forget it."

"Hoity-toity, you are giving yourself airs."

"I propose," said Captain Johnson, swallowing his rage with difficulty, "that we refuse to give our butter to this swindler, and instead band together to form a dairy cooperative."

"A dairy cooperative?"

The idea electrified the mood of the crowd.

"How could we," shouted someone?

"Between us, we have three-hundred-and-ten cows, plenty of labour and timber. If we divide the company into nine-hundred one-pound shares, we could build a factory and form the first cooperative dairy company in the Westcoast."

A great cheer arose until Henry Haws shouted:

"How would we sell our produce?"

"We could pack it in casks and store it in a pit until the *Charley* comes to take it to Westport."

By now, the cheers were loud and long.

Amid the excitement, several motions were moved and accepted, and by the time we dispersed, the butcher, Meyrick Jones, was Secretary of the Karamea Dairy Company, and I was one of the many shareholders.

Riding on the first flush of enthusiasm, we built the factory within weeks. We sold our milk to the Co-op for three pennies a gallon, and butter was stored in the pit we dug in the bank beside the factory. I would like to say the venture was a success from the start, but the reality was different.

"The difficulty is putting butter on the market in good condition," said Robert, twisting his precious cap between his hands. "No matter how hard we try, much of the butter is rancid by the time the *Charley* gets here."

"The idea of a dairy company is sound."

"I know, Dad." Robert pulled a rueful face. "But without our own steamer, we are sunk."

And so we were. We struggled on a little longer, but after a mere four seasons, we admitted defeat, and went back to swapping butter for goods with Hubert Dolphin and our neighbours.

To Own a Fig Tree

Robert buys a boat

Sometime after the collapse of the dairy company, Robert and I were in Little Wanganui when Captain Bloomfield brought his fishing smack up the river. There was nothing unusual about a boat on the river, what caught my son's eye was the for-sale painted on the *SS Picton*'s side.

"There is Karamea's salvation," he said, pointing at the steamer. He twitched his hat and morphed into Captain Johnson. "With her I'll destroy isolation and assist the dairy industry."

"You can't afford to buy that boat!" I said, my mind reeling at the grandiose words.

"No, but the Karamea Steamship Company can."

"There is no Karamea Steamship Company."

"There will be once I form it. Twenty-two investors ought to be enough."

"Like the Karamea Dairy Company? That was hardly a booming success."

Captain Johnson deflated into Robert.

"A horse without legs is no use. It failed because we did not have a steamer. Transport once a month or less is no good. We had to store the butter for too long. When we have our own delivery system, things will be different."

My eldest son was a strong man with an unusually forceful character. I could feel myself being sucked into his vision as we watched the *SS Picton* chug to the wharf.

"Stanley Allen is interested in buying some of my land," I said, succumbing to the inevitable. "I don't need all of my twenty-five acres."

"Now you're thinking, Dad. Let's go and talk to the captain."

We wandered along the timber boards of the dock until we got close to the vessel.

"Ahoy, *Picton*," called Robert, twitching his hat again. "Captain Johnson requesting permission to board."

"Welcome, gentlemen," said a thin man coming out of the cab, "I'm Captain Bloomfield. He dropped a gangplank onto the wharf and we walked over it and into the boat.

"I see your fishing smack is for sale," said Captain Johnson, getting straight to the point.

"I'm not the owner," said Captain Bloomfield, "she is owned by John Hornby, a saw miller in Picton. If you are interested in her you will need to see the harbour-master of Westport, he is in charge of negotiations."

"Captain Leech, I know him well! He helped me gain my Certificate of Competence by procuring work for me aboard vessels trading along the coast. Perhaps you could show me around before I see him?"

"Certainly." Captain Bloomfield pointed at the bow and swept his hand around to the stern. "As you see, she's an open type launch with no mast, forty-one foot long, nine by four wide."

Captain Johnson adjusted his cap and nodded. "Where was she built?"

"Wellington in 1880, by David Robertson and Company,"

To Own a Fig Tree

said Captain Bloomfield, leading the way into the cab and below deck. "Two eight-horse-power engines," he said, as we peered at the pistons. "The boiler's good, but she's rather shallow in the draught, I'm afraid."

"Shallow is exactly what I am after," said Captain Johnson, examining the fish-well in the dim light. He tapped the side of the boat and squinted at a small leak. "I want her for Karamea."

"Karamea!" Captain Bloomfield's eyebrows shot up. "Rather you than me, that bar is treacherous."

"The bar is difficult, but not impassable," Captain Johnson said in a preoccupied tone. He picked at a spot of rot with his pocketknife. "What's the price John Hornby wants for her?"

"I'm not sure. You would have to ask Captain Leech. All I can tell you is Hornby wants out, and will sell cheap."

My son's eyes glinted. He put away his knife and rubbed his moustache with the side of his index finger. "My only concern is she may be too small for the Dairy Company's needs," he said, forgetting to be a captain in his desire for a bargain.

"Yes, yes, too small," I whispered from the side of my mouth. "Keep looking, Bob, something better will come up."

"Don't be so hasty," hissed Robert, as we climbed back into the light. "If the price is right, we can make-do."

I trailed behind him as he pottered about the deck, looking at the condition of the vessel and gear. At last, he had seen enough.

"Thank you, Captain Bloomfield," he said, tipping his cap. "I'll be in touch."

When we got out of earshot, Robert let out a yell of joy and threw his cap into the air.

"Finally, my own steamer."

W.E. Hamilton

"You don't have her yet, Son. You have to get the backing of the settlers, negotiate an acceptable price, and make her seaworthy!"

"Details, details," said Robert, dismissing them with a wave of his hand. "I have more chance of getting a steamship than you have of getting Mum a fig tree today."

"God sends his gifts at the perfect time," I said, as we continued on our way to Westport. "Perhaps he will choose to bless your mother on her sixty-second birthday with a fig tree."

"And perhaps he won't," sneered Robert, picking up a stick

"I think you are right about the steamer being too small," I said, changing the subject.

Robert slashed at a bush on the edge of the dusty road.

"We might get away with it."

"Get away with it! You need to do better than that!"

"Relax Dad, I can make it bigger if I have to."

"Make it bigger," I spluttered, "how can you possibly make it bigger?"

Robert snapped the stick in half.

"I have my ways."

And that was all he would tell me.

At Westport, we parted and went in separate directions. After attending to our business, we met again.

"I see I have been more successful than you," said Robert, looking meaningfully at the quince tree I carried.

"It was not the right time for the fig."

"So, it would seem."

"How did you get on?" I said, as we started our long journey home.

"Wonderfully. Captain Leech and I came to an arrangement

over the ship, and he's given me a month to get the money."

"That's good…I think," I said hesitantly.

"Of course, it's good. Moreover, as harbour-master, he's going to request that the Marine Department in Wellington officially recognizes the Karamea Steamship Company as a coastal trader."

I clapped Robert on the back.

"Captain Leech is a good friend to you."

"That's not all he's done. He's negotiating for us to take over the mail run between Karamea and Westport, and pick up coal from Mokihinui."

My eyes grew wide.

"That will make all the difference."

Robert nodded.

"It's a sound venture. We ferry butter and home produce to Westport, and bring back supplies, coals, and Her Majesty's mail. You should have brought two trees, Dad, for soon you will plant one to mark your part ownership in the *Picton*."

"I'll make-do," I said, as we trudged home.

Two days later, I sold some land to Stanley Allen.

"I'd like a plant as a memento before I go, if you don't mind, Stanley."

"Certainly, take what you want," he said, shaking my hand.

"I don't feel good about this," said Anderina, as we dug out the green grape. "It's a big risk."

"Moving to New Zealand was a big risk too," I said, wrapping the roots in a wet sack. "But it paid off."

Anderina clipped away the long gangling branches. "You're right. I'm glad we didn't stay. They say *Zetland* is full of ruined crofts; the tilled strips and gardens are smothered in kingcups and rushes."

"You can't remove twelve hundred people without it impacting the country," I said, picking up the grape by its thick stem. "We had a tiny window of opportunity, which we took. The steamer is the same thing."

"No, it's not," said Anderina, looking at the sold land with regret. "We had nothing to lose by leaving *Zetland*."

"Nothing material. We lost family, friends, and could have lost our lives."

"I suppose so," said Anderina, as we herded the cows out and shut the gate for the last time. "We don't have a large family to feed anymore.

"That's right," I agreed, "less is better. A full twenty-five acres is too much for an old couple to manage."

On Sunday (between the morning and afternoon church meetings) the family gathered and we transplanted the green grape.

"I knew I could get twenty-two men interested in the ship," said Robert, digging a hole at the other end of the grape trellis.

"My two boys," said Anderina, looking ready to burst with pride, "Captain Robert Johnson, Master of the Karamea Steamship Company, and Chairman John Johnson. Who would have thought it?"

"Oh Mum, we are not boys anymore," said John, embarrassed. "I'm thirty-five and Bob is forty!"

"You'll always be boys to me," said Anderina, peeling the sacking off the vine's roots.

"How will you get the *Picton* here, Bob?" said Willie, getting the conversation back on track. "You only have a provisional captain's ticket."

To Own a Fig Tree

"John and Morris McNabb will come with me overland to Little Wanganui. Once they have the *Picton* seaworthy, Captain Bloomfield will bring her as far as the Karamea entrance, and then Morris (with John as pilot) will take her up the river."

"Can I come?"

"Of course, Willie. Another man would be a big help."

"What will you do, Daddy," said Dan?

"Go to Westport, and once I have bought the ship, I'll stay there until my captain's ticket is confirmed," said Robert, dropping the vine into the hole, "and arrange for builders to construct a terminal for our company."

"Won't that cost a lot, my dear," said Elizabeth, swapping little Sarah onto her other hip.

"Fifty pounds for the new wharf at Westport."

"*Fifty pounds!*" Anderina exclaimed.

Robert shovelled dirt around the roots.

"Oh, Mum, that's not bad. We can use Johnson's Landing as one terminal, so it is only half the cost."

"I suppose you know what you are doing."

Robert put down the spade and trod around the stalk gently.

"I certainly do," said Captain Johnson, straightening his cap.

———

W.E. Hamilton

The Settlers Get a Boat

Early Monday morning, Robert, John, Willie, and Morris McNabb set off over the Rough and Tumble Track. For the next couple of weeks, the question on everyone's mind was, when will we see our ship? At last, we heard the whistle we were waiting for.

"THE *PICTON'S* HERE, ANDERINA" I shouted, throwing my pitchfork down. I grabbed the half-full sack of potatoes and shambled as swiftly as I could to the house. The door flew open and my wife hobbled down the steps quicker than I thought possible.

"Oh, Robert, how exciting!" She rammed her hat on her head. "Just think, our very own ship!"

"Karamea's ship," I corrected, as I dropped the sack inside. "We share her with twenty-one others."

"Yes, yes, there is no need to get picky over details."

"Are you going to keep your apron on, dear?"

"Mercy me, no!" Anderina tore it off, rolled it into a ball and threw it onto the doorstep.

My eyebrows shot up at this unexpected behaviour.

"Aren't you going to hang it up like you usually do?"

"No time for that. I don't want to miss seeing our ship come up the river."

"Neither do I," I said, as we hurried down our driveway and turned towards the coast.

To Own a Fig Tree

"Everyone is going to see the new arrival," I said, looking at all the people and canoes heading towards Johnson's Landing, "the last time the track and river were so busy was the annual sports day and picnic."

"Even Mrs Pettit has let the children out of school for the event," said Anderina, waving to the teacher in charge of a crocodile line of children.

"I should think so," I said, as we neared the wharf. "This is a historic moment for Karamea. They will remember it for the rest of their lives."

"They will indeed," said Elizabeth, overhearing me as she came down the pathway of her house.

"Come to Granny, Georgie," said Anderina, holding her hand out to the three-year-old hanging onto his mother's skirts. George considered her with owl eyes as he sucked his thumb.

"Go to Granny," said his mother, hitching up the baby on her hip.

George's sturdy little legs remained rooted to the ground behind his barricade of gathered calico.

"It's all the people," said Elizabeth, jerking her head towards the crowded wharf. "The make him clingy."

"Come to Granddad," I said, marching over and swinging him up.

George pulled his thumb from his mouth, and squealed with laughter as he whooshed through the air before landing astride my neck. "Now, young fella," I said, gripping his ankles. "You can watch your Daddy's ship come in."

The chugging of the steamer's engine was growing louder every minute, and we jumped as the whistle sounded once more. "Here she comes!"

And sure enough, rounding a bend in the river crept the *Picton*, with Morris McNabb behind the wheel and John out front.

"Why's *Nuncle* John waving his hands, *Ganddad*!" lisped George.

"He's signalling to Mr McNabb where it is safe or dangerous to take the boat."

"What's *Nuncle* Willie doing?"

"He's getting ready to throw the rope to the men on the wharf as soon as they get here."

"Why?"

"They tie it up to stop it floating up and down the river with the tide."

"Oh." He lapsed into silence as we watched the *Picton* reverse her engines and drift slowly towards the dock. As soon as she bumped the pile, a great cheer arose.

"I'll hold Sarah if you want to go on board and look around," Anderina said to Elizabeth.

"Thanks, Granny Johnson." Elizabeth handed her the baby. "What a pity Robert is missing this," she said, as we joined the queue.

"Getting his captain's ticket confirmed is his priority. He will be back as soon as possible."

And so he was. The excitement had hardly waned when he came over the Rough and Tumble. He called in at our place before he got home, for our house was on the way. As he eased his boots off and sank into a chair, I said:

"Did you have any trouble?"

"No, everything went pretty smoothly. Our Westport terminal is built, and I am now officially Captain Robert

To Own a Fig Tree

Johnson, the fully licenced captain of the *Picton*. Has she arrived here yet?"

"Yesterday. She's safely docked at Johnson's Landing."

"Yesterday!" Robert leapt up and was about to rush out the door, but Anderina stopped him.

"There is plenty of time for you to see your boat. Sit down and have a cup of tea before you finish your journey, for you have had a long hike."

"I suppose an extra half-hour will not hurt," said Robert, sinking back into the chair. "A cup of tea will be welcome. What do the settlers think of their investment?"

"They are delighted. Everyone is eager to try her out as soon as possible."

"As am I," said Robert, taking the cup Anderina handed him. "I'll tell the children to bring the cart around tomorrow for your butter."

"That would be good, Son," I said.

We chatted a while longer, and when he had drunk his fill and eaten a large slab of his mother's plum cake, he took his leave.

The bush telegraph was no less effective in 1893, than in 1875. By the time the bull dragged my load to Johnson's Landing early the next morning, the butter and produce of the whole community was already on board the *Picton*. Instead of happy faces, however, the settlers stood about glumly.

"Turn around and take your butter back home, Dad," said Robert, halting me. He rubbed a hand over his face. "It is as I feared, she is too short and down in the bow when loaded."

"Why did you buy her if you knew this would be a problem?" said Morris McNabb angrily.

"Because the price was right and we can fix her."
"How?"
"We will cut her in half and extend her."
"This is no time for silly jokes, Brother," said John.
Robert twitched his hat.
"I am not joking," said Captain Johnson, putting his thumbs in his waistcoat pocket and leaning against the bull. "If we extend her fifteen feet, she will carry more cargo and cut through the water faster."
There was a flabbergasted silence, so Captain Johnson continued. "We'll do most of the work ourselves, but we will need a shipwright to do the caulking."
"I had a letter from Samuel Friend the other day," Morris said suddenly.
"How is he getting on in Nelson?" I said.
"Much better. Both he and Frederick Liley are doing pretty well now. They feel they made a great mistake going to Karamea."
Impatience flicked Captain Johnson back into Robert.
"Yes, yes, that is all very nice, can we stick to solving the problem of the *Picton*?"
"I am. Sam mentioned that one of the brethren in the Nelson congregation is a shipwright."
Robert's eyes lit up.
"What was his name?"
Morris scratched behind the bull's horns absentmindedly as he tried to remember.
"Something beginning with Bal."
"Baldwin?"
"No." Morris wrinkled his nose and squinted into the

To Own a Fig Tree

distance. "Bal…Balk…Balkham. *Balkham, that's it!*"

Robert adjusted his cap.

"Be a good chap, McNabb, and write that name down for me. I shall need it when I get to Nelson. While I'm gone, William and John get the *Picton* onto land. When I get back, we will cut her up."

Willie stopped whistling under his breath. "How are we going to do that, Bob?"

"You and John are clever fellows," said Captain Johnson, with a dismissive wave of his hand. "You'll think of something." He took the paper Morris handed him and put it in his pocket. "I'll see you in a couple of weeks, I'm off to Nelson."

He marched up the path and into his house.

"That's not the way to Nelson," said Morris McNabb.

"I expect that Dad's gone to get a clean shirt," said Bobby, leading the bull back and forth in a hundred-point-turn. "I'll take you home Granddad when I get this thing turned around."

It was slow and awkward getting the unwieldy contraption to face the opposite direction. By the time the bull pointed the right way, the settlers had collected their butter and produce off the *Picton*, and one by one were melting away. While we waited, my sons and I puzzled over the problem Robert had left us to solve.

"There is a spot a mile and a half upstream where the bank slopes gently to the water," said Willie, "we could build a slipway there."

"I know the spot," said John. "It's ideal."

"How are you going to pull the ship up the slipway?" I said. "I doubt a hundred men could pull her onto land."

"Remember the big capstan on the *Ocean Mail*?" said John,

gazing at the ground with a faraway look in his eyes.

"Vaguely," said Willie.

"We could make one like it, and use the bull to turn it."

William stopped whistling and his mouth dropped open. "But that thing was huge!"

"No, it wasn't, it was big but it wasn't huge," I said, clapping him on the back.

"It was taller than me!"

"Son, you were only four. The capstan was about the size of that stump over there."

John's head jerked up and his eyes focused.

"That's it!"

"That's what?"

"We will make the capstan from a tree stump."

"It needs to turn!"

"Yes, yes, I wasn't suggesting we leave it in the ground. We cut a hole down through the centre of the bole, saw it free from its base, and then drive a sapling through both pieces."

"Like the wheels and axles of Robert's cart?" said Willie.

"Yes, only it turns horizontally instead of vertically."

"I think that would work," I said, visualizing it in my mind. "Provided you have lots of mutton fat to grease the moving parts, and a bar for the bull to pull."

"Another sapling driven into the side should do it," said John.

"Don't wait, Bobby," I said, "take the butter home and put it back in the pit for me, there's a good boy. Tell Granny I've gone for a walk with your uncles."

Bobby nodded and William, John, and I turned and made our way towards the spot for the slipway. After hunting about

To Own a Fig Tree

for a bit, we found what we were looking for.

"That one will do," said John, pointing to a tall stump at the top of a gentle slope. "Let's get our tools, Willie."

"I'll leave you boys to it," I said. "My days of working a twelve-foot saw through a tree are over. Let me know how you get on."

"Righto, Dad. We'll keep you posted."

They waved and we parted company.

W.E. Hamilton

Captain Johnson Solves the Problem

It was a busy time of year for the garden. I did not see John and Willie until the bush telegraph alerted me that they were hauling the *Picton* out of the water. Despite hurrying, Anderina and I were the last to arrive at the crowded 'boatyard.'

"We missed it," said Anderina with disappointment in her voice.

"At least it is safely on land," said a familiar voice.

And turning, we saw Robert and a stranger.

"Hello, Bob," said Anderina, kissing his cheek. "You got home at the right time."

"So it would seem." He motioned towards the stranger at his side. "This is Mr Balkham, the shipwright."

"Welcome, Mr Balkham," I said, "I'm Robert Johnson and this is my wife, Anderina."

"My parents," said Robert.

The man smiled.

"I guessed as much."

"The name is a tip-off," I said.

"And the beard, and the nose, and the height," said Anderina smiling.

"This is a good-sized crowd," said Balkham, looking at the people watching Willie unhook the bull from the capstan.

"I'm sorry about that," said Robert. "I'm afraid in such an

isolated place anything unusual is turned into a sideshow."

"Even you, Sir," added Anderina, "will be a subject of great curiosity."

Balkham's eyes lit up and he rubbed his hands together. "Wonderful. I shall caulk the ship by day and preach the gospel by night."

Robert looked horrified.

"You can't do that! Not everyone is a believer."

"All the more necessary," said Balkham. "Second-Timothy-four-two."

Robert looked puzzled. "What do you mean by, second-timothy-four-two?"

"It's a bible verse," I said, embarrassed by my son's lack of knowledge.

"Preach the word; be ready in season and out of season; correct, rebuke, and encourage with great patience and teaching," quoted Balkham.

"Yes, well, we'll see about that," said Robert, noncommittally. "Come and meet my brothers."

Balkham nodded and picked up his toolkit as Robert lifted two wooden boxes.

"What's in there?" I said, noticing Robert's burden for the first time.

"Copper nails and bolts," said Robert, as we made our way through the milling people. "I instructed James Black and David Grayney to cut me a good supply of yellow pine and black birch lumber before I left, so we can make an immediate start."

Anderina pulled me back as we neared Willie and John.

"I don't think I can bear to watch them hack our investment

apart."

She had a point. My legs felt wobbly at the thought.

"Robert," I called, "your mother and I are going home. Let us know when you have the *Picton* done."

"Alright, Dad. I'll send the children with updates."

"They have sawed through the deck," said Harriet, when she milked the cows on Tuesday morning. "And Mr Balkham stood on the roof of the cabin and preached for an hour in the evening."

On Wednesday, she told us they were cutting up the starboard side, and on Friday they sawed down the Portside.

We didn't sleep well that night.

"Won't it fall over?" Anderina worried in the wee hours of the morning.

"I expect they will prop the sides up somehow."

"They are pulling it apart today," said Dan, a week later as he turned the handle of the butter churn vigorously.

"Half a farm is a lot to risk," said my wife, as she handed him a piece of toffee.

"The boat looks funny," giggled Anderina Alice, when her turn to milk rolled around. "It has a bow and stern but only a few boards between them. Mr Balkham didn't preach last night."

"He must have needed a rest."

Anderina Alice finished stripping out the cow and picked up the pail of milk. "No. He was too busy baptising sinners in the river."

"The Lord be praised," I said, "that is worth losing a farm for."

"I told you I had a bad feeling about it, Robert!"

To Own a Fig Tree

"Don't worry Granny," said Anderina Alice, "the ship is coming along fine."

"Dad and Uncle John have almost finished extending the boat," said Dan, on butter churning day. He pulled a nail and bolt from his pocket and held them up for my inspection. "The *Picton* is held together with one-hundred-and-fifty pounds of these."

I let out a whistle of appreciation as I took them from him.

"One-hundred-and-fifty pounds of these wee beasties. Fancy that!"

Dan was gratified by my interest.

"When Dad launches her, she'll be so heavy with copper she'll sink to the bottom."

"I knew it was doomed!" groaned Anderina. "Our boys are not boat builders."

"Don't fuss, woman," I said, handing the precious mementoes back to my grandson. "They have both built houses and are good with their hands."

Yet despite my brave words, I did not sleep well until Robert came to see us on May the thirtieth.

"Order your memorial tree, Dad, the new-and-improved-*Picton* is docked at Johnson's Landing."

Anderina's face split into a wide smile.

"There, what did I tell you, Robert?" she said, with the air of a prophetess. "I knew everything would turn out fine."

W.E. Hamilton

Safety Precautions are for the Rich

The entire community turned out to see the *SS Picton* set off on her maiden voyage. Anderina and I stood with Elizabeth by her gate and gazed at the crowd spilling down the hill and onto the wharf. Barbara Pettit and the school children were gathered nearby. Anderina leaned forward and tapped the teacher on her shoulder.

"I like the flags and the bunting on the gangplank, Barbara," she said, "they add to the gala spirit."

Mrs Pettit turned and smiled. "They were a class project. It is the perfect time to teach about shipping and New Zealand's exports."

"Very sensible," I said. "I hope you mentioned Karamea's dairy trade to Westport."

"Of course, and the lumber trade."

I nodded.

"If I was twenty years younger, I'd go into the railway sleeper business myself."

Georgie, who was sitting on my shoulders, patted my hat to get my attention.

"Look Ganddad, Nuncle John is lifting the gangplank and untying the boat."

"They are about to go," I said, gripping his ankles firmly.

The whistle blew, and instantly the school children waved

To Own a Fig Tree

their flags and shouted: "Yahoo."

"Wave to Daddy," said Elizabeth, wobbling little Sarah's hand.

The steamer's engine growled and the water foamed, and as she pulled away from the dock a great cheer arose.

"There she goes," Anderina said, dabbing her eyes. "We have very clever sons."

"We do indeed," I said. "The new and improved *SS Picton* sits like a duck on the water. Beautifully balanced even with a full load."

We watched as our ship slid down the river. Just before she rounded the bend and disappeared, she blew her whistle in farewell. The crowd hung about for a few minutes, staring at the empty water before melting away. Elizabeth turned to Anderina and me.

"I must get back; I am cooking applesauce. Would you like to come in for a cup of tea before you go home?"

"We'd love to," said Anderina, taking the baby from our daughter-in-law's arms.

Elizabeth smoothed her apron over her swollen belly, and we followed her up the path and into the house.

The kitchen oozed the comforting smell of stewing apples. Elizabeth swung the kettle over the fire before lifting the lid off a large iron pot.

"Just in time," she said, lumbering over to the fire and stirring the apples with a wooden spoon. "Five more minutes and they would have stuck to the bottom." She placed a low milking stool before the fire.

"Put George down here," she said to me, pointing at the stool.

W.E. Hamilton

I stood Georgie on the stool before taking a chair at the table.

"I want you to be a good boy and stir the sauce, Georgie," said Elizabeth, putting the spoon in his hand. "Go around and around like this." She covered his fist and together they stirred the apples.

Anderina watched with growing anxiety. "He's very young for that, Elizabeth."

"Nonsense. It is good to teach young'uns to work from an early age. I couldn't manage if they didn't help out. I get so tired when I am pregnant."

"Of course," said Anderina, jiggling Sarah. "All my children started milking cows at three, but fire is an entirely different matter."

"He'll be fine," said Elizabeth, lifting the singing kettle off the crane. "He is a smart little fellow. He won't come to any harm."

"I feel sure your mother (God rest her soul) would agree with me if she were still with us."

"Don't interfere, Anderina," I said, frowning at her. "We have had our time of raising children. Things are done differently nowadays."

"I suppose so." Anderina chewed on her bottom lip in an unconvinced manner.

Elizabeth's shoulders sagged and her mouth drooped. "Dear Mother. I still miss her." She set the kettle on the table absentmindedly as she eased herself into a chair. "Forty-five… only two years older than me. Far too young to die."

"Pioneering life is hard on women."

"It can be," sighed Elizabeth. "Poor Father has not been

lucky with wives. His second wife, Elspeth Coutts, did not live long either. I only hope Jane has more stamina; three wives are too many to lose."

"She will be fine," I said, patting Elizabeth on the hand. "She comes from sturdy stock. The Moffatts are a healthy lot."

"It's nice Elspeth got a husband, even though it wasn't for long," said Anderina, her mind slipping back to earlier days. "Who did Catherine marry?"

"Someone in Nelson," said Elizabeth, "and Clementina married a sailor called Andrew Jackson."

Anderina's face lit up.

"That's right, I remember now."

"Benjamin would have been pleased," I said. "He braved the voyage in his old age to see his girls get husbands, and his son released from the burden of looking after them."

We all fell silent thinking of poor Peter.

"You could do with an iron stove like Mary Simpson's big black range, Elizabeth," said Anderina, shifting the subject back to the fireplace. "They are much safer than naked flames."

Elizabeth roused herself and poured hot water into the teapot.

"I'd love one but they're too expensive," she said, spooning tea leaves into the teapot. "Mary only got it because she bakes for all the flaxies[43] and saw millers."

She got up, took Sarah from Anderina and popped her in a highchair.

"You bake almost as much as she does, keeping your big brood fed," said Anderina, laying cups on the table.

"It doesn't count, because I am not making money with my

---

43   Flax workers

baking." Elizabeth tied a slice of apple in muslin and placed it in Sarah's chubby fist. "Suck on this, poppet."

"When do you expect Robert back?" said Anderina, pouring the tea.

Elizabeth took a cake tin from the cupboard over the sink bench.

"I have no idea. It depends how quickly they unload and load, and what the seas and weather are like." She opened the tin and cut the cake into generous slabs. "I worry about him going over that treacherous bar," she said, lifting slices onto a plate. "Hoisting three white balls up the flagstaff to warn him of danger, is a scant precaution."

I pulled a face.

"The Marine Department in Wellington only reluctantly recognizes our steamer service. They consider beacons and navigational aids are an unwarranted expense for such a small unimportant service."

"That's the problem with being poor," said Elizabeth, lifting George off the stool and handing him a piece of cake. "Safety precautions are for the rich. The rest of us have to make do as best we can."

To Own a Fig Tree

Shipwreck

It was February, 1896, and Anderina was in the kitchen tying toffee onto a branchy twig.

"What on earth are you doing?"

"Making a toffee tree for Sarah's birthday."

"Why?"

"The little pet says she doesn't want another banana palm, she wants a toffee tree, so I'm making her one."

"Does she know a toffee tree won't grow?"

"Of course not. She is only turning four."

I raised an eyebrow.

"Don't look at me like that, Robert. It will be fun. After we plant it, the children can pick a piece of 'fruit' off Sarah's toffee tree."

"You do realize, they will all want toffee trees for their birthdays after this!"

"The orchard is huge, and grandchildren are coming thick and fast; we can afford to slow up on the planting."

I was saved from replying by Robert clumping onto the veranda.

"Hello, anybody home?"

"We're in the kitchen, son, come on in."

"If your boots are dirty, take them off," his mother added.

There was a pause before Robert walked through the door on stockinged feet.

"What are you doing, Mum?

"Making a toffee tree for your daughter's birthday on Sunday."

"Is this instead of the mythical fig tree?"

"Fig trees are real," I said, "and God will send our fig tree at the perfect time."

"Yeah, yeah, whatever; believe what you like if it keeps you happy, Dad."

Ignoring his sarcasm, I pointed to the wooden box slung on a long strap over his shoulder.

"What have you got there?"

"They're a present for Sarah," he said, slipping out from under the strap and putting the box on the table. "I don't want her to see them. Would you keep them here until her party?"

"Of course," I said, peering through the chicken wire in the lid. "What are they?"

"Homing pigeons." He took a bag from his pocket and dropped a few grains of corn through the mesh.

"Cute little things," I said. "They'll make nice pets. Bobby and I could build Sarah a dovecote for her birthday."

"Pets!" Robert looked scandalized. "We don't have room for pets! With them, I will send Elizabeth messages when I'm at sea."

"I thought they were for Sarah?" said Anderina, breaking another piece of toffee from the pan.

"She can feed and care for them when I am home," said Robert airily.

"Clever idea," I said, "not a bad safety precaution either. Have you had any luck with your complaints against the lack of efficiency among the signalmen along the coast?"

To Own a Fig Tree

"No. The Wellington Marine Department answers in boring memoranda. His face darkened. "For three years I have laboriously reported the state of the five rivers in Karamea, and are they interested? No! Last month I complained about the silting caused by gravel washing down the mountains in the Little Wanganui and Karamea river, and sent lengthy reports showing how to resolve the problem by dynamiting."

"Are they going to do anything about it?" I said.

Robert's voice rose to a high falsetto as he quoted:

"'Fill out another form and send it to another department.'" His voice dropped back to normal. "We go around in circles. Ships are on the brink of disaster every day, but the only thing they get excited about is my spelling mistakes!"

"Never mind, dear. Have a piece of toffee."

Robert took a piece from his mother and popped the sweet shard into his mouth.

"I wish my problems were so easily solved. The rate those rivers are silting up, the *Picton* will be lost before you plant Sarah's toffee tree."

He got up and walked to the front door. "I will see you on Sunday," he said, putting his boots back on. "Where is the meeting held this week?"

"Thomas Lineham's place," said Anderina. "Try not to look so bored; it is not a good example to your children."

"Well, it is boring. We just sit around the bread and wine[44] every Sunday," said Robert defensively. "The singing is cheerful, I'll grant you that, but I don't agree with much of the preaching. Perhaps I won't bother going this Sunday."

Then before we could think of a reply, he waved cheerily

---

44   The communion ritual

and was off.

"Oh, Robert," said Anderina in dismay. "What do you make of that?"

"It is a great pity one of our children does not see beyond the surface of things," I said, sadly. "We must pray for him."

Despite his bold threat, Robert was at the meeting as usual. As usual, the family gathered at our place for a potluck lunch, and the orchard rang with shouts and laughter like it did every Sunday afternoon. The pigeons were a great success, and the toffee tree was very popular.

"So much better than a banana palm, said the birthday girl.

"Can I have a gumball tree when I turn four?" said little Lily Margret.

"I want a lollypop tree," said Arthur Thomas.

"What would you like, Georgie?" I asked.

"A stink bomb."

His mother turned a suspicious eye on him.

"Why do you want a stink bomb?"

"To put in the teacher's desk."

"George Cooper Johnson! I don't know what has got into you these days!" said Elizabeth, throwing her hands in the air.

"Boys will be boys," said Robert indulgently.

Elizabeth glowered at her husband. "Take him with you next time you do the mail run. You might change your tune then."

"I can't do that my love," said Robert, his face turning hard. "It's far too dangerous. The river is so silted up my next trip may be my last."

"That is a very gloomy prediction," said Anderina, "I hope you are wrong."

To Own a Fig Tree

"Surely not!" cried Elizabeth. "If it is that bad you should not keep taking the boat out."

"I exaggerate," said Robert, quickly backtracking. "The river is bad but I am more than a match for it."

And so, it seemed. For despite the ever-present hazard of shifting gravel, the gallant little *SS Picton* found her way back and forth over the treacherous bar, time and time again. Then on the ninth of June, 1896, disaster struck, and the *SS Picton* became stranded on the beach. Robert's face was white and strained when he broke the news to us.

"I'm afraid she's gone, Dad," he said, slumping in a kitchen chair. "My steamer, your farm, the settler's first major asset."

"Don't trouble yourself on our account, son," I said. "We couldn't have coped with a whole twenty-five acres. What we have left is more than enough for our needs."

"The main thing is nobody was drowned," said Anderina, patting him on his back.

Robert put his elbows on the table and dropped his head into his hands. "My name will be mud with the settlers."

"Nobody will blame you. These things happen when the sea is heavy."

"It wasn't just the sea, Dad, a coil of rope fouled the propeller while we were crossing the bar." He lifted his head and stared at me with a troubled face. "How did it happen? I am very strict about keeping everything shipshape; ropes in particular."

I had no answer, so I nodded sympathetically.

"I lost the steering, of course, at just the worst possible moment, and the sea drove us onto the North Spit."

"At least nobody was drowned," repeated Anderina.

"Is she salvageable?"

"No. She's a total wreck, ribs and pieces of decking are strewn all along the beach. Come and see."

I put on my boots and we walked along the edge of the river to the scene of the wreck.

"Back in the bad old days in *Zetland*, my father would have taken this home to fix his roof," I said, kicking a curved beam on the sand. "This was the nearest we got to trees."

"I remember; the roof was our only insurance against homelessness."

"That's right." I sat on the beam. "Since then, God has delivered us from three-hundred years of bondage, and given us land and houses. What is the loss of a boat against that? You have a promising future; you'll get another steamer one day."

Robert sat beside me and stared at the river for a long time.

"I suppose so," he said at last.

We planted a weeping willow tree by the river in memory of the *SS Picton*, and all Karamea mourned.

To Own a Fig Tree

Tragedy

Not long after losing the *Picton*, Captain Leech sent word of a steamer for sale.

"*The SS Admiral was expressly built for the river trade and sounds right for Karamea,*" said Robert, reading the captain's letter aloud. "*It has two, fifty-horse-power engines, and schooner rigging.*"

"Schooner rigging," I said. "You could cross the Tasmin with schooner rigging."

"I will have to," said Robert, "for she's currently in Sydney."

"Sydney!" Anderina's face was a mask of horror. "That is a long way away."

"Nonsense, Mother, I used to sail further than that when I was a lad in Shetland."

"When do you go, son?"

"Tomorrow. When I get to Westport, Captain Leech is going to loan me a suit to wear, and advise me on the best way to acquire the SS Admiral. After that, I will catch the steamer to Wellington and a ship to Sydney."

"What does Elizabeth think about this?" said Anderina.

"She is supportive provided I take the pigeons to inform her of my progress. She will manage alright for the older children are a great help around the farm."

"What about Georgie?" I said with a chuckle.

"I have promised to bring him back the treat of a lifetime if he chips in and does his chores without making his usual fuss."

"You should not bribe him into good behaviour," said Anderina.

"It's not really a bribe; I've always wanted a monkey."

"A monkey!"

"Yes, I've heard of a place where they sell them in Sydney."

"What use is a monkey? You can't eat or work it."

"Oh, Dad," said Robert, airily, "don't be so old-fashioned. It's high time the children had a pet."

In our close community, you could not sneeze in a cave without it becoming public knowledge. The bush telegraph got wind of Robert's quest, and at daybreak, all Karamea was gathered at Johnson's Landing to see him off on his great adventure.

"Wave Daddy goodbye, Wallace," said Elizabeth, wobbling the hand of the baby on her hip.

"Be a good boy, Norman," said Robert, "ruffling the hair of the toddler clinging to his mother's skirts.

He turned to the six-year-old walking along the edge of the wharf.

"Do your chores nicely, Georgie, and I will bring you back something special."

"What about me, Daddy?" said Sarah. "Will you bring me something nice for stirring the porridge every morning?"

"Georgie's present will be fun for everyone," said her father, swinging her high into the air.

"This is for you, Captain Johnson," said Meyrick Jones, stepping forward and handing Robert a piece of paper. "You might find a reference useful."

Robert scanned the document, which read as follows:

To Own a Fig Tree

> ### To Whom It May Concern
>
> The Karamea shipping Company Ltd have much pleasure in testifying that Captain Robert Johnson has served as master of our steamer (the SS Picton) for two years and eight months, and during that time he crossed the Karamea, Little Wanganui, Mokihinui and Westport bars two-hundred-and-sixty-six times with the said mail steamer.
> His sobriety, good conduct, daring, and skill, as a seaman in command is hard to be found, and he has executed his duties incumbent on him as Master during all that time with great satisfaction, and as being an agent of our company in money matters has been true to his trust.
>
> (Excerpt taken from, Robert Johnson 'The Captain'
> by Peter Johnston)

Robert wiped his hand over his face and said in a gruff tone:

"That means a lot to me. Thank you very much."

Then someone called: "Three cheers for Captain Johnson," and we hip-hip-hoorayed him gustily.

"You need to go if you want to get to Little Wanganui before nightfall," said Anderina, when the noise settled down.

"Be careful, love," said Elizabeth, kissing her bearded man goodbye. "I could not bear it if something terrible should happen to you."

"Nothing terrible will happen," said Robert confidently, as he waved and set off.

Now that there was nothing more to see, the crowd melted away.

George tugged at my hand.

"Come and help me gather moss."

"Don't you have school today?"

"Oh Granddad," he giggled, "it's the holidays."

"So, it is. I had forgotten. What do you want moss for?"

"The Chinaman who has the little shop opposite the Holy Trinity Church, of course."

"Old Chung, who lives at 'Peking'?"

"Yes, if we clean and dry it, he gives us two pennies a pound for it."

I ruffled Georgie's hair.

"And what would you do with two pennies, young scamp?"

"Buy sweets," said George without hesitation.

I winked at him.

"Now that is important. Do you know of the big patch of moss on the South Terrace?"

George's eyes grew wide.

"No."

"It's near here, just at the top of the track that goes up the hill from your house."

"Show me, Granddad, show me?"

"Well, it depends on what your mother and grandmother say. They may have chores for you and me."

"I'd be glad to have him taken out from under my feet," said Elizabeth, "I'm making marmalade today."

"Would you like some help?" said Anderina.

"I never say no to help," said Elizabeth, turning towards the house. "If you just hold the baby, you will do me a great

To Own a Fig Tree

service."

"Mum, can I have a flour sack for the moss?" said George, as we walked up the path.

"No. You need a new shirt; it's hard enough bleaching words off the bag, without adding moss stains."

George's mouth drooped.

"A bucket would be better," I said, "it's easier to fill."

"Come on Granddad," said George, his face lighting up. "We'll get one from the cowshed."

We collected the milking pail, and made our way along the track that wound its way up the steep hill.

"Where is the moss, Granddad?" said George, when we arrived at the top.

I bent over and held my knees with my hands as I puffed. "Let me have a breather first," I gasped. "I'm not as young as I once was."

"How old are you, Granddad? - a hundred?"

"No, only seventy-one, and I can still fell trees. Just not as many as I could twenty years ago."

I straightened up and stared at the panoramic view before me. "It sure is beautiful."

"I can see Market Cross, the Dairy Factory, and the new bridge across the Karamea River," said George.

"Yes," I shifted my eyes downward. "And there is Harriet picking lemons in your garden."

"Helloo, Harriet," shouted George, waving his arms and jumping up and down.

Harriet waved back before disappearing inside the house.

"I'm glad I am not Sarah, stirring the marmalade," said George, watching the smoke rising from the chimney.

"It might not be Sarah."

"Yes, it will be. Stirring is Sarah's job. My jobs are milking and collecting the eggs." He rattled the bucket impatiently. "Have you had a big enough rest, Granddad?"

"It will do." I walked a short distance from the edge of the plateau. "Now if I remember rightly, there was a big patch of moss under these trees. Scout about and hopefully we will find some."

My memory did not fail me. Within minutes, we found what we were looking for. We took our time filling the bucket, for it was a pleasant job and we were not in a hurry to finish.

"Tell me stories about Dad and the Shetlands, Granddad."

"Alright. Have I told you about the boat race?"

"No."

"One time, your father was rowing out to the fishing grounds with five other men, when another boat drew alongside them and they started racing. They went neck and neck for miles, with neither boat drawing ahead. Finally, the man at the steering oar shouted:"

"Put your back into it, Johnson."

"If I pull any harder, I will break the oar, said your father."

"Don't be stupid, you can't break it."

"So, your father pulled harder." I paused and looked at George. "And what do you think happened?"

"He broke the oar?"

"That's right, your father is such a strong man he broke the oar."

"Tell me another one, Granddad."

"This one is not about your father. This is about another Johnson. The British Navy knows Shetland Islanders are expert

To Own a Fig Tree

seamen. Every year, the press gangs came and took more men than they were entitled to. One day they stole a boatload of men. While the British were rowing their prisoners out to the ship, a Johnson pointed to the man at the steering oar and said:"

"Can that man swim?"

"Then he swung across the boat with his shoulders on one side and his feet on the other, and pulling hard, broke the boat in half."

"Did he get away, Granddad?"

"I should think he did! The British were too busy trying to save themselves from drowning to worry about their prisoners. The Shetlanders swam to the shore and escaped."

"Tell me another one."

"Do you know the story about the greedy man that ate a dead mouse by mistake?"

"No."

"Well, the Johnsons put a dead mouse in his porridge as a practical joke, and when he was about to eat it, they tried to stop him but…"

Suddenly, frightful screams ripped through the air.

George and I forgot the story, forgot the moss, forgot everything, as we rushed to the edge of the plateau and stared at the house below. A dreadful scene met our eyes. Bobby and John were running down the wharf to the store shouting: "HELP, HELP!" While Margret and Daniel tore about the garden, wailing and crying. Harriet ran out of the back door, and looking up the hill screamed:

"GRANDDAD, GRANDDAD, COME QUICKLY!"

At this, an icy wave of terror washed over me, and George burst into tears as we hurried down the track as fast as we could. I saw glimpses through the trees, of men pouring out of the store, pounding up the path, and rushing into the house. Then there was a lull in noise and activity before a team of men burst from the front door. They were running, and a child burnt beyond recognition lay on a stretcher between them.

"Shut your eyes, George," I commanded, stepping in front of the small boy. "Don't open them until I say you can."

I put my hand over his eyes and hurried him past the cowshed.

By the time I got to the back of the house, the rescue team had disappeared.

"You can look now, George," I said, opening the back door and stepping into the kitchen.

"Robert, thank goodness you have come," said Anderina, rushing to greet me.

"What's happened?"

"There's been a terrible accident. Sarah has been badly burnt."

"My child, my child," Elizabeth sobbed. "It happened so quickly!"

"What happened?"

"Sarah's skirt flicked into the fire and she was instantly engulfed in flames. You warned me it would happen, Anderina. Oh, why did I not listen?"

"Don't blame yourself, Elizabeth," said Anderina, putting her arm around her. "It was just one of those things. She has stirred the pot hundreds of times without coming to harm before."

"Where are they taking Sarah?" I said.

"To Doctor Jenkins."

To Own a Fig Tree

"Over the Rough and Tumble?"

"No, around the coast, for it is quicker. A team is running relays with her."

"Sit down, Lizzy. I'll make you a cup of tea," said Anderina, unsure what else to do.

Elizabeth ripped off her apron and reached for her hat. "No. I must follow them."

"There is nothing you can do." Anderina gently pushed her into a nearby chair. "The way is too far for you in your condition. You don't want to miscarry."

"If only I knew what was happening," sobbed Elizabeth, wringing her hands.

"Robert took the homing pigeons with him," I said suddenly. "If they catch up with him at Little Wanganui, he will send word of Sarah."

"Yes, yes, he will," said Elizabeth, "I will wait on the veranda for his message."

I took charge of the children while Anderina and Elizabeth scanned the sky for a pigeon.

The awful news spread like wildfire throughout the community. We did not go home at milking time. Instead, kind neighbours milked our cows, fed the chickens, and brought food. Somehow, Elizabeth's marmalade was made, and the kitchen full of cakes and stew by nightfall. The practical gifts were expressions of deep sympathy, but none of us felt like eating; our only desire was to see the pigeon. At last, it came. Elizabeth caught the bird and took the tiny roll from its leg with a trembling hand.

"Here, Granddad Johnson. I cannot bear to read it for I fear it is bad news."

I unrolled the scroll and read the message aloud.

"Sarah passed away at Mokihinui. Body currently at Doctor Jenkins. I will come home after burying her in Westport. Love Robert."

Elizabeth collapsed into grief.

As there was nothing I could do, and Robert needed me, I left Anderina to comfort the grieving family as best she could. Then Willie, John, Laurence, and I made our way sadly to Westport. The journey was quiet. Only the crunching of our feet on the stony track disturbed the tranquillity of the bush. Even William was silent, his ever-present whistling was missing.

The funeral was small, and I never attended a more tragic one. The Reverend Dart tried to soothe our agonized souls with comforting words, but solace was impossible. Finally, he motioned the pallbearers to lower the small coffin into the ground, and finished with the familiar words:

"Ashes to ashes, dust to dust. We commit little Sarah Johnson to the ground, looking for that blessed hope when the dead in Christ shall rise."

When he finished, the others fell back and Robert and I were left standing beside the grave.

"She was so young," said Robert, in broken tones.

"She will not come back to us," I said slowly, "but we will see her again in heaven."

Robert's eyes stared into mine with intensity.

"Do you really believe that, Dad?"

"With all my heart!"

He looked at me for a long time before dropping his eyes. I knew he wanted to be alone, so I withdrew. I left him silently staring at the coffin in the ground, and made my way into town.

To Own a Fig Tree

"Why, God, why?" I silently cried, as I trudged along the streets.

There was no answer, perhaps there would never be an answer this side of the grave, but at the Trading Depot, I found God's comfort. The shadows were long by the time I got back to the cemetery. Robert had not moved. I put my comfort behind a tombstone and walked over to my grieving son.

"Come, Robert," I said, drawing him away from the grave. "Follow me."

He came without resistance, like a small boy.

"I have something for you."

He stood with his head hanging as I took God's gift from its hiding place.

"Let us plant a memorial for Sarah, and a symbol of hope," I said. And into his hands, I placed a little fig tree.

W.E. Hamilton

Glossary

Aotearoa. *The Maori name for New Zealand*
Bampot. *A Glasgow term for a stupid person*
Bivouac. *A temporary shelter improvised from bush materials*
Bulwark. *The part of a ship's side that rises above the deck*
But and ben *A simple two-roomed cottage*
Daibodi. *A fish trap made of cornstalks*
Factor. *Merchant or agent*
Flaxies. *Slang for flax workers*
Jackeen. *A derogatory Irish name for a city dweller*
Kiwi. *A flightless native New Zealand bird*
Line. *Equator*
Morepork. *A native New Zealand owl*
Ponga. *A large tree fern*
Saith. *A codfish*
Sixern. *A six-man traditional fishing boat propelled by oars*
Thirl. *To pierce a body part. (Biblical implications of enslavement.)*
Toetoe. *A native New Zealand plant similar to pampas grass*
Toonie-dog. *Town dog*
Toon. *Town*
Weka. *A flightless hen sized bird*
Zetland. *The old name for Shetland*

References

- The Robert Johnsons and Karamea by Elva Bett
- Karamea A Story of Success by Dulcie McNabb
- The Special Settlements of Jackson's Bay and Karamea thesis by Jennifer Mary Curtis
- Shipping Records
- Notes of Whalsay from the Shetland times
- Life on Board by Te Ara Encyclopedia of New Zealand
- Shetland: Descriptive and Historical by Robert Cowlie, M.A, M.D Aberdeen 1871
- Truck or Semi-Serfdom in the Shetland Isles (1871) Verbatim Reprint of the Report of the Commissioners by Kessinger's Legacy Reprints
- Shipboard: the 19th-century emigrant experience by State Library of NSW Australia
- Arrival of the Ocean Mail by Colonist, Volume XVII, issue 1838 November 1874 page 2
- The Diary of Henry Herringshaw
- Emigration Regulations- Hints for emigrants
- Notes on New Zealand for the use of Emigrants by Reverend Barclay
- Advice to Single Women. Chambers Journal Feb 1872
- History of Braemar. The Development of Mental and Intellectual Health Services in Nelson by Miriam Clark

W.E. Hamilton

- A to Js Online Appendix to the Journals of the House of Representatives- 1877 Session 1. D 07 Karamea Special Settlers. (Report by Mr A MacKay.)
- Robert Johnson 'The Captain' by Peter Johnston

About the Author

Wendy Hamilton is a New Zealander who moved to Australia in 2014.

Wendy Hamilton is a descendant of Robert and Anderina Johnson, through the William's line.

Nowadays, Wendy and her husband, Ian, live in Mittagong in The Southern Highlands of NSW. She spends her days writing and illustrating. Wendy is a diverse writer. This is her third historical book. Her other works include books on home-schooling, parenting, life in New Zealand, children's novels, and picture books.

If you enjoyed "To Own a Fig Tree"
please leave a review on Amazon

You may be interested in Wendy's other books,
Shipwrecks and Bush Felling and The Spot the War Forgot.

SHIPWRECKS AND BUSH FELLING

Is the true story of George Meredith who in 1845 goes to sea at eleven, is shipwrecked twice, rescues a princess, and runs away to the gold rush in Melbourne. In New Zealand he meets a girl at the Lyttleton docks, marries her the next day, and carves out a life for himself and his family in the New Zealand bush.

Can be found on Amazon
or at www.zealauspublishing.com

THE SPOT THE WAR FORGOT

Is a remarkable story based on a series of real events that took place during World War One. In a time of great turmoil, three-hundred-and-twenty-five German mariners, six women, and seven little girls found peace and joy in Berrima. While the sword devoured Europe, the internees built huts along the river, made boats, had a theatre and orchestra, and turned the surrounding countryside into a Garden of Eden. Amid a sea of fighting and hatred, Australians, Germans, and guards forgot they were enemies in a little spot south of Sydney. One of the few positive stories of the first world war. The Berrima POW Camp gives new meaning to the term the Great War and is a badge of honour on Australia's sleeve.

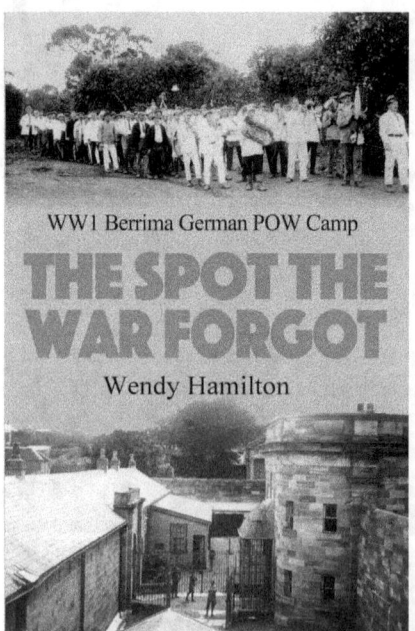

Can be found on Amazon
or at www.zealauspublishing.com